D0567540

LODGE
CAST IRON
NATION

GREAT AMERICAN COOKING FROM COAST TO COAST

LODGE
CAST IRON
NATION

GREAT AMERICAN COOKING FROM COAST TO COAST

COMPILED AND EDITED BY
PAM HOENIG

Oxmoor House®

CONTENTS

PREFACE

There is something soulful about a cast iron skillet. When I pick up my favorite skillet, I feel an emotional connection. It may sound corny, but it is true.

When I place well-floured chicken pieces in sizzling oil or taste sweet butter melting on hot-out-of-the-pan cornbread, it brings the memory of my grandmother back to life.

When I sauté shallots, bacon, and chopped farmers' market vegetables to make a "hash bed" for a piece of crispy cast iron-cooked fish, I am back in Los Angeles with my good friend and co-author, Bob Blumer (see page 156 for the Country Ham and Fig Pizza from our book, *Pizza on the Grill*).

I love that you can take a neglected pan that is pockmarked with rust and re-season it until it's as good as it was in its heyday. And if someone accidently misuses that pan (shame on them!), it can be re-surfaced and re-seasoned and resuscitated yet again. If that doesn't make you believe that these pots and pans and molds have a living spirit, I don't know what will.

I love that Lodge cast iron pots and pans have stayed a constant in kitchens all across America for more than 100 years, and that many people have passed down their pans as family heirlooms. Others like me have picked up pans—with a silent rich history—at yard sales and antique stores. The only thing that has changed at Lodge in all these years just makes the cast iron even better! New Lodge pans are seasoned in the foundry, and it would take 10 years of cooking sausage and bacon to develop—putting the "Lodge" in logical!

Obviously, I have a deep relationship with my cast iron pans. That long-standing relationship is the main reason that I am excited to have been a part of both the first Lodge cookbook and this new one. I don't feel the same way about most of my kitchen equipment, but my cast iron pans are like my favorite pair of cowboy boots—they get better and more dear to me with every use. It also helps that the family behind the foundry includes some of the best people I have ever met.

I've known Bob Kellermann and his wife, Cheryl, for almost as long as I have been cooking professionally. Bob is always dapper, and his bow ties mirror his smiling face. He is the epitome of a Southern gentleman and loves cast iron as much as he loves his family—which makes sense because Lodge Manufacturing is his family's multi-generational business. And Cheryl is the very definition of a firecracker! She is no doubt the best-dressed woman in Tennessee—and her sharp wit and unwavering warmth match her good taste, making her the belle of every room she graces.

Together, the Kellermanns are fun with a capital F, hardworking, welcoming, gracious, and the very best of all things Southern. The Kellermanns embody life—just like their cast iron pieces embody life.

Elizabeth

Chef Elizabeth A. Karmel
June 2, 2013

FOREWORD

There is nothing more enjoyable than being asked to write about something you love. Remaining tempered in one's exuberance is one of life's great challenges, so rather than a "traditional introduction," I consider this piece a love letter to the good people who make Lodge cast iron cookware roll off the line every single day.

Thank you all. What you do is wonderful. You make our lives richer and riper.

The resurgence of the use of cast iron cookware over the past couple of decades speaks to a number of things, like nostalgia, simplicity, and craftsmanship, among others. But to me, more than anything else, it smacks of good sense, because cast iron cookware offers great value for the dollar, durability (so much so that pieces get passed down from generation to generation), and unparalleled performance on the stove, in the oven, on the grill, or over a campfire. And the remarkable transition Lodge has made under the leadership of Bob Kellermann and Henry Lodge (great-grandsons of the company founder, Joseph Lodge) in response to this rise in popularity has been accomplished by remaining committed to the outstanding qualities that define Lodge cast iron cookware.

In the early 1990s, as the government was making the manufacture of these sorts of materials more financially challenging through the implementation of new regulations, a lot of manufacturing was outsourced to foreign markets in order to manage costs. But Lodge planted their flag. Instead of deciding to manufacture their products more cheaply overseas and ship them back to the U.S. for distribution, Bob and Henry led the charge for investment in and modernization of the plant in South Pittsburg, Tennessee, and have ultimately ended up being the sole manufacturer of cast iron cookware in the United States.

In doing so, Lodge remains the main employer in South Pittsburg, employing a good 15% of the entire population and sustaining the life of a little Southern town that, in all likelihood, would have withered on the vine. And in the process, Lodge Manufacturing has established permanent brand recognition of a true Southern icon.

As significant as its commitment to modernization and keeping manufacturing in the U.S. have been to the survival of Lodge Manufacturing Company, it is the thoughtful and elegant extension of the product line that has given the company wings in the past two decades. The elegance of the Tableware Cast Iron Mini Servers and the durability and versatility of the black seasoned steel line of sauté and paella pans have helped establish a greater legitimacy of American cast iron in the modern kitchen.

Lodge is at work every day in every one of our five restaurants. We converted from aluminum pans to black steel the minute they were available, and we have stocked the cast iron mini servers for tabletop use since they were developed. I don't want to imagine what our kitchens and dining rooms would look like without Lodge.

As hard as Lodge works at its cast iron, equal attention is given to "non-iron" projects, like this book. The fine folks at Oxmoor House, editor Pam Hoenig, and Lodge Public Relations Manager Mark Kelly put together a wonderful collection of recipes with the first Lodge book, *The Lodge Cast Iron Cookbook*. This sophomore effort has been driven by Lodge's mantra—the first one was great; let's make the next one even better.

Lodge Cast Iron Nation is for a new generation of cast iron cookery lovers. The recipes are fascinating, delicious, and designed to be accessible to everyone. Curated from Lodge's generous network of professional cooks, chefs, and enthusiasts, these recipes illustrate just how versatile and user-friendly cast iron cookware is. From casseroles to chili, skillet pies to fried fish, eggs any way you want them to French toast and crepes, *Lodge Cast Iron Nation* once again shouts loudly, "Cast iron ain't just for cornbread!"

Now take this book and your favorite Dutch oven, or skillet, or griddle and get to work. I'm making myself hungry.

Chef John Currence
City Restaurant Group, Oxford, Mississippi
July 22, 2013

WELCOME!

In 1876 my great-grandfather, Joseph Lodge, sought permanent work. His search had led him on a 10-year journey through the United States, to Cuba and to South America, then back to Pennsylvania. At age 28 he went south to investigate the "iron business." From Chattanooga, Tennessee, he walked 30 miles to South Pittsburg, a small industrial town on the banks of the Tennessee River. There he found employment, married his Pennsylvania fiancée, and began to put down roots. Twenty years later, in 1896, Joseph started the Blacklock Foundry, later renamed Lodge Manufacturing Company. And so my family's journey with cast iron cookware began.

Many Lodge-Kellermann family recipes use what was available in the home. There were no large or small eggs, just fresh eggs from the chicken house. The same for milk: there were two choices, fresh milk and buttermilk. Blossom, the family cow, lived on the lot next to the home that Joseph Lodge built. Butter was churned on the back porch.

In our family, each dish brings with it memories of family and friends and holidays, and the recipes are passed along in the tradition of sharing good food cooked in "our local product."

We grew up with cast iron. We fourth-generation children played in the foundry when our fathers worked on Saturday mornings. When we left home to find our way in the world, we left armed with a skillet and a Dutch oven for our kitchens. Whenever we were given a piece of cast iron passed on by our mother or grandmother, we had a family treasure. My favorite Dutch oven is the one with which my mother started keeping house in 1935.

If Joseph Lodge had known in 1876 what the future held, his 30-mile walk would have been a happy one. He sought a hometown for himself and his wife-to-be. He would be pleased to know his great-grandchildren still live in South Pittsburg and his company still makes quality products for cooks everywhere.

So it is with great pleasure and humility that I offer this collection of recipes. Just like the cast iron cookware in which they were prepared, our family's recipes should always be shared. May your journey with Lodge cast iron be a happy one.

—Carolyn Kellermann Millhiser

Joseph Lodge holding
William Leslie Kellermann;
Susan Catherine Lodge;
Charles Richard "Dick" Kellermann Jr.;
Joseph Lodge Kellermann;
Francis Kellermann;
William Leslie Kellermann.

Dick and Lynda Kellermann on their Kentucky farm.

Fred Millhiser and grandson Matthew Millhiser fishing on the Eastern Shore of Maryland.

Three generations of Lodge family cooks: (L to R) Granny "Pat" Lodge, Sarah Lodge and Masey Lodge Stubblefield.

John Lodge at the U.S. Coast Guard Academy, New London, CT, 1945

Chicken Piquant,
page 36

LODGE·KELLERMANN
FAMILY FAVORITES

LODGE FAMILY TREE

The following recipes are family-favorites from five generations

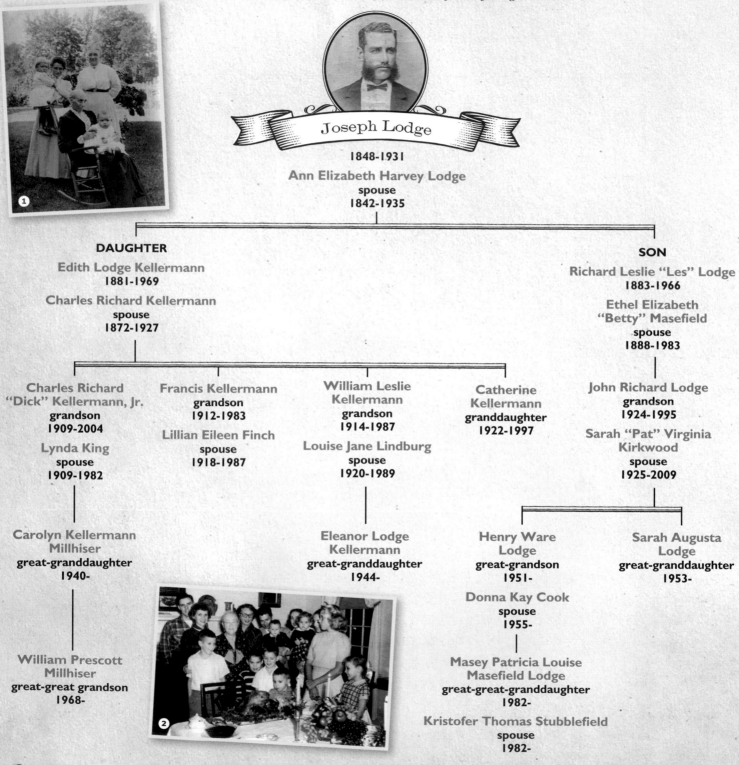

Joseph Lodge
1848-1931
Ann Elizabeth Harvey Lodge
spouse
1842-1935

DAUGHTER
Edith Lodge Kellermann
1881-1969
Charles Richard Kellermann
spouse
1872-1927

SON
Richard Leslie "Les" Lodge
1883-1966
Ethel Elizabeth
"Betty" Masefield
spouse
1888-1983

Charles Richard
"Dick" Kellermann, Jr.
grandson
1909-2004
Lynda King
spouse
1909-1982

Francis Kellermann
grandson
1912-1983
Lillian Eileen Finch
spouse
1918-1987

William Leslie
Kellermann
grandson
1914-1987
Louise Jane Lindburg
spouse
1920-1989

Catherine
Kellermann
granddaughter
1922-1997

John Richard Lodge
grandson
1924-1995
Sarah "Pat" Virginia
Kirkwood
spouse
1925-2009

Carolyn Kellermann
Millhiser
great-granddaughter
1940-

Eleanor Lodge
Kellermann
great-granddaughter
1944-

Henry Ware
Lodge
great-grandson
1951-
Donna Kay Cook
spouse
1955-

Sarah Augusta
Lodge
great-granddaughter
1953-

William Prescott
Millhiser
great-great grandson
1968-

Masey Patricia Louise
Masefield Lodge
great-great-granddaughter
1982-
Kristofer Thomas Stubblefield
spouse
1982-

❶ Edith Lodge Kellermann holding Charles Richard "Dick" Kellermann, Jr.; Martha Brinton "Aunt Mattie" Lodge; Susan Catherine Maison Lodge holding Joseph Lodge Kellermann.

❷ At a mid-1950s Thanksgiving celebration. **Top Row (L to R):** John Lodge, Alice Kirkwood, Greatie Miriam (Cooke) Spratling, Margaret (Spratling) Erskine, Howard Syler (holding Richard Syler), Miriam Ann Syler, Sarah Lodge being held by Sarah "Pat" Kirkwood Lodge and Bonnie Erskine. **Bottom Row (L to R):** Kenneth Kirkwood, Jr., Dick Lodge, E.H Kirkwood, Henry Lodge, and Nancy Kirkwood.

Crisp Biscuits, page 16

CRISP BISCUITS

Vegetable oil
1 cup all-purpose flour (measured before sifting)
1 teaspoon baking powder
½ teaspoon salt
¼ teaspoon baking soda
¼ teaspoon sugar
¼ cup vegetable shortening
⅓ cup buttermilk

1. Preheat the oven to 400°. Lightly oil a Lodge 14-inch cast iron round baking pan.

2. Sift the dry ingredients into a medium bowl. Cut in the shortening with a pastry blender until the mixture resembles coarse meal. Add the buttermilk all at once, and stir until the mixture is well dampened.

3. Turn the dough onto a lightly floured board. Roll out to ⅓- to ½-inch thickness, and cut with a 3-inch round cutter. Pat the scraps together, and cut out more biscuits. Place the biscuits ½ inch apart on the prepared baking pan. Bake until the tops are golden brown, about 15 minutes. **Makes 6 biscuits**

Lynda King Kellermann (1909-1982) shared with her mother, Eula Renfro King, a love for cooking for her family. Every morning Eula made these **Crisp Biscuits** for breakfast on her Barren County, Kentucky, farm. She knew exactly how many sticks of wood to put into the firebox of the woodstove to bake a proper biscuit. Years later, Lynda carried on her mother's breakfast tradition by regularly making pancakes for her husband and children. In 1974, she added these **Oatmeal Buttermilk Pancakes** to her line-up after clipping the recipe from an issue of *Southern Living*.

OATMEAL BUTTERMILK PANCAKES

2 cups quick-cooking oats
½ teaspoon baking soda
2½ cups buttermilk
1 cup all-purpose flour
2 tablespoons sugar
2 teaspoons baking powder
1 teaspoon salt
⅓ cup salad oil
2 large eggs, beaten

1. In a large bowl, combine the oats, baking soda, and buttermilk. Let stand 5 minutes.

2. In a small bowl, combine the flour, sugar, baking powder, and salt. Add the flour mixture to the oat mixture along with the oil and eggs. Stir until blended.

3. Lightly oil a Lodge Reversible Pro Grid Iron Griddle. Place over medium heat. Wait a few minutes, then fling a drop of water onto the griddle; if the water dances, the griddle's ready! For each pancake, pour about ¼ cup batter onto the griddle. Cook until golden brown on both sides, turning only once.
Makes 14 to 16 (3-inch) pancakes

Lodge-Kellermann Family Memories

Whenever Lynda prepared pancakes, her husband, Charles Richard "Dick" Kellermann, Jr. (1909-2004), would tell his children how his mother, Edith Kellermann (1881-1969), used pancakes to play a practical joke on her seven children. On April 1, she would cut rounds of white flannel, dip them in the pancake batter, and cook them up like pancakes. Each child's serving included at least one of these "special" pancakes. When each child discovered the flannel cake, their mama would gleefully exclaim "April Fool!"

Oatmeal Buttermilk Pancakes

Lodge-Kellermann Family Memories

Sarah "Pat" Kirkwood Lodge grew up in the home of her grandmother near Auburn, Alabama. After she and John Richard Lodge married in 1948, they began their life together in married student housing at the University of the South in Sewanee, Tennessee, where John was an undergraduate student and then a student in the School of Theology. Their life together took them to Tennessee, Alabama, Georgia, and even Alaska, where John served Episcopal congregations. Pat collected recipes from good cooks in communities everywhere the Lodge family lived.

Bran Muffins

BRAN MUFFINS

6 cups All-Bran cereal	4 large eggs, beaten
2 cups boiling water	1 quart buttermilk
1 cup (2 sticks) salted butter, melted	5 cups bleached all-purpose flour
	5 teaspoons baking soda
2 cups sugar	2 teaspoons salt

1. Put 2 cups of the cereal in a large bowl. Pour the boiling water over cereal, and let stand a few minutes. Mix in the melted butter, sugar, eggs, buttermilk, and the remaining 4 cups cereal.

2. In another large bowl, sift the flour, baking soda, and salt together. Add to the wet mixture, mixing thoroughly.

3. Using a well-buttered Lodge cast iron muffin pan, you can bake however many muffins you like or transfer the batter to an airtight container and refrigerate for up to 1 week. The batter is good to go as soon as it is mixed.

4. When you are ready to bake, preheat the oven to 425°. Fill the wells of the muffin pan to just below the tops. Bake 15 to 20 minutes. Poke a broom straw or toothpick into the muffins. If it comes out clean, the muffins are ready.

Makes 36 muffins

arah "Pat" Kirkwood Lodge (1925-2009), who was married to founder Joseph Lodge's grandson, John Richard Lodge (1924-1995), often made quick breads like Pumpkin Bread to serve for breakfast and at afternoon tea or to give new neighbors. It is believed that this bran muffin recipe came from the Hemlock Inn in North Carolina, one of Pat and John's favorite places to visit.

PUMPKIN BREAD

1 (16-ounce) can pumpkin puree (about 1⅔ cups)	2 teaspoons baking soda
	1 teaspoon baking powder
3 cups sugar	1 teaspoon ground nutmeg
1 cup vegetable oil	1 teaspoon ground cinnamon
4 large eggs, beaten	1 teaspoon ground allspice
3½ cups all-purpose flour	½ teaspoon ground cloves
2 teaspoons salt	⅔ cup orange juice

1. Preheat the oven to 350°. Grease two Lodge 10 x 5 x 3-inch cast iron loaf pans.

2. In a large bowl, combine the pumpkin, sugar, oil, and eggs, and beat until fluffy.

3. In a medium bowl, sift the dry ingredients together. Add the dry ingredients to the pumpkin mixture alternately with the orange juice.

4. Divide the batter between the two prepared loaf pans. Bake about 45 minutes. Let cool in the pans for 10 minutes before unmolding onto a plate.

Makes 2 loaves

KENTUCKY STATE FAIR PRIZE-WINNING ROLLS

1 cup whole milk, scalded
⅔ cup sugar
⅔ cup vegetable shortening
1 tablespoon salt
1 cup mashed potatoes (mash them with some of their cooking water—they should be kind of soupy)

1 (¼-ounce) envelope active dry yeast
½ cup lukewarm water (about 110°)
2 large eggs (if you'd like a lighter roll, separate the eggs and use only the whites), well beaten
5 to 5½ cups all-purpose flour
Butter

1. In a large bowl, combine the scalded milk, sugar, shortening, salt, and mashed potatoes until well mixed. In a small bowl, dissolve the yeast in the lukewarm water.

2. When the milk has cooled to lukewarm, add the eggs, dissolved yeast, and enough of the flour to make a soft dough.

3. Put the dough in a bowl greased with butter. Grease the top of the dough. Cover with plastic wrap, and refrigerate overnight or up to 2 days.

4. Using your hands, form the rolls to be about 2 inches in diameter and about 1 inch high, then place them about 1 inch apart on a Lodge 14-inch cast iron round baking pan. Let them rise, uncovered, until doubled in size, about 1 hour. (You can also freeze the rolls once formed. If you do, let them thaw at room temperature for 3 hours before baking.)

5. Preheat the oven to 400°. Bake the rolls until golden brown on top, about 20 minutes. **Makes 20 rolls**

Lodge-Kellermann Family Memories

In 1932, Lynda King Kellermann came to South Pittsburg, Tennessee, to teach home economics and French at the high school. Elizabeth Lodge Kellermann, granddaughter of Joseph Lodge, suggested her oldest brother, Dick, have a date with her new teacher, the shy Miss King. During their courtship, Dick would throw pebbles at the bedroom window to get her to come downstairs. Lynda and Charles Richard "Dick" Kellermann were married in June 1935 on the King farm.

Glazed Ham Balls

GLAZED HAM BALLS

¾ pound ground pork
½ pound ground fresh or cooked ham
⅔ cup quick-cooking oats
1 large egg, beaten
½ cup whole milk
⅓ cup firmly packed light brown
  sugar

2 tablespoons all-purpose flour
1 teaspoon dry mustard
⅔ cup fruit juice (orange,
  pineapple, or peach)
2 tablespoons cider vinegar
⅓ cup dark corn syrup
6 whole cloves

1. Preheat the oven to 300°.

2. In a medium bowl, mix the ground meats, oats, egg, and milk together until well combined. Mold the mixture into balls about the size of a walnut, and arrange in a single layer in a Lodge 12-inch cast iron skillet. Bake for 45 minutes. Carefully drain off any fat in the skillet.

3. Combine the remaining ingredients in a Lodge Chef Skillet, and cook over medium heat, stirring almost constantly, until the brown sugar, flour, and mustard are dissolved and the sauce is slightly thickened. Pour the sauce over the ham balls, and bake another 20 minutes, basting once or twice. **Serves 4 to 5**

DEVILED CRABMEAT

Vegetable oil
½ cup (1 stick) salted butter, divided
½ cup minced onion
½ cup minced celery
¼ cup minced green bell pepper
1 tablespoon chopped fresh parsley
2 cups soft breadcrumbs, buttered
½ cup whole milk or heavy cream
2 large eggs, beaten
1 large egg, hard-cooked, peeled,
  and chopped

1 tablespoon vinegar
1 tablespoon Worcestershire sauce
1 teaspoon salt
¼ teaspoon dried thyme
Dash of cayenne pepper
Few drops of Tabasco sauce
Few drops of fresh lemon juice
1 pound lump crabmeat, picked
  over for shells and cartilage

1. Preheat the oven to 425°. Oil 10 Lodge 9-ounce cast iron oval mini servers.

2. Melt 6 tablespoons of the butter in a Lodge 12-inch cast iron skillet over medium-low heat. Add the next 4 ingredients, and cook until softened.

3. In a medium bowl, combine 1 cup of the breadcrumbs, the milk, raw and cooked eggs, vinegar, and next 6 ingredients with the sautéed vegetables. Add the crabmeat, and combine gently, trying not to break up the crabmeat too much.

4. Divide the mixture among the prepared mini servers. Cover with the remaining 1 cup breadcrumbs. Melt reserved 2 tablespoons butter; drizzle over breadcrumbs. Bake until bubbling, 10 to 15 minutes. **Serves 10**

Carolyn Kellermann Millhiser remembers the delicious crab dish from the vacations spent with her inlaws at the Eastern Shore of Maryland or at Virginia Beach, Virginia. Frederick Millhiser would catch and pick the crabs, and Priscilla would prepare the deviled crab dish.

CHICKEN CROQUETTES

2 or 3 tablespoons salted butter
¼ cup all-purpose flour
Salt and black pepper
1 cup whole milk
2 cups cooked chicken, cut into very small pieces

1 tablespoon Worcestershire sauce
½ cup chopped fresh parsley
1 large egg, beaten
½ cup fine buttered breadcrumbs
Vegetable oil

1. Melt the butter in a Lodge 8-inch cast iron skillet over medium heat. Add the flour and salt and pepper to taste, and stir for a few minutes, but don't let the roux color at all. Slowly pour in the milk, stirring all the while, and continue to stir until the white sauce thickens, about 5 minutes. Stir in the chicken, Worcestershire, and parsley.

2. Transfer the mixture to a medium bowl, and refrigerate. Put the beaten egg in a small bowl and the crumbs on a plate. When the chicken mixture is cool, for each croquette, take a rounded tablespoon of the mixture; first dredge it in the crumbs, then coat with the beaten egg, then dredge again in the crumbs. Refrigerate the croquettes in a single layer in a covered dish for several hours to firm up.

3. In a Lodge 10-inch cast iron skillet, heat 1 inch of oil over medium to high heat. When the oil is hot, fry the croquettes in batches (you don't want to crowd them in the pan), turning them often, until they are golden brown. Drain on paper towels. **Serves 6 to 8**

Lodge-Kellermann Family Memories

Edith Lodge Kellermann's niece, Elizabeth Lodge Sherwood, remembers watching her aunt make these croquettes during the 1930s, and her oldest granddaughter, Carolyn Kellermann Millhiser, remembers the same croquette recipe being prepared by her grandmother for luncheons 15 or 20 years later.

Edith's table would be set with flowers from her garden, round hand-crocheted place mats, white linen napkins in silver napkin rings, individual salt cellars, and blue willow china. "Gramma" taught her grandchildren how to set a table with the silverware placed the width of a thumb from the edge of the table. The tea wagon was to the right of the hostess at the head of the table. Once the dishes were served, they, along with pitchers of iced tea and ice water, were left on the tea wagon within easy reach if anyone wanted seconds.

e sure to serve this dip with plenty of Fritos Scoops or tortilla chips," says Sarah Augusta Lodge, great-granddaughter of Joseph Lodge.

CORN DIP

2 (11-ounce) cans Mexicorn (corn kernels with red and green peppers)
1 (10-ounce) can shoepeg corn
3 green onions, chopped

1 cup sour cream
1 cup mayonnaise
1 tablespoon ground cumin
Fresh lime juice to taste
Salt and black pepper to taste

1. Drain the corn. Combine all the ingredients in a Lodge 5-quart cast iron Dutch oven, and heat through over medium-low heat.

2. When ready to serve, transfer to two Lodge 1-pint cast iron Country Kettles. **Makes 6 cups**

a cooking secret from Sarah

To save time, make this dip the day ahead, and then heat right before serving. A squeeze of lime juice is the key to its fresh flavor.

Lentils have a definite affinity for curry spices, which form a fragrant, savory broth when combined with the tomatoes in this recipe from **William Prescott Millhiser**, great-great grandson of Joseph Lodge. William likes to serve this spooned over hot mashed sweet potatoes. This recipe is adapted from *Vegetariana* by **Nava Atlas**.

CURRIED LENTILS
WITH SPINACH AND
MASHED SWEET POTATOES

1 cup dried lentils, rinsed and picked over

1 tablespoon safflower oil

2 garlic cloves, minced

½ pound fresh spinach leaves, stemmed, washed well, and chopped

1 (14-ounce) can peeled whole plum tomatoes, undrained, chopped

2 teaspoons good-quality curry powder, store-bought or home-made, or more or less to taste

½ teaspoon grated peeled fresh ginger

¼ teaspoon ground cinnamon

¼ teaspoon ground nutmeg

Hot mashed sweet potatoes

1. Place the lentils in a small saucepan, add water to cover generously, and bring to a boil. Reduce the heat to a simmer, and cook until the lentils are tender but still keep their shape, 6 to 10 minutes, then drain.

2. Heat the oil in a Lodge 5-quart cast iron Dutch oven over medium-low heat. Add the garlic, and cook, stirring, for 1 minute. Add the spinach, cover, and steam until it wilts, 6 to 10 minutes.

3. Add the lentils, tomatoes, and spices; cover and simmer over very low heat for 20 minutes, allowing the flavors to meld. Serve over the mashed sweet potatoes. **Serves 4 to 6**

a cooking secret from **William**

Look for a good-quality curry powder at specialty markets or online.

A CAST IRON JOURNEY

William P. "Will" Millhiser

*Member, Lodge Manufacturing Co. Board of Directors, 2010-present,
grandson of Charles Richard "Dick" Kellermann, Jr. (President of Lodge, 1949-1973), and
great-great grandson of Joseph Lodge (Founder of Lodge, 1896)*

My first cast iron skillet arrived 20 years ago, the same year I was questioning a career in corporate America and a meat-centered diet. Shortly after obtaining the skillet—and doing some soul searching—I decided to quit my job and become a vegetarian. So I packed my skillet, camping gear, and skis into my Honda to "go west, young man, go west and grow up with the country." I began to wonder what it was like in 1876 when my great-great grandfather Joe Lodge began his 11-year odyssey by foot, rail, and boat from Philadelphia to New Orleans to Cuba to New York to Argentina to Peru to Panama to South Pittsburg, Tennessee. My journey seemed less glamorous.

After two and a half days along Interstate 80, I arrived in Salt Lake City, stayed the winter, and became a professional ski instructor—skiing by day and exploring the art of cast iron vegetarian cooking by night. The skillet taught me that cast iron isn't only for cooking meat. It's great for sautéing vegetables, mixing rice and beans, simmering curries, baking small pizzas, and much more. The experience also revealed that cast iron cookware is like a pair of skis: Both need to be seasoned regularly for peak performance, but, unlike skis, it's impossible to hurt a cast iron skillet. For example, the kind of "rookie mistakes" that leave burn marks on stainless steel aren't even visible on cast iron.

It was in Salt Lake City that I discovered my favorite vegetarian recipe for cast iron cooking in Nava Atlas's 1993 book *Vegetariana* (Little, Brown & Co.; now out of print): Curried Lentils with Spinach, reproduced with slight modifications here.

After collecting dozens of cast iron pieces over the past 20 years, I now realize that my second piece is the favorite. It's a 5-quart Dutch oven acquired during the 1996 Lodge Manufacturing Company Centennial Celebration. I love it for four reasons. First, its 10¼-inch diameter means the lid fits the number 8 skillet perfectly. Second is its versatility; a Dutch oven does everything the cast iron skillet can, and more. For instance, it's ideal for baking long, slow-rise bread recipes and stews. Third is the portability of the Dutch oven. We live in Manhattan and often attend potluck dinner parties. My approach is always the same: Cook a hearty dish in the Dutch oven, put on the lid, and carry the warm vessel on the subway. Finally is the industrial design; I'm not sure any other object in the kitchen blends as much functionality with elegant simplicity. Look at the profile of any Lodge Dutch oven, paying careful attention to the angles and curves. Aesthetically, it is a work of art belonging on the shelf at the Museum of Modern Art next to the minimalist designs of Dieter Rams and Jony Ive.

Upside-Down Meatloaf

This recipe is from *Taste/Son of Best of Taste*, a collection of recipes from the "Taste" section of the newspaper that *The Minneapolis Star* published in 1974. It has always been a favorite of Eleanor Lodge Kellermann's family, served with cornbread.

UPSIDE-DOWN MEATLOAF

Vegetable or olive oil
½ cup firmly packed light brown sugar
½ cup ketchup
1½ pounds ground beef
¾ cup crushed cracker crumbs

1 small onion, grated
¾ cup whole milk
2 large eggs, beaten
1½ teaspoons salt
¼ teaspoon black pepper
¼ teaspoon ground ginger

1. Preheat the oven to 350°.

2. Oil a Lodge 10 x 5 x 3-inch cast iron loaf pan. Press the brown sugar evenly over the bottom, then evenly spread the ketchup over the sugar.

3. In a medium bowl, mix the remaining ingredients together, and shape into a loaf. Press firmly into the pan. Bake for 1 hour.

4. Remove from the oven. Let the meatloaf cool in the pan for 5 to 10 minutes. Turn the pan upside down onto a serving platter to unmold the loaf. Cut into slices to serve. Can be reheated. **Serves 4 to 6**

Lodge-Kellermann Family Memories

Sarah "Pat" Kirkwood Lodge's daughter, Sarah Augusta Lodge, remembers, "Mother cooked a well-balanced meal six nights of every week." Pork Chops with Tomato Rice was one of the John Lodge family's favorites. Sarah thinks it was one of her mother's favorites as well, as the ingredients are few. Pat could fix the vegetables and salad while the entrée was simmering in the skillet.

PORK CHOPS WITH TOMATO RICE

4 thick-cut pork chops
½ teaspoon salt
Black pepper
1 (16-ounce) can stewed tomatoes, undrained

½ cup water
½ cup long-grain rice

1. Heat a Lodge 12-inch cast iron skillet over medium heat until hot. Brown the pork chops on both sides in the hot pan. Sprinkle with the salt and season to taste with pepper. Add the tomatoes and water to the skillet; sprinkle in the rice.

2. Cover the skillet tightly, reduce the heat to low, and cook until the chops are tender, 50 to 60 minutes. Add more water, if necessary, to keep the chops from sticking. **Serves 4**

"This beautiful recipe," says Masey Lodge Stubblefield, great-great granddaughter of Joseph Lodge and daughter of current Lodge President, Henry Lodge, and wife, Donna, "was born out of a Friday night in which junk food cravings were high, and spring was in full force. It blew us away with its smoky, crispy crust topped with a variety of hot and cold fresh veggies and greens."

GRILLED PIZZA

6 plum tomatoes, skewered and charred on the grill, about 5 minutes per side
3 garlic cloves, minced
Salt and black pepper
1 red onion, sliced
Shiitake mushrooms, stems discarded
½ pound Italian sausage, casings removed

1 pound refrigerated pizza dough
2 tablespoons olive oil
Fresh mozzarella cheese, thinly sliced, cut into small pieces, or shredded
Chopped fresh basil or baby arugula mixed with a dash of olive oil, salt, and fresh lemon juice

1. In a medium bowl, combine the grilled tomatoes, garlic, and salt and pepper to taste, mixing and crushing the tomatoes into a sauce. Set aside.

2. Grill the onion and mushrooms directly on the grill or using a Lodge Reversible Pro Grid Iron Griddle. As you finish grilling them, transfer to a Lodge 9-ounce cast iron oval mini server on the top rack of the grill to keep warm. Meanwhile, cook the sausage in a Lodge 8-inch cast iron skillet on the side of the grill or attached burner until no longer pink, breaking into small pieces.

3. Lightly flour a work surface and the pizza dough; roll it out ½ inch thick, trimming off any excess. (Masey recommends brushing any dough trimmings with oil and garlic powder and popping them in the toaster oven for about 5 minutes on 350° for a delightful snack/appetizer.) Brush one side of dough with some of the oil, and place on a Lodge 14-inch cast iron round baking pan, oil side down, and grill for 2 to 3 minutes.

4. Remove the pan from the grill, brush the top side of the dough with oil, and flip it over. Top the grilled side of the dough with the tomato sauce, then scatter your choice of the grilled toppings and sausage over the top. Finally, cover with mozzarella. Place the pan back on the grill, close the lid, and cook for 4 to 5 minutes. If the mozzarella hasn't melted, remove the pizza from the grill, and stick under the broiler for another few minutes to melt.

5. Top with the basil or dressed arugula, and serve. **Makes one 14-inch pizza; serves 4**

Lodge-Kellermann Family Memories

As a young Lodge, my father, Henry Lodge, talked about having to eat quickly with three other siblings around the table. Apparently, with my grandmother's cooking (Sarah "Pat" Kirkwood Lodge), things disappeared quickly and you didn't want to be the last person left to fill your plate. It appears in our new generations that this behavior of gobbling up food might be a genetic predisposition. It is most commonly witnessed at Thanksgiving when the pumpkin pie arrives.

Everyone in the Lodge family loves food, but more important, we always seem to be on a quest to find some new way to thrill our taste buds. Luckily, this tends to lead me to search for healthy alternatives to the junk food I love. In this way, I find myself often standing in front of a grill. As it happened, I got lucky enough to marry a fellow griller, Kris Stubblefield. We both share a passion for the fire-breathing beast and the way that it can transform food. In fact, I have found that the best way to introduce new veggies to my meat-and-potato-loving husband is via the grill.

—Masey Lodge Stubblefield

Lodge-Kellermann Family Memories

For almost as long as I can remember, I've been in a kitchen. Running a single-parent household in Sewanee, Tennessee, it was hard for my mother, Lynn Stubblefield, to get dinner on the table, what with my brother, Nick, and me running amuck, as little boys do. She combatted this by Tom Sawyer-ing us into becoming her "countertop height" sous chefs. With the help of a kitchen chair, I could stir a skillet with the best of them. The first dish I learned to prepare was my great-grandmother's Baked Spaghetti. I still believe it to be the best spaghetti I've had.

My early education in the kitchen transformed into a passion for cooking, and I was lucky enough to marry Masey. Fortunately for me, she shares my excitement for cooking, and if we are so blessed, we hope to pass that on to our children. Until that day, we'll share the responsibilities of sous chef.

—*Kris Stubblefield*

A recipe passed down from his great-grandmother Dorothea Elizabeth Johnson, this is the first dish Kris Stubblefield learned how to make when he was growing up.

BAKED SPAGHETTI

2 tablespoons olive oil
4 large garlic cloves, minced
2 large yellow onions, chopped
1½ teaspoons salt, divided
2 pounds 80% lean ground beef
1 (28-ounce) can crushed tomatoes
1 (16-ounce) can tomato sauce
2 tablespoons balsamic vinegar or dry red wine
2 tablespoons sugar
1 tablespoon garlic powder
1 tablespoon dried basil
1 tablespoon dried tarragon
1 teaspoon red pepper flakes, or more to taste
16 ounces angel hair pasta
Mozzarella cheese as needed

1. Heat a Lodge 12-inch cast iron skillet over medium heat. Add the oil, garlic, onions, and ¼ teaspoon of the salt, and cook, stirring a few times, until the onions are softened, 8 to 10 minutes. Add the ground beef, and cook until no longer pink, breaking up any clumps of meat. Drain off any excess fat.

2. In a Lodge 5-quart cast iron Dutch oven, combine the tomatoes, tomato sauce, vinegar, sugar, garlic powder, basil, tarragon, red pepper, and remaining 1¼ teaspoons salt. Simmer over medium to medium-low heat for 10 to 15 minutes, then stir in the browned ground beef. Wipe out the skillet, and set aside.

3. Preheat the oven to 350°. Put a large pot of water on to boil.

4. Cook the pasta according to package directions. Drain and pour the pasta into the skillet you used to cook the beef. Pour the spaghetti sauce over the pasta. Shred as much mozzarella as you like over the top, covering the sauce. Bake until the cheese is melted and starts to brown, 15 to 20 minutes.
Serves 6

In 1963 Catherine Kellermann (1922-1997), the youngest child of Edith (1881-1969) and Charles Richard Kellermann (1872-1927), returned to South Pittsburg, Tennessee, to live with her elderly mother in the Lodge home. In the ensuing years, Catherine opened her home to her 18 nieces and nephews and their children, especially during the gathering of the Lodge family for the annual shareholders meeting. Chicken Piquant was her signature dish for small family gatherings.

CHICKEN PIQUANT

1 pound fresh mushrooms, sliced	¼ cup soy sauce
4 skin-on, bone-in chicken breasts or leg quarters	2 tablespoons olive oil
	2 tablespoons light brown sugar
2 tablespoons cornstarch or all-purpose flour	1 garlic clove, crushed
	¼ teaspoon dried oregano
¼ cup water	Hot cooked white rice
¾ cup rosé wine	

1. Preheat the oven to 350°.

2. Lightly oil a Lodge 12-inch cast iron skillet. Scatter the mushrooms evenly over the bottom. Set the chicken pieces on top.

3. In a small bowl, mix the cornstarch and water together. Mix in the wine, soy sauce, 2 tablespoons oil, brown sugar, garlic, and oregano, and pour over the chicken. Bake, uncovered, until the chicken is tender and cooked through, 1 to 1½ hours, basting with the pan juices occasionally. Serve with rice. **Serves 4**

A FAMILY TREASURE

Carolyn Kellermann Millhiser

*Daughter of Charles Richard "Dick" Kellermann, Jr. (President of Lodge, 1949-1973)
and great-granddaughter of Joseph Lodge*

When I was a child in South Pittsburg, Tennessee, in the 1940s, my first piece of Lodge cast iron was given to me by my father. It was a salesman's sample of a "preserving kettle" with a lid. In the 1930s, Lodge made a deep Dutch oven with a lip (in size 8 only) to be used as an all-around cooking vessel. I was too young at the time to start cooking and much less ready for making jams, jellies, and pickled vegetables. This pot quickly became one of my favorite toys, as I often filled it with sand, berries, and leaves when I played with my dolls under the shade trees in the yards of my parents or my next-door grandmother, Edith Lodge Kellermann.

It wasn't until years later when I received my next Dutch oven, a number 8, which Lodge still makes. When I acquired the new, larger pot, I had long since graduated from "cooking" sand and berries! But, I never parted ways with my original kettle, and it is still a part of my cast iron collection today.

Since then, I finished school, moved to New Jersey, married, had two sons, and started the tradition of cooking family suppers. I made many Sunday dinners in that Dutch oven, including my favorite comfort food, baked chicken with dressing.

After 38 years, I came home to Tennessee. In 2000, my husband and I moved into the home that Joseph Lodge built in 1877. My father, Dick Kellermann, still lived next door in the house where he was born in 1909 and where I grew up. After his death I finally got my real "preserving kettle"…the deep Dutch oven with which my parents started housekeeping in 1935. At the time, my father just casually went into the warehouse part of the plant and picked up the deep Dutch oven along with a number 8 skillet and a chicken fryer to equip their kitchen for cooking. I watched my mother prepare some of our most memorable family meals in that pot. I love all of my cast iron pieces, but my real "preserving kettle" is my favorite—it reminds me the most of my upbringing, and I use it the most often.

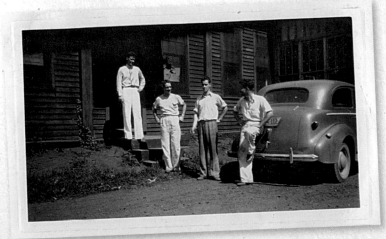

Kellermann boys: (left to right) Francis, Dick, Harvey, Leslie at entrance to Lodge office

My grandparents on my father's side, Priscilla Bacon Millhiser (1911-2008) and Frederick Millhiser (1910-1998), enjoyed vacationing on the Eastern Shore of Maryland and Delaware, with its abundant regional seafood and white beaches," remembers William Prescott Millhiser, member of the Lodge Board of Directors. "They would rent a cottage, and their sons and families would come to visit. Great fun was had by all. Grandpa would fish in the surf; his grandsons would play in the waves."

BAY COUNTRY
OYSTERS & FISH

¼ cup (½ stick) margarine or salted butter
1 cup finely chopped onion
1 pound flounder fillets, each cut into 4 pieces
1 (4-ounce) can sliced mushrooms, drained and juice reserved
½ pint (8 ounces) shucked oysters, drained and liquor reserved
½ cup liquid (combination of juice and liquor from mushrooms and oysters)
¼ cup dry sherry
½ teaspoon salt
⅛ teaspoon black pepper
Hot cooked white or wild rice

1. Melt the margarine in a Lodge 12-inch cast iron skillet over medium heat. Add the onion, and cook, stirring, until glazed, 8 to 10 minutes.

2. Spread the onion evenly in the skillet. Lay the fish fillets over the onion. Spread the mushrooms over the fish. In a small bowl, combine the mushroom and oyster liquid, sherry, salt, and pepper. Pour over the fish and mushrooms. Cover and simmer over medium heat until the fish flakes easily when tested with a fork, 5 to 8 minutes.

3. Add the oysters to the skillet, and simmer, uncovered, basting frequently with the pan juices, until the edges of the oysters curl, about 5 minutes. Serve in a bowl over rice. **Serves 4**

This recipe from Cathy Black comes from her sister, Tammy Lee of Madisonville, Tennessee. Her husband's aunt, Cathy Lee Plenge, gave Tammy the recipe. Aunt Cathy lives in Phoenix, Arizona, and has a huge garden with lots of zucchini, so she has many zucchini recipes. This is Tammy's favorite soup recipe. She can't wait for the zucchini crop to come in each summer so she can make it.

ZUCCHINI SOUP

6   small zucchini, trimmed and
    shredded
Salt
1   tablespoon olive oil
2   tablespoons salted butter
2   medium onions, finely minced
1   garlic clove, minced

5   cups chicken stock or broth
2   tablespoons chopped fresh herbs
    of your choice (oregano, basil,
    parsley, chives)
2   tablespoons fresh lemon juice
Freshly ground black pepper

1. Place the shredded zucchini in a colander over a bowl, sprinkle with salt, and allow to drain for about 30 minutes.

2. Heat the oil and butter together in a Lodge 5-quart cast iron Dutch oven over medium heat until the butter melts. Add the onions and garlic, and cook, stirring a few times, until the onions are golden, about 10 minutes.

3. Dry the zucchini on paper towels, and add to the onion mixture. Cook over low heat for about 5 minutes. Add the stock, and simmer for 15 minutes.

4. Using an immersion blender, puree the soup in the pot. Let the soup cool a little. Stir in the herbs and lemon juice, and season with salt and pepper to taste. Reheat and serve. **Serves 4 to 6**

In Lynda King Kellermann's recipe collection, there is a recipe for Creole Cabbage with the notation "Mrs. D. F. Hobbs Fayetteville, Tenn." Mrs. Hobbs was the wife of the family where Lynda boarded when she was teaching home economics. Mrs. Hobbs and her brother, Robert Buchanan, owned *The Lincoln County News.* In the 1940 U.S. Census, Mrs. Hobbs' occupation is listed as social editor of a rural newspaper.

CREOLE CABBAGE

2 tablespoons vegetable oil or bacon drippings

1 medium head cabbage, cored and shredded

1 medium green bell pepper, seeded and chopped

1 medium onion, chopped

1 (15-ounce) can diced tomatoes, undrained, or 3 cups diced fresh tomatoes

Salt

Cayenne pepper

1. Heat the oil in a Lodge 12-inch cast iron skillet over medium heat. Add the cabbage, bell pepper, and onion, and stir to combine. Pour over the tomatoes and season with salt and cayenne to taste. Simmer until the cabbage, onion, and pepper are tender, 20 to 30 minutes. **Serves 6**

Isabelle Bishop (Mrs. Samuel Blaine Bishop, 1891-1989), a Kellermann family friend, sent over this sweet potato dish after a death in the Kellermann family. The recipe immediately became a favorite of the family of Carolyn Kellermann Millhiser. The recipe continues to be a family favorite, and brothers William and Richard Millhiser frequently take Miss Isabelle's Sweet Potato Casserole to friends' gatherings.

Lodge-Kellermann Family Memories

Isabelle Bishop, known for her good Southern dishes, was a charter member of the Marion County Chapter 424 of Eastern Star. She served for many years as the chairman of baked goods sales for the Parent-Teacher Association's annual Country Fair.

Her son George says, "I only enjoyed the results of her cooking. Mother's granddaughters faithfully use this recipe for their traditional Thanksgiving and Christmas dinners.

"Mother was raised on a small farm in McMinn County, and their home was without electricity or running water. She and her three sisters (all excellent cooks) learned to cook on a wood stove. Sweet potatoes were one of the many vegetables that were raised on the farm and were either canned or stored in the cellar (the sweet potatoes were placed under straw, if my memory is correct)."

SWEET POTATO CASSEROLE

3 cups mashed cooked sweet potatoes
1 cup granulated sugar
2 large eggs
½ cup whole milk
½ teaspoon salt
1 teaspoon vanilla extract

1 cup firmly packed light brown sugar
½ cup bleached all-purpose flour
1 cup chopped pecans
¼ cup (½ stick) salted butter or margarine, melted

1. Preheat the oven to 400°. Grease a Lodge Color 3-quart covered casserole or 2 Lodge oval mini servers.

2. In a large bowl, combine the sweet potatoes, granulated sugar, eggs, milk, salt, and vanilla. Pour into the prepared casserole or mini servers.

3. In a small bowl, combine the brown sugar, flour, pecans, and melted butter until well mixed. Sprinkle evenly over the top of the casserole. Bake until the topping browns, 30 to 40 minutes. **Serves 5 to 8**

This recipe was handed down from my great-grandmother to my grandmother, to my mother, to me," says Billie Jobyna Cline Hill, who worked as a secretary at Lodge for almost 60 years. "I still have the original paper written in my great-grandmother's hand on January 1, 1900. My grandmother made notes in the margin about using only cast iron for the icing." Double the icing recipe if you would like to ice the top and side of the cake instead of just using it as a filling.

JULIA CLINE'S JAM CAKE

Cake:
½ cup (1 stick) salted butter, melted
2 cups sugar
6 large egg yolks
2 cups buttermilk
2 teaspoons baking soda
3 cups all-purpose flour
3 tablespoons unsweetened cocoa powder (Billie uses Hershey's)
2 teaspoons ground cinnamon
2 teaspoons ground cloves
2 teaspoons ground nutmeg
2 teaspoons ground allspice
2 cups jam (Billie usually makes it with blackberry)
1 cup dark raisins

Icing:
1 cup whole milk
2 cups sugar
½ cup (1 stick) salted butter
Pinch of baking soda

1. Preheat the oven to 325°. Place a Lodge 10-inch cast iron skillet on a sheet of wax paper, and draw the outline of the bottom of the skillet. Repeat with two more sheets of wax paper. Cut out the circles, and fit into the bottoms of three 10-inch cast iron skillets (if you have only two skillets, you can bake two layers together, then bake the last layer once they come out of the oven). This is necessary, as the cake has a tendency to stick because of the jam.

2. In a large bowl, beat the melted butter and sugar together. Add the egg yolks, one at a time, beating well after each addition. Set aside. In another bowl, mix the buttermilk and baking soda together; let it rise for 4 minutes, then mix well. Whisk the flour, cocoa, and spices together. Add the flour mixture to the butter mixture alternately with the buttermilk mixture, mixing well. Stir in the jam and raisins. Divide the batter evenly among the three prepared skillets. Bake for 30 minutes. Poke a toothpick into each cake; if it doesn't stick, the cake is done. Unmold immediately after removing from the oven. Peel off the wax paper.

3. Combine the milk, sugar, butter, and baking soda in a deep Lodge 10-inch cast iron skillet (it must be cast iron or the filling won't turn out). Cook over medium heat until the temperature of the mixture reaches the hard-ball stage on a candy thermometer, 20 to 25 minutes. (To test, use a teaspoon to take a little of the mixture, and put it in a glass of cold water; it should form a ball.)

4. Set one cake layer on a cake plate. Smooth half the icing over the layer. Set another layer on top of the icing, and smooth the remainder of the icing over it. Top with the final cake layer. **Makes one 3-layer (10-inch) cake**

Lodge-Kellermann Family Memories

In 1951 Charles Richard "Dick" Kellermann, Jr. called Grace Dean Havron, the English teacher at South Pittsburg High School, as he needed to hire a secretary. Mrs. Havron recommended Billie Jobyna Cline Hill, who had graduated third in her class the previous year. Billie graduated from McKenzie Business College on Friday, May 11, 1951, and went to work as a secretary at Lodge on Monday, May 14, 1951. She worked at Lodge almost 60 years and was secretary to four presidents. "Richard Leslie Lodge (1883-1966) was president when Dick hired me but had retired before I finished school and came to work," remembers Billie.

FRUIT AND NUT SQUARES

1 cup sifted all-purpose flour	½ cup raisins
1 teaspoon baking soda	½ cup (1 stick) margarine or butter
½ teaspoon ground cinnamon	2 large eggs, beaten
1 cup water	1 teaspoon vanilla extract
½ cup chopped pitted prunes	½ cup nuts of your choice, chopped
½ cup chopped pitted dates	

1. Preheat the oven to 350°. Grease a Lodge 10½-inch cast iron square skillet.

2. Sift the flour, baking soda, and cinnamon into a small bowl. Set aside.

3. In a 3-quart saucepan, bring the water, prunes, dates, and raisins to a boil. Reduce the heat to low, and simmer for 4 minutes. Remove from the heat. Add the margarine, and stir until melted. Let cool, then stir in the beaten eggs, vanilla, and nuts. Add the flour mixture, and stir until well blended.

4. Pour the batter into the prepared skillet. Bake until a toothpick inserted in the center comes out clean, about 30 minutes. Let cool, then cut into 2-inch squares. The squares freeze well. **Makes 16 (2-inch) squares**

hese two desserts are from long-time Lodge family friends. The Fruit and Nut Squares recipe is from Nancy E. Coppinger Holtcamp, who moved to Marion County in the 1860s. The Luscious Squares recipe is from Wilma Leona Neff (1909-1976), a librarian at South Pittsburg High School who was a wonderful cook. Her recipe was published in the December 1974 issue of *Southern Living,* a first for South Pittsburg.

LUSCIOUS SQUARES

½ cup (1 stick) salted butter or margarine, softened	2 tablespoons all-purpose flour
1 cup all-purpose flour	1 cup English walnuts or pecans, chopped
2 tablespoons granulated sugar	2 tablespoons salted butter, melted
2 large eggs, beaten	2 or 3 tablespoons milk
1½ cups firmly packed light brown sugar	1 to 1½ cups confectioners' sugar

1. Preheat the oven to 400°. Grease a Lodge 10½-inch cast iron square skillet.

2. In a medium bowl, combine the butter, flour, and granulated sugar; mix until smooth and creamy. Spread the dough evenly in the prepared skillet. Bake until lightly browned, about 10 minutes. Remove from oven.

3. While the pastry bakes, combine the eggs, brown sugar, and flour in another medium bowl; mix until smooth. Stir in the walnuts.

4. Reduce the oven temperature to 350°. Pour the filling evenly over the browned crust, and bake for 30 to 35 minutes.

5. While the filling bakes, combine the melted butter, milk, and confectioners' sugar in a small bowl, stirring well. When the filling is done, spread the glaze over it while still hot. Let cool, and cut into squares. **Makes about 36 squares**

Luscious Squares

This is a pie that Carolyn Kellermann Millhiser's mother, Lynda King Kellermann, would make. It uses staple ingredients found in a Southern kitchen pantry—eggs, milk, and butter from the farm; and flour, cornmeal, and vanilla from the store. Cornmeal is what distinguishes the pie from other custard pies.

CHESS PIE

5   large egg yolks
2   cups sugar
1   cup whole milk
½   cup (1 stick) salted butter (do not substitute), melted

1   tablespoon all-purpose flour
1   tablespoon white cornmeal
1   teaspoon vanilla extract
2   unbaked 8-inch piecrusts (recipe follows)

1. Preheat the oven to 400°.

2. In a large bowl, beat together the egg yolks and half the sugar, then beat in the remaining sugar. Beat in the milk, melted butter, flour, cornmeal, and vanilla.

3. Fit the piecrusts into two Lodge 8-inch cast iron skillets, and trim the edges. Divide the filling between the two piecrusts. Bake until the crusts are lightly browned and the filling is bubbling up (it won't look entirely set at this point). Remove from the oven, and let cool on a wire rack until the filling sets.
Makes two 8-inch pies

FLAKY PASTRY

3   cups bleached all-purpose flour
1   teaspoon salt
1   teaspoon sugar

1   large egg
Milk as needed
1   cup vegetable shortening

1. Sift the dry ingredients together in a bowl. Place the egg in a measuring cup, and add enough milk to make ½ cup; beat together. Cut the shortening into the dry ingredients with a pastry cutter until the pieces are about the size of peas. Slowly add the milk mixture, mixing thoroughly. Roll the mixture into 2 balls (for two crusts), and chill at least 30 minutes before rolling out. (At this point, you can wrap the dough in wax paper, then aluminum foil, and refrigerate for up to 4 days, or freeze up to 3 weeks.)

2. On a lightly floured counter, roll the dough out thinly with a floured pin. Fit each crust into a Lodge 9-inch cast iron skillet. If the crust is to be blind baked, bake it in a preheated 450° oven for 12 to 15 minutes.
Makes two 9-inch crusts

Fried Kentucky Country Ham
with Newsom Family Red-eye
Gravy, page 76

BREAKFAST

TOMATO AND EGG

Marco Fossati, executive chef of Quattro, located at the Four Seasons in Palo Alto, California, was recently inspired to add his favorite childhood dish to the brunch menu. Simply called Tomato and Egg, it was known to rouse Marco from bed on Saturday mornings and send him bounding into the kitchen. Featuring fresh organic eggs (purchased from the family-run cage-free Glaum Egg Ranch) roasted in a cast iron skillet, this dish has quickly become a hotel favorite, too.

3 cups Salsa di Pelati (recipe follows)
8 large organic eggs
8 thin slices Tuscan-style country bread, toasted
3 tablespoons freshly grated Parmigiano-Reggiano cheese
1 tablespoon chopped fresh basil
Freshly ground black pepper
Tuscan extra virgin olive oil for drizzling

1. Preheat the oven to 325°.

2. Divide the marinara between two Lodge 10-inch cast iron skillets, and bring to a simmer over medium heat. Reduce the heat to low, and crack 4 eggs into the sauce in each skillet. Place the skillets in the oven, and bake until the egg whites are opaque but the yolks are still soft, 7 to 9 minutes.

3. For each serving, place 2 slices of toasted bread in a large shallow soup bowl or Lodge 5-inch cast iron mini server. Spoon marinara and an egg onto each piece of toast. Sprinkle with Parmesan, basil, and a grinding of fresh pepper; drizzle with a little oil. **Serves 4**

SALSA DI PELATI
Marinara

2 medium yellow onions, finely chopped
3 garlic cloves, sliced
¼ cup olive oil
2 (28-ounce) cans peeled whole San Marzano tomatoes, undrained, chopped
16 fresh basil leaves

1. In a Lodge 5-quart cast iron Dutch oven, sweat the onions and garlic in the oil over medium heat until translucent, about 5 minutes.

2. Stir in the tomatoes, and simmer, uncovered, for about 1½ hours, adjusting the heat to prevent scorching and stirring occasionally.

3. Turn the heat off and stir in the basil. Let steep as the sauce cools completely. Remove the basil before using. **Makes about 6 cups**

The late summer garden at Rick and Lora Lea Misterly's Quillisas-cut Farm in Rice, Washington, provides an abundance of peppers and tomatoes. During the farm-to-table retreats offered at the farm, Chef Kären Jurgensen serves this dish to take the chill off the cool mornings. Serve these eggs straight from the pan with tortillas or hearty rye toasts.

ROSEMARY AND BAY-POACHED PEPPERS AND EGGS

1 ½ pounds mixed chiles and peppers (some hot, some sweet)
¼ cup extra virgin olive oil
2 garlic cloves, slivered
1 cup dry white wine
½ cup tomato sauce of your choice
2 sprigs fresh rosemary
2 bay leaves
½ teaspoon cracked black peppercorns
6 large eggs
Kosher salt and freshly ground black pepper

1. Seed and cut the chiles and peppers into small dice.

2. Place the oil, chiles, peppers, and garlic in a Lodge 10-inch cast iron skillet, and sweat lightly over medium-low heat for about 3 minutes. Add the wine, and simmer for 5 minutes. Stir in the tomato sauce, rosemary, bay leaves, and cracked pepper. Simmer gently for 15 minutes, adding water to the level of the peppers if the sauce reduces too much before the peppers are tender. Check the mixture for seasoning. The peppers should be saucy but not soupy.

3. Keeping the heat at medium-low, quickly crack the eggs into the pan, evenly spacing them. Lightly salt and pepper the tops of the eggs. Cover the pan, and cook the eggs 3 to 5 minutes, to whatever degree of doneness you prefer.

Serves 6

Big Bad Breakfast, in Oxford, Mississippi, was chef John Currence's response to pondering the "most important meal of the day." BBB is an all-natural, locally sourced breakfast concept that Currence says applies the same philosophies to breakfast as he does to lunch and dinner at his white linen venues. Eggs in Purgatory is a nod to his liberal arts education. The poached eggs sit in a spicy tomato sauce, surrounded by red. "It screamed hell to me," says the chef. Dante would clean his plate, certainly.

EGGS IN PURGATORY

Grits:

3   cups whole milk

1   cup chicken stock (store-bought is fine)

2   teaspoons kosher salt

1   cup stone-ground grits

6   tablespoons (¾ stick) unsalted butter, cut into pieces

¼   cup cream cheese, softened

½   cup grated Parmesan cheese

2   teaspoons ground white pepper

Sauce:

2   cups tomato sauce of your choice

¼   cup chopped crisp-cooked bacon

1   teaspoon red pepper flakes

Eggs:

¼   cup distilled white vinegar

4   large eggs

¼   cup grated Parmesan cheese

1. Make the grits: Bring the milk, stock, and salt to a boil in a medium saucepan over high heat. Reduce the heat to low; whisk in the grits, stirring constantly until they are cooked through, 12 to 15 minutes. Once the grits begin to thicken, stir with a wooden spoon instead of the whisk. Turn off the heat, and blend in the butter, cream cheese, Parmesan, and white pepper. Adjust the seasonings, if needed.

2. Make the sauce: Combine the tomato sauce, bacon, and red pepper in a small saucepan. Heat through over medium heat; keep warm.

3. In a shallow sauté pan, bring 2 to 3 inches of water to a simmer with the vinegar.

4. While the water heats, begin assembling the dish. Divide the grits among four Lodge 5-inch cast iron round bowl mini servers. Make a well in the center of the grits in each server. Ladle the tomato sauce into the wells. Preheat the broiler.

5. Crack the eggs directly into the simmering water. Use a spoon to keep them separated, and slowly spoon water over the tops of the eggs. As soon as the whites turn opaque, remove each egg with a slotted spoon, and drain briefly. Place a poached egg on top of the sauce in each server. Sprinkle them evenly with the Parmesan, and place under the broiler until the cheese melts.

Serves 4

a cooking secret from John

There are a variety of tricks that help eggs set up when poaching. I've found that adding vinegar to the water helps the egg white set quickly around the yolk and ensures a nice shape is formed, which prevents the yolk from overcooking.

CHILAQUILES WITH FRIED EGGS AND TOMATILLO SALSA

Chilaquiles:

2 to 3 tablespoons peanut or vegetable oil

12 (6-inch) corn tortillas, each cut into 6 wedges

1 recipe Tomatillo Salsa (recipe follows)

½ cup grated queso fresco or a high-moisture Monterey Jack cheese

½ cup goat cheese, separated into small pieces

1 to 2 tablespoons unsalted butter or nonstick cooking spray

6 large eggs, preferably farm-fresh

Kosher salt and freshly ground black pepper to taste

Garnishes:

6 to 12 tablespoons crumbled goat cheese

12 small sprigs fresh cilantro

12 tablespoons crème fraîche

6 slices ripe avocado

6 lime wedges

1. Heat the oil in a Lodge 10- or 12-inch cast iron skillet over medium-high heat. When the oil is almost smoking, add the tortillas, breaking them apart, and cook, stirring, until crispy. Drain any excess oil from the skillet, then pour the tomatillo salsa over the tortillas, and mix well. Add the queso fresco and ½ cup goat cheese, and mix lightly. Reduce the heat to low.

2. Heat a Lodge 12-inch cast iron griddle over medium-low heat. Heat 6 serving plates in a warm oven.

3. Melt the butter over the surface of the griddle, or remove from the heat, and coat with cooking spray. Gently break the eggs onto the griddle, trying to keep them separate from one another. Cook them sunny side up, and season with salt and pepper to taste. Just before the eggs finish cooking, stir the chilaquiles, and place a portion of the mixture in the center of each warm plate. Top with a fried egg, sprinkle with 1 to 2 tablespoons goat cheese, and tuck in 2 sprigs cilantro. Drizzle 2 tablespoons crème fraîche over all, and top with a slice of avocado. Serve a lime wedge on the side, if desired. **Serves 6**

One of my favorite breakfast memories as a kid growing up in Minneapolis was my dad serving me blood sausage. He served the Russian-style kind with buckwheat in it. He cut it on an angle and slowly sautéed it in a Lodge cast iron pan until it was crispy on both cut sides and tender and hot inside," remembers Cindy Pawlcyn, Napa Valley-based chef/restaurateur, caterer, and cookbook author. Cindy's all-time favorite breakfast is the corn tortilla casserole chilaquiles. It's perfect for brunch, as it will hold well in a warm oven, and both the salsa and corn chips can be made ahead. "My garden has more tomatillos than tomatoes, so I always do a green tomatillo version," she says, but you can easily substitute red tomatoes.

TOMATILLO SALSA

4 cups tomatillos, peeled from their papery husks

4 garlic cloves, peeled

½ medium onion, roughly chopped

3 serrano chiles

1 cup water

¼ to ½ teaspoon kosher salt, to taste

2 tablespoons peanut or vegetable oil

1. In a blender, puree the tomatillos, garlic, onion, chiles, water, and salt until smooth. Heat the oil in a Lodge 10-inch cast iron skillet over medium-high heat for about 2 minutes, then add the puree—it will splatter, so be careful. Cook until heated through, 3 to 4 minutes. Keep warm until needed.

Makes 4½ to 5 cups

SPINACH, TOMATO, AND BACON FRITTATA

This recipe from Amy Beth Edelman, chef and co-owner of Night Kitchen Bakery in Philadelphia, is perfect for a holiday brunch or served to guests as a light lunch.

Nonstick cooking spray
1 pound sliced bacon
4 ounces fresh baby spinach
¼ cup halved cherry tomatoes
15 medium eggs

1 tablespoon kosher salt
1 teaspoon freshly ground black pepper
2 cups (8 ounces) grated white Cheddar cheese

1. Preheat the oven to 350°. Coat a Lodge 9-inch cast iron skillet with cooking spray. Set aside.

2. In a deep Lodge 12-inch cast iron skillet, fry the bacon over medium-high heat until crisp (you may need to do this in several batches). Remove to paper towels to drain.

3. Pour all the bacon fat out of the skillet except for 1 tablespoon. Add the spinach and tomatoes, and cook over medium heat, stirring a few times, until the spinach wilts and the tomatoes heat through.

4. In a large bowl, scramble the eggs, and season with the salt and pepper. Pour into prepared skillet. Transfer the spinach and tomatoes to the prepared skillet. Evenly sprinkle the cheese over the top. Crumble the bacon, and sprinkle over the cheese.

5. Bake the frittata until the center is set, 25 to 30 minutes. Let rest on top of the stove for 10 minutes before cutting into wedges to serve. **Serves 6 to 8**

how Amy Beth makes a frittata

1. For the best flavor, build depth and dimension during each cooking step. Start by browning bacon and reserving the browned bits. Sauté the aromatic spinach and tomatoes in the bacon grease to intensify their flavors and to dissolve the browned bits in the pan.

2. I add salt and pepper to the eggs after the eggs have been beaten with a whisk. This step guarantees the seasoning will be evenly dispersed.

3. For an added hit of flavor, use just one skillet, and pour the egg mixture over the spinach and tomatoes. Sprinkle with crumbled bacon and cheese.

4. After baking, let the frittata rest on top of the stove for 10 minutes to let the eggs set and the flavors meld.

"Our cast iron skillet is particularly special to my husband, Mark, and me because close friends gave it to us as a wedding gift. We use it all the time, and in the six years we've been married, it has taken on that lovely seasoned quality that we know will just get better and better—kind of like our relationship!" says Beth Lipton, food director of *Health* and *All You* magazines. "Weekend breakfasts are a big deal at our house, and we always grab the cast iron skillet when making hearty frittatas like this one."

SMOKED SALMON AND SCALLION FRITTATA

4 scallions or green onions, trimmed
2 tablespoons olive oil
1 medium sweet onion, such as Vidalia, roughly chopped
Salt and freshly ground black pepper

8 large eggs
½ cup whole milk
4 ounces smoked salmon (see kitchen note), chopped
1 (3-ounce) package cream cheese, softened, pulled into pieces

1. Preheat the oven to 375°.

2. Roughly chop the white and light green parts of the scallions. If desired, slice the dark green parts of 2 scallions, and set aside for garnish.

3. Warm the oil in a Lodge 10-inch cast iron skillet over medium-high heat. Add the onion and white and light green parts of the scallions, sprinkle lightly with salt, and season generously with pepper. Cook, stirring occasionally, until just tender, 3 to 5 minutes.

4. In a large bowl, whisk together the eggs and milk until well blended. Pour into the skillet. Scatter the salmon pieces and bits of cream cheese all over the top of the frittata. Season with more pepper, if desired. Cook the frittata on the stove without stirring for 3 minutes, then transfer the skillet to the oven. Bake until the frittata is nearly set in the center, about 10 minutes.

5. Turn the oven to low broil, and cook until the frittata is just set in the center, 1 to 2 minutes longer.

6. Remove the skillet from the oven, and let stand for 5 minutes. Sprinkle with the reserved scallion greens, if desired; cut into wedges, and serve.

Serves 4 to 6

kitchen note:

Buy the most flavorful smoked salmon you can get. Beth likes the wild sockeye salmon from Trader Joe's. Snipped chives or a light sprinkling of fresh dill would make a pretty and flavorful garnish instead of the scallion greens.

This is one of the most popular dishes Ina Pinkney offers at Ina's, her breakfast mecca in Chicago. At the restaurant, a slice of it is served up set on a pool of marinara sauce.

THE BREAKFAST QUEEN'S PASTA FRITTATA

Olive oil
¾ cup chopped onion
2 garlic cloves, minced
¾ cup thinly sliced red bell pepper
1½ cups sliced mushrooms
1½ cups thick-cut julienned zucchini
1 teaspoon dried oregano
Salt and freshly ground black pepper
to taste
9 extra-large eggs

½ cup whole milk
1½ cups (6 ounces) shredded sharp
white Cheddar cheese
½ cup grated Parmesan cheese, plus
more for serving
2 (8-ounce) packages cream
cheese, softened and pulled into
bite-size pieces
3 cups leftover cooked spaghetti

1. Preheat the oven to 350°.

2. In a Lodge 10-inch cast iron skillet, heat just enough oil to coat the bottom of the pan over medium heat. Add the onion and garlic, and cook, stirring a few times, until the onion is softened, about 5 minutes. Add the bell pepper, mushrooms, and zucchini, and cook, stirring a few times, until softened, 6 to 10 minutes. Add the oregano, and season with salt and pepper to taste; transfer the mixture to a bowl. (If the vegetables have given off a lot of liquid, drain off most of it.) Wipe out the skillet, and brush lightly with oil. Cut a piece of parchment to size, and place in the bottom of the pan. Brush with oil. Set aside.

3. In large bowl, using an electric mixer on low speed, beat the eggs, milk, 1½ teaspoons salt, and 1 teaspoon pepper. Add the Cheddar and Parmesan, and blend on low. With the mixer running, add the cream cheese, a few pieces at a time, beating until blended.

4. Put the spaghetti in the prepared skillet. Spoon in the vegetables. Pour in the egg mixture. Mix with your hands so that all the components are equally distributed within the pan. Pat down so that as much as possible of the solids are covered with liquid. Bake until firm to the touch and lightly browned, 30 to 40 minutes. It will puff up when baking, then settle as it cools.

5. Cut into wedges, and serve immediately sprinkled with some freshly grated Parmesan. This is also good served the next day. Wait until the frittata is cool, invert it onto a plate, remove parchment, and turn right-side up. Refrigerate and, when cold, cut into portions. Wrap them well, and refrigerate. The next day, unwrap the wedges, place on a baking sheet lined with parchment paper, and reheat for 10 to 15 minutes at 400°. **Serves 8 to 10**

Inspired by her purchase of a Lodge muffin pan, California-based private chef June Pagan came up with the idea for these breakfast popovers. "As I prepared the batter, it occurred to me that if I added purple corn flour to the mix, I could kick up the nutritional profile by boosting the polyphenol content. At the same time I would naturally enrich the flavor and color. It worked better than expected. Although they were not quite as light as traditional popovers, there was a nice trade-off: the rich flavor of the centuries-old maize—untouched by modern science," remarks June.

PURPLE CORN FLOUR POPOVERS

3 large eggs, lightly beaten
1 cup 2% milk
3 tablespoons grapeseed oil or other non-GMO vegetable oil, plus extra to brush the pan

¾ cup organic unbleached all-purpose flour
¼ cup purple corn flour (June uses Suntava brand)
½ teaspoon fine sea salt

1. In a large bowl or blender, combine all the ingredients until well mixed. Let the batter sit at room temperature for 20 minutes to set up.

2. Preheat the oven to 400°.

3. Brush the wells of a Lodge cast iron muffin pan with oil. Once the batter has set up, place the pan in the oven for 2 minutes.

4. Reblend the batter, then pour into the muffin pan, filling each well three-quarters full. Bake for 15 minutes, then reduce the oven temperature to 325°, and continue to bake until the popovers are lightly browned at the edges, about another 20 minutes. They should be springy to the touch.

5. Remove from the oven, and carefully lift out the popovers. Serve immediately while you finish baking up the rest of the batter (remember to reheat the oven and muffin pan to 400° before baking). **Makes 10 to 12 popovers**

CAST IRON AND THE URBAN SURVIVAL KITCHEN

June Pagan

Private chef and founder of Urban Survival Kitchen, Los Angeles, California

Part of my battery of tools as an urban private chef is my collection of contemporary stainless steel pots and pans. Although they are quite nice to cook with, there is a certain coldness about them. Down deep, my "country" heart belongs to my 10-inch cast iron skillet, which always sits proudly on my stove as the "go-to" pan for all of my comfort cooking.

When I think about the fact that I have had this pan for over 30 years, so many memorable meals come to mind: pan-cooking right on deck, fish plucked straight from the waters off Long Island; catering many a New England-style seafood dinner in the galley of the historic presidential yacht, the U.S.S. *Sequoia*, while cruising on the Potomac River; preparing chicken Milanese for Al Pacino in the kitchen of a Frank Lloyd Wright house; and making fried country tomatoes for the cast of *Steel*

Magnolias in an antebellum house in Louisiana. The list goes on and on.

Lodge cast iron is a thing of domestic beauty. Treat it right and you will have a loyal travel companion. Like a rare wine, it develops with time and, with minimal care, it will remain rugged and built to last.

I chose the cast iron pan as part of the logo for the Urban Survival Kitchen, a culinary health program that teaches budget-conscious students how to FACE the future by preparing food that is Flavorful, Affordable, Clean, and Eco-conscious. Cast iron is easy to use and maintain, and it should have a prominent role in the urban kitchen because it is affordable, healthful in that it provides iron, and represents a tradition of reliable service for the cook's kitchen.

repes were always a special treat when Connecticut-based marketing consultant and blogger (www.myMEGusta.com) Mary Ellen Griffin visited her grandparents. Originally from rural Quebec, they had emigrated to New England. Her grandmother's crepes weren't the lacy type you might find in Parisian bistros. Hers were hearty, perfect for breakfast on a cold winter morning.

MEME'S FRENCH CANADIAN FARMHOUSE CREPES

1	large egg		Dash of salt
½	cup milk	1	tablespoon lard or vegetable oil
⅓	cup all-purpose flour		Pure maple syrup

1. In a small bowl, whisk together the egg, milk, flour, and salt until smooth.

2. Set a Lodge 9-inch cast iron skillet over high heat. When the pan is VERY hot, add the lard, and swirl to coat the pan with it. Pour in half the crepe mixture (about 3 ounces), and swirl the pan to coat the bottom with the batter. The crepe will cook quickly, in less than a minute per side. Using a fork and knife, as soon as the batter starts to solidify, lift the crepe up, and rotate it to ensure even browning. Once browned, flip the crepe. Rotate it in the same way; when evenly browned, remove it to a warm plate, stacking between sheets of wax paper to prevent sticking, and repeat with the remaining crepe batter.

3. Serve immediately with maple syrup. **Serves 1 (makes 2 crepes)**

GRIDDLED CORN CAKES

These crispy corn cakes come from Mary Sue Milliken, chef/co-owner of Border Grill (with locations in Santa Monica, Los Angeles, and Las Vegas). The savory cheese in the dough balances the sweetness of corn. Says Mary Sue, "I love them for a weekend brunch because they are not overly sweet, quick to prepare, and gluten free. Split them hot off the griddle, and spread with a little cream cheese and honey for breakfast."

1 cup crème fraîche (known as crema in Mexican cuisine)
1 cup high-quality canned (drained) or frozen (thawed) corn kernels
½ teaspoon baking powder
½ teaspoon sugar
¼ teaspoon salt
1 cup masarepa (see kitchen note)
½ cup grated Mexican Manchego or Monterey Jack cheese
½ cup grated Cotija or similar salty cheese
Unsalted butter, for frying

1. In a small, heavy saucepan, bring the crème fraîche to a boil. Carefully pour into a blender, add the corn, and puree until smooth. Pour into a large bowl, and whisk in the baking powder, sugar, and salt. Fold in the masarepa and cheeses, then, using your hands, mix until a uniform dough is formed.

2. Place the dough between two large sheets of parchment or wax paper. Roll out with a rolling pin until about ½ inch thick. Using a round cutter, cut into 3-inch rounds. Reroll the scraps of dough together, and cut out more rounds.

3. Melt a teaspoon of butter in a Lodge 10-inch cast iron skillet over medium-low heat. Place two or three corn-dough rounds in the skillet, and cook until puffed up a bit and browned on both sides, making sure the inside is fully cooked, about 2 minutes per side. Transfer the corn cakes to a plate as they are cooked. Add more butter to the skillet as needed, and continue frying until all the corn cakes are done. **Makes 6 to 8 (3-inch) corn cakes, 3 to 4 servings**

kitchen note:

Masarepa is a precooked cornmeal that allows the corn cakes to be light and fluffy. It can be found in specialty Latin food stores and is sometimes referred to as *masa al instante* or *harina precocida*. Masarepa flour is also used to make the traditional South American corn cakes called arepas, the inspiration for Mary Sue's griddled cakes. Arepas are similar to gorditas or sopes, which are also traditionally found in Central and South America.

I n Glastonbury, Connecticut, apple season was a big deal for Cecily McAndrews, associate food editor at *All You* magazine. "As a kid, I reliably had an apple in my lunch box from late August through October. However, my real favorite was my mom's tarte tatin, a sophisticated French upside-down apple tart. It was magic: She'd flip the pan to reveal deeply caramelized apples, just this side of burnt. She made it for dinner parties, and it always meant something delicious was coming," remembers Cecily. Here, she reimagines her favorite French treat for breakfast, adding bacon and maple in a truly American twist.

CARAMELIZED APPLE-BACON FRENCH TOAST

5 large eggs
2 cups whole or low-fat milk
1 tablespoon granulated sugar
½ teaspoon ground cinnamon
¼ teaspoon kosher salt
1 teaspoon vanilla extract
5½ cups lightly packed cubed (¾ inch) sourdough bread
8 ounces thick-cut bacon, sliced across into ½-inch slivers

3 large Granny Smith apples (about 2 pounds)
2 tablespoons unsalted butter
¼ cup maple sugar, or 2 tablespoons packed light brown sugar plus 1 tablespoon pure maple syrup
Pure maple syrup (optional)

1. Preheat the oven to 375°. In a large bowl, whisk together the eggs, milk, granulated sugar, cinnamon, salt, and vanilla. Add the bread, and stir.

2. In a Lodge 12-inch cast iron skillet over medium heat, cook the bacon until crisp, stirring occasionally. While the bacon cooks, peel, core, and slice the apples into quarters, then cut each quarter into thirds. Scoop the bacon into a small bowl, and set aside. Drain all but 1 tablespoon of fat from the skillet.

3. With the skillet still over medium heat, melt the butter in the hot bacon fat. Sprinkle the maple sugar over the pan or add the brown sugar and syrup, and stir to dissolve; add the sliced apples. Stir to coat; then, using a spoon, arrange the apples so that as much apple as possible is touching the bottom of the pan. Cook, undisturbed, for about 10 minutes. Every few minutes, peek at the bottom of an apple—it should be caramelized, with a deep golden color.

4. Sprinkle half the crisped bacon over the apples. Pour the bread mixture over the top, arranging the cubes evenly. Sprinkle the remaining bacon over the bread mixture, and place the skillet in the oven.

5. Bake until the custard is set and the bread cubes on top are toasty, about 30 minutes. Flip the French toast onto a serving plate, and let sit for 5 minutes to firm up. Serve hot or at room temperature, with maple syrup, if desired.

Serves 6 to 8

Ninth-generation Southerner Rebecca Lang lives in Athens, Georgia, and is a cooking instructor and author. Her fancy version of French toast is as comforting and rich as it is beautiful. Right out of the oven, it's puffed high above the skillet edge, calling for a memorable morning around the table.

SORGHUM FRENCH TOAST

¼ cup (½ stick) unsalted butter, cut into 8 pieces, plus ½ table-spoon unsalted butter
10 ounces challah bread
1¼ cups whole milk
¾ cup heavy cream
8 large eggs
¼ cup sorghum syrup (see kitchen note)
⅓ cup granulated sugar
2 tablespoons vanilla extract
⅛ teaspoon salt
½ teaspoon ground cinnamon
⅛ teaspoon ground allspice
⅛ teaspoon ground nutmeg
⅛ teaspoon ground ginger
2 teaspoons confectioners' sugar

1. Grease a Lodge 9-inch cast iron skillet with the ½ tablespoon butter.

2. Cut the bread into 1-inch-thick slices. Cut each slice into 6 pieces. Arrange in the skillet in a single layer, crust sides up.

3. In a large bowl, whisk together the milk, cream, eggs, sorghum syrup, granulated sugar, vanilla, and salt. Pour evenly over the bread. Refrigerate for 45 minutes.

4. Remove the skillet from the refrigerator, and let sit at room temperature for 20 minutes. Preheat the oven to 350°.

5. In a small bowl, combine the spices. Sprinkle over the bread. Arrange the pieces of butter evenly over the top. Bake until puffed and golden brown, about 45 minutes.

6. Remove from the oven. Use a small sieve or tea strainer to dust the confectioners' sugar over the top. Serve immediately, straight from the skillet.
Serves 6 to 8

kitchen note:

Sorghum syrup pours like honey and tastes milder than molasses. The coveted dark golden syrup can be found at Southern roadside stands and upscale grocery stores. If you can't find it, use maple syrup.

a cooking secret from Rebecca

Don't be tempted to skimp on the bread and egg mixture soaking time. To achieve this dish's signature soft, creamy center, you'll want to give the mixture at least 45 minutes to penetrate the bread.

Cast Iron Memories

My Grandma Harper used two cast iron skillets all her life, until she gave them to me when I got married. That was over 60 years ago, so the skillets must be well over a century old. I recently gave the larger one to the Queen of Woks, Grace Young. I kept the smaller one.

Both had traveled with Grandma from Nebraska to Colorado to Southern California, where she and Grandpa raised me. She made beef hash then pretty much the way I make it now, except when I was a kid the beef she used came out of a can, whether it was Dinty Moore's Beef Stew or Hormel's Corned Beef or that tireless staple, Spam.

The chief virtue of hash is that it's thrifty. I use steak, but leftover meats of any kind will do, particularly those you don't want to overcook but just mix and crisp up. Kicking it off with bacon adds magic flavor and texture. Grandma Harper was not looking for such niceties. Thrift was her god. She always had a can of saved bacon fat near her stove, ready for whatever she decided to fry in her skillets. And so do I.

Of course, when I'm no longer able to fry, I will give my remaining skillet to my traveler daughter, to carry on the tradition, since my hunter son has long had his own set of cast iron skillets.

—*Betty Fussell*

When California-based food historian and author Betty Fussell wants to make hash, she uses cast iron. Once it gets hot, it stays hot. And, of course, cast iron provides the perfect nonstick surface. Once seasoned, it stays seasoned. "Unless, of course," Betty says, "you ruin it with soap and water, but I don't know anyone foolish enough to do that."

BEEF-BACON HASH

3   slices bacon
½   cup finely chopped onion
2   cups new potatoes, cut into ½-inch cubes and parboiled 5 minutes
1   cup cubed (½-inch) leftover cooked beef or other meat
2   garlic cloves, minced

1   tablespoon fresh thyme leaves or ½ teaspoon dried
Sea salt and freshly ground black pepper (Betty likes to add a lot of pepper)
¼   cup (or more) fresh flat-leaf parsley leaves, chopped

1. In a Lodge cast iron skillet (preferably 10 inches in diameter or more), fry the bacon until crisp. Remove the bacon to a paper towel to drain, and pour off all but a thin layer of fat.

2. Add the onion to the skillet, and cook for 2 to 3 minutes over medium heat, stirring.

3. Turn the heat up under the skillet, and add the potatoes in a single layer (you may need to brown the potatoes in two batches, depending on the size of the skillet). Cook until the potatoes are browned on both sides, about 5 minutes.

4. Add the beef, and lower the heat slightly. Add the garlic and thyme, season with salt and pepper to taste, mix well, and heat thoroughly.

5. Remove the pan from the heat, and add the parsley. Crumble the bacon (or cut into small pieces), and add to the hash. Mix well, and serve hot or at room temperature. **Serves 4**

Stuffed tomatoes are hearty and satisfying, like a whole meal unto themselves. Minneapolis-based lifestyle expert Ross Sveback wanted to come up with a rendition for breakfast. "I immediately knew maple syrup had to be in it, along with sage, and the rest was easy." Ross likes to serve these in individual Lodge 6½-inch cast iron skillets with poached eggs.

SAUSAGE AND MAPLE STUFFED TOMATOES

6 to 8 ripe medium tomatoes
Kosher salt
1 pound bulk country-blend pork sausage (don't use Italian seasoned)
1 medium onion, cut into ½-inch dice
4 garlic cloves, minced
7 to 8 ounces button mushrooms, cut into ½-inch dice

2 tablespoons olive oil
½ cup pure maple syrup (Ross likes to use Burton's Maplewood Farm)
2 cups plain dry breadcrumbs
2 tablespoons chopped fresh sage
1 cup (4 ounces) grated Parmesan cheese
Coarsely ground black pepper to taste

1. Core the tomatoes and, using a melon baller, scoop out the insides. Sprinkle salt on the inside of each tomato, and set upside down for 30 minutes on a wire rack set over the sink or a baking sheet to catch the juice.

2. While the tomatoes drain, cook the sausage in a Lodge 12-inch cast iron skillet over medium heat until no longer pink, breaking it into small pieces. Using a slotted spoon, transfer it to paper towels. Do not drain the fat from the pan. Add the onion and garlic, and cook, stirring a few times, until translucent, 4 to 5 minutes. Add the mushrooms and oil, and cook, stirring occasionally, until the mushrooms have released their moisture, about 10 minutes.

3. In a medium bowl, combine the sausage and mushroom mixture. Add the maple syrup, breadcrumbs, sage, cheese, and salt and pepper to taste.

4. Using your hands, evenly divide the filling among the tomatoes, gently pushing the filling in to pack it, and press a roughly ¼-cup mound on top of each tomato. Place the stuffed tomatoes on a baking sheet. At this point, you can cover the tomatoes with plastic wrap and refrigerate until ready to bake or overnight.

5. If you have refrigerated the tomatoes, pull them out 30 minutes before you intend to bake them to take the chill off. Preheat the oven to 375°. Replace the plastic wrap with aluminum foil, and bake, covered, for 30 minutes. Remove the foil, and bake for an additional 10 to 15 minutes. Serve hot. **Serves 6 to 8**

a cooking secret from Ross

Keeping the tomatoes covered two-thirds of the way through, then uncovering lets them steam-cook and not get overly browned and tough on top.

This recipe comes by way of Nancy Newsom Mahaffey, from Princeton, Kentucky. For a milder or less salty taste, Nancy recommends soaking the sliced ham in lukewarm water or sweet milk for up to 30 minutes before frying.

FRIED KENTUCKY COUNTRY HAM WITH NEWSOM FAMILY RED-EYE GRAVY

2 center slices (about ¼ inch thick) or 4 smaller boneless slices country ham	¾ cup hot brewed coffee 1 teaspoon brown sugar

1. Fry the ham: Trim off the hard outer edge of the ham and remove the rind. DO NOT TRIM THE FAT. This adds flavor, and no other fat will be needed for cooking.

2. Place the ham in a Lodge 12-inch cast iron skillet, turning the lean part away from what will be the hottest point of the skillet. Add just enough water to cover the bottom of the pan. Let the water evaporate over medium-low heat, then fry the ham slowly over medium to low heat. Do not overfry, as this will make the ham hard, dry, and tough. Turn the slices often. Country ham is usually done when the fat is transparent and beginning to brown. If you'd like to brown the ham just before taking it out of the pan, turn up the heat as necessary and very quickly turn the ham to brown it as you prefer. Remove the ham to serving plates.

3. Make the gravy: Pour the pan drippings into a small bowl (see kitchen note). Return the skillet to medium heat. When the skillet is hot, pour in the coffee, stirring the side and bottom of the skillet to loosen all the browned bits from frying the ham. Stir into the coffee, and cook for 3 to 5 minutes, maintaining just enough heat for the coffee to bubble. Add the brown sugar, and stir in well.

4. Pour the coffee into the center of the bowl with the drippings. Do not stir. You will see a "red eye" in the center of the bowl. That's where the term "red-eye" gravy comes from. Serve the gravy on the side with a ladle for diners to help themselves. **Serves 2 to 4**

kitchen note:

If you end up with less than 2 tablespoons of drippings, the next time you want to make red-eye gravy, cook some extra fat or skins along with the slices. Nancy says that old-timers will tell you that young hams (less than 10 months old) do not make red-eye gravy.

HAND-CRAFTED HAM

Nancy Newsom Mahaffey

Artisan ham maker and store owner, Princeton, Kentucky

Nancy Newsom Mahaffey, also known as "The Ham Lady," is the third-generation owner of Newsom's Old Mill Store and Colonel Bill Newsom's Aged Kentucky Country Hams. Nancy's grandfather, H.C. (Hosea Cleveland) Newsom, opened the mill store in 1917. "My father, Colonel Bill Newsom, who always wanted to be known simply as 'Bill,' used this recipe for country ham and red-eye gravy since at least the 1930s. I'm sure he must have learned it from his father and mother—H.C. and Ora Lee Newsom—for in my grandparents' day and in my dad's day, the days of the Great Depression, nothing was ever wasted," recalls Nancy. "I'm sure that the recipe for red-eye gravy was developed during the early days of my family, previous to 1900."

Newsom country hams continue an unbroken chain of curing tradition, dating back to the landing of a Newsom forefather in Jamestown, Virginia, in the 1640s. It is their mission to continue the preservation of the lost art of artisanal ham curing—an ambient weather cure that requires time and know-how. Newsom country hams are rubbed with salt and brown sugar (no nitrates permitted), hand washed, then hung to smoke over hickory wood. A few years ago, one of their hams was placed in a museum in Aracena, Spain, as part of the Fifth World Congress of Dry Cured Hams, where it still hangs.

This dish, more than any other, takes me back to my childhood," says Kelly English, chef-owner of Restaurant Iris in Memphis. "My dad would make the family a Dutch oven full of grillades that we would eat on all Sunday. It appears now on our brunch menu at Restaurant Iris." Serve grillades over stone-ground grits and poached eggs.

MY FATHER'S GRILLADES

2   pounds pork loin, clean of all fat and silverskin
Kosher salt and freshly ground black pepper
Sodium-free Creole or Cajun seasoning
3   cups all-purpose flour
1   cup canola oil
1½ cups (3 sticks) unsalted butter
2   large onions, finely chopped
2   large green bell peppers, seeded and finely chopped

3   celery ribs, finely chopped
2½ tablespoons minced garlic
2   large ripe tomatoes, diced
2   tablespoons chopped fresh thyme
3   quarts beef stock (if not home-made, use reduced-sodium organic)
2   tablespoons Worcestershire sauce
1   bay leaf

1. Slice the pork into very thin medallions (almost scaloppine). Vigorously season with salt, pepper, and Creole seasoning on both sides. Lightly season the flour with the same three seasonings, and dredge the pork in it, tapping off any excess.

2. Heat the oil in a Lodge 15-inch cast iron skillet over medium heat. Dip the corner of one of the dredged pork medallions in the oil; if it begins to "fry," then the oil is ready; if it doesn't, wait until it does. When the oil is ready, sear the medallions until nicely browned on both sides. You may need to do this in batches; don't crowd the pan. As the pork is browned, transfer it to a plate.

3. Drain the oil from the skillet (don't wipe the skillet clean). Set the pan over medium-low heat, and add the butter. When it has melted, add 2 cups of the seasoned dredging flour, and stir with a wooden spoon to make a dark roux. Do not try to rush through this; if you take your time, your guests will be able to tell (if you don't, they'll know that as well). Slowly cook the roux, stirring every minute or two and scraping all the edges (never walk away from the pot).

4. Once the roux has taken on the color of semi dark chocolate (this could take an hour), add the onions, bell peppers, and celery (collectively referred to as "the trinity" in South Louisiana). Cook your trinity, stirring, until it has softened. Add the garlic, tomatoes, and thyme, and cook, stirring, until you can smell the garlic. Whisk in the stock, and add the Worcestershire and bay leaf. Season to taste with salt, pepper, and Creole seasoning. Bring to a simmer and add the seared pork. Cover the skillet (with aluminum foil if you don't have a lid) and place in a preheated 250° oven until the pork is tender, 1 to 1½ hours.
Serves 8

Beef Stew with Herbed Dumplings,
page 86

SOUPS & SANDWICHES

GRILLED CAST IRON SEAFOOD STEW

This recipe from Ryan Prewitt, who runs the kitchen at Pêche Seafood Grill in New Orleans, is a great dish to serve at a summer party. Be sure to search out the highest quality seafood—it really makes a difference. Ask your fishmonger to remove and discard the scales and gills. Ideally, you take home the fish bones, head, and fillets.

1 recipe Slow-Cooked Onions and Tomatoes (recipe follows)
2 tablespoons vegetable oil
5 pounds 16/20 count shrimp, preferably with heads on, peeled and deveined; reserve shells and heads for seafood broth
2 yellow onions, cut into small dice
2 carrots, cut into small dice
5 celery ribs, cut into small dice
2 tablespoons tomato paste
1 ripe tomato, cut into medium dice
Leaves from 1 bunch fresh flat-leaf parsley, chopped; reserve stems for seafood broth
1 whole snapper (2 to 3 pounds), scaled, gutted, and fillets removed; reserve head and bones for seafood broth

4 quarts cold water
3 bay leaves
3 dried chiles, such as chile arbol
1 recipe Roasted Garlic and Jalapeño Aïoli (recipe follows)
1 tablespoon kosher salt
2 teaspoons freshly ground black pepper
½ teaspoon cayenne pepper
5 pounds mussels, scrubbed and debearded (discard any that won't close)
Wood chips, soaked
1 pound jumbo lump crabmeat, picked over for shells and cartilage
1 bunch green onions, thinly sliced
Toasted slices French bread
Hot sauce to taste

1. Make the Slow-Cooked Onions and Tomatoes.

2. While the onions and tomatoes cook, make the seafood broth. Heat the oil in a large stockpot over high heat. Add the shrimp shells, and sauté until they turn bright red and take on a toasted aroma. Add the onions, carrots, and celery, and cook until the vegetables soften, about 5 minutes, stirring regularly. Stir in the tomato paste, and cook for 5 minutes. Add the tomato and parsley stems, along with the fish bones and head from the snapper. Add the water, bay leaves, and dried chiles, and bring to a simmer. Continue to simmer for 45 minutes, then strain through a fine mesh strainer, and set aside. Discard solids.

3. While the broth simmers, make the Roasted Garlic and Jalapeño Aïoli.

4. Build a charcoal fire in a grill with a lid. When the coals have burned to an even white, nestle a Lodge 9-quart cast iron Dutch oven in the embers. Transfer the Slow-Cooked Onions and Tomatoes and seafood broth to the pot, and stir in the salt, black pepper, and cayenne; let come to a simmer.

5. Meanwhile, cut the snapper fillets into 2-inch squares. When the mixture is simmering, add the fish to the pot, along with the shrimp and mussels. Throw some soaked wood chips (any hardwood variety is fine) on the fire, and close the lid. Cook for about 5 minutes, then stir. Continue cooking with the grill lid down until the mussels have opened and the fish and shrimp are cooked. (Discard any mussels that will not open.) Gently stir in the crabmeat, green onions, and chopped parsley. Heat thoroughly. Ladle the stew into bowls, and serve with slabs of toasted bread and the aïoli on the side for diners to drizzle over the top of their stew as they prefer. Add hot sauce as you like. **Serves 8**

SLOW-COOKED ONIONS AND TOMATOES

¼ cup olive oil
1 pound slab bacon, cut into medium dice
3 yellow onions, cut into small dice
2 ripe tomatoes, cut into small dice
1 head garlic, cloves peeled and minced
2 jalapeño chiles, seeded and minced

1. Heat the oil in a Lodge 5-quart cast iron Dutch oven over medium-low heat for 5 minutes. Add the bacon, and render for about 5 minutes, stirring occasionally. Add the onions, and cook, stirring occasionally, until they are very soft and a deep golden brown, about 20 minutes.

2. Add the tomatoes, garlic, and jalapeños, and cook very slowly over low heat until all the liquid is cooked out of the tomatoes, about another 30 minutes. The vegetables should be completely soft and cooked into a juicy paste. **Makes about 2 cups**

ROASTED GARLIC AND JALAPEÑO AÏOLI

10 garlic cloves, peeled
¾ cup vegetable oil
1 jalapeño chile, seeded and diced
1 tablespoon fresh lemon juice
1 large egg yolk
1 teaspoon kosher salt
¼ teaspoon freshly ground black pepper

1. Heat the garlic in the oil in a small saucepan over low heat. Cook very slowly until the garlic is completely tender, about 30 minutes. Do not allow the garlic to brown. Strain the oil into a heatproof glass, and let cool to room temperature; set the garlic cloves aside.

2. When the oil has cooled, place the garlic cloves, jalapeño, lemon juice, egg yolk, salt, and pepper in a blender, and puree until smooth. With the machine running, very slowly pour the oil in a steady stream through the hole in the top of the lid. Process until the mixture thickens to a mayonnaise-like consistency. Refrigerate, tightly covered, until ready to use. Any leftover aïoli will last for 4 to 5 days in the refrigerator. **Makes about 1 cup**

Shortcut Roasted Garlic and Jalapeño Aïoli:
Cook the garlic as directed in step 1, and strain. Reserve the oil for another use. In a blender, puree the garlic with the jalapeño, lemon juice, salt, and pepper. Combine the puree with 1 cup mayonnaise.

NORTH CAROLINA DOWN EAST CLAM CHOWDER

No, not Down East Maine, but North Carolina. All along its Outer Banks and Southern Outer Banks is home to this style of chowder. Somewhat akin to the chowders of Rhode Island, this style is more about the clams than the thick, cream-based chowders of New England. "It's a type of chowder," says Fred Thompson, a cookbook author, resident of Raleigh, North Carolina, and publisher of *Edible Piedmont,* "that you'll find at a local's home."

¼ pound salt pork or slab bacon, sliced ¼ inch thick
½ cup chopped onion
4 cups water, or half water and half clam juice
1 teaspoon salt
¼ teaspoon freshly ground black pepper
1 quart coarsely chopped chowder clams

4 cups diced (½-inch) potatoes
2 dozen small clams in the shell, scrubbed (farm-raised from North Carolina are perfect)
Milk, half-and-half, or light or heavy cream, as desired
Sliced white bread (optional)
Chopped fresh flat-leaf parsley for garnish
Oyster crackers

1. Cook the salt pork in a Lodge 5-quart cast iron Dutch oven over medium heat until crisp. Remove the pork, and discard, reserving the rendered fat in the pot. Add the onion, and cook until tender (but don't let it color), about 5 minutes, stirring a few times. Pour in the water, then add the salt and pepper. Bring to a boil. Add the chowder clams, reduce the heat to low, and slowly simmer, uncovered, until the clams are tender, about 1 hour.

2. Add the potatoes, increase the heat to medium, and simmer until they are tender, about 20 minutes. During the last 10 minutes, add the clams in the shell, and cover the pot. Add the milk, if using, right before serving, but give it enough time to warm (a couple of minutes usually works).

3. If you like, set a slice of bread in the bottom of each large shallow serving bowl, then ladle in the chowder, making sure to get a couple of the shell clams. Sprinkle with parsley, and serve with oyster crackers. **Serves 10 to 12**

how Fred makes chowder

1. The key to a good chowder is timing. Wait until the potatoes are fork tender before adding the clams in the shell, because they don't take long to cook.

2. Be careful not to overcook the clams. They will be completely cooked when their shells open wide (about 10 minutes). Discard shells that remain closed.

3. To thicken this chowder like the locals do, place a slice of white bread in the bottom of each serving bowl before ladling the chowder into the bowl.

The key to making this stew, says Massachusetts-based cookbook author and barbecue expert Mike Stines, is to do all the prep work ahead of time and have everything ready when it's needed. "If you dice the meat and vegetables into bite-size pieces," declares Mike, "you shouldn't need a knife for the stew." This stew, like any stew or chili, is better after standing for a day, but even without a nap in the fridge, it's tasty.

BEEF STEW
WITH HERBED DUMPLINGS

Beef Stew:
2 tablespoons vegetable shortening
1½ pounds beef chuck, trimmed of fat and cut into ¾-inch cubes (about 1 pound trimmed)
1 pound beef top round, trimmed of fat and cut into ¾-inch cubes
1 tablespoon smoked paprika
Coarse kosher salt and freshly ground black pepper
1½ teaspoons finely minced garlic
¼ cup tomato paste
¼ cup dark roux, plus more as needed
4 bay leaves
1 teaspoon dried rosemary, crushed
1 teaspoon dried basil
1 teaspoon dried thyme
1 teaspoon ground cumin
¼ teaspoon ground allspice
8 to 10 cups beef stock
2 tablespoons Worcestershire sauce
2 teaspoons sugar
½ cup chopped flat-leaf parsley
2 tablespoons seeded and finely diced hot chiles (1 medium jalapeño or 3 serranos)

¼ teaspoon finely diced fresh bird's eye chiles (do not seed; about 1 chile)
¾ cup chopped yellow onion
2 cups Baby Bliss or small Yukon Gold potatoes, quartered
1½ cups peeled parsnips or yams, cut into bite-size dice
1 cup peeled carrots, cut into bite-size rounds
1 cup thinly sliced leeks (white and light green parts)
1 cup peeled turnip, cut into bite-size dice
1½ cups celery, cut into bite-size pieces
¾ cup quartered button or small cremini mushrooms
¾ cup seeded and chopped red, green, or orange bell pepper
Herbed Dumplings (optional):
2 cups Bisquick baking mix
⅔ cup whole milk
2 tablespoons minced fresh flat-leaf parsley
1 tablespoon poppy or caraway seeds

1. Melt the shortening in a Lodge 7-quart cast iron Dutch oven over medium-high heat. Brown the meat well on all sides in batches. (Don't crowd the meat in the pan or it will steam and not brown.) Remove the meat to a plate as it is browned. When all the meat has been browned, return it to the pot, and season with the paprika and salt and pepper to taste. Add the garlic and tomato paste, and cook briefly, stirring to coat the meat with the paste. Add the roux, and cook, stirring, for 3 minutes. Add the bay leaves, rosemary, basil, thyme, cumin, allspice, and 4 cups of the stock. Stir to combine. Add the Worcestershire, sugar, and ¼ cup of the parsley. Add another 2 cups stock, and bring to a boil. Cover, reduce the heat to a simmer, and cook, stirring occasionally, until the meat is barely tender, about 45 minutes. Add the chiles, onion, potatoes, parsnips, carrots, leeks, and turnip. Add more stock and roux, if necessary, to cover the vegetables (add 1 tablespoon roux for every 2 cups stock). Cover and simmer for 20 minutes.

2. Add the celery, and cook for another 10 minutes. Add the mushrooms and bell pepper, and cook until the vegetables are tender, about another 5 minutes.

3. If serving with dumplings, spoon out enough liquid into a small saucepan so the vegetables and meat are exposed. Keep the reserved liquid simmering over low heat while you make the dumpling dough. Keep the stew at a low boil.

4. In a medium bowl, combine all the dumpling ingredients until well mixed. Using two tablespoons, form the dough into oval-shaped, heaping tablespoon-size dumplings, and drop onto the stew. (The dough will come off the spoons easier if the spoons are dipped in hot stock or water before forming.) Once all the dumplings have been added to the pot, cover and cook until a toothpick inserted into the dumplings comes out cleanly, 15 to 18 minutes. Transfer the dumplings to a warm plate, and keep warm in a low oven until ready to serve.

5. Return the reserved liquid to the pot, and stir to combine. Ladle the stew into warm serving bowls, and set several dumplings on top. Garnish with a sprinkling of the remaining ¼ cup parsley, if desired. **Serves 6**

a cooking secret from Mike

You can make your own dark roux (cook flour and unsalted butter or vegetable shortening together in a one-to-one ratio over medium-low heat, stirring constantly, until it is the color of chocolate, which can take an hour or more) or buy it ready made—I like Savoie's Old Fashioned Roux, which you can purchase online.

HAWAIIAN-STYLE BEEF STEW

What makes this beef stew particularly Hawaiian is that, despite the potatoes in the stew, it will always be served over a bed of medium-grain white rice. Native Hawaiians enjoy beef stew served over poi, cooked taro root pounded to a paste-like consistency. The addition of shoyu (soy sauce) to beef stew instead of sea or kosher salt is also a nod to the ethnic mix that is Hawai'i. If you are eating beef stew with chopsticks, you are definitely in Hawai'i, as culinary product specialist Ann Hall Every discovered when she first relocated to Honolulu.

1 cup all-purpose flour, seasoned with sea or kosher salt and freshly ground black pepper
2½ pounds beef chuck (preferably grass-fed), trimmed of fat and cut into 2-inch cubes
1 (1-inch-thick) slice beef shank (preferably grass-fed)
3 tablespoons vegetable oil, or more as needed
3 large carrots, cut in half length wise, each half cut diagonally into 3 pieces
3 celery ribs, cut diagonally into 2-inch pieces
2 medium Maui or other sweet onions, quartered
8 small Yukon Gold potatoes, scrubbed clean and cut in half
6 garlic cloves, coarsely chopped
3 dried bay leaves (if using fresh bay leaves, use 2)
1 (28-ounce) can crushed tomatoes (preferably organic)
2 cups beef broth (preferably low-sodium organic)
1 tablespoon soy sauce, or more to taste
1 tablespoon freshly ground black pepper, or more to taste
2 to 3 dashes of hot sauce (optional)
2 cups medium-grain white rice, cooked according to package directions
4 to 6 sprigs fresh cilantro

1. Place the seasoned flour in a large shallow dish. Dredge the beef cubes and slice of beef shank in the flour, shaking off any excess.

2. Heat the oil in a Lodge 7-quart cast iron Dutch oven over medium heat until it is hot but not smoking. Add the beef cubes and slice of shank to the hot oil, and brown on all sides; brown the beef cubes in two or more batches to avoid crowding the pan. Remove the beef to a plate as it is browned.

3. If needed, add 1 or 2 additional tablespoons oil to the pot, then add the carrots, celery, onions, and potatoes. Cook, uncovered, over medium-low heat until the vegetables are lightly browned, stirring occasionally, about 10 minutes. Add the garlic, cover, and cook another 5 minutes.

4. Remove the vegetables to a clean plate; return the browned beef cubes and the meat of the beef shank (discard the bone) to the Dutch oven along with the bay leaves and tomatoes. Add enough broth to just cover the beef; raise the heat to medium-high, and bring the stew to a low boil for 2 minutes. Reduce the heat to medium-low, cover, and cook for 1½ hours.

5. Return the vegetables to the pot, and stir to combine with the beef. Taste the liquid for seasoning, and add soy sauce and black pepper to taste. Add the hot sauce, if desired. Cover and cook until the vegetables are tender, about another hour. Remove the bay leaves before serving.

6. An hour or so before the stew is finished cooking, start the rice. Serve the stew ladled over rice (a soup bowl works well). Garnish each serving with a sprig of cilantro. **Serves 4 to 6**

When cookbook editor **Pam Hoenig** was growing up, chili was
one of her very favorite dinners and one of the first
recipes she asked her mother, **Phyllis Hoenig**, for after
moving into her first apartment. The recipe has evolved over the years.
Initially it derived all its heat from chili powder, but now it's powered
by a combination of chili powder, cumin, and ancho and chipotle chile
powders. Bittersweet chocolate adds another layer of deep flavor. It's a
cold-weather favorite of her husband, **Chris**, and son, **Liam**.

MY MOM'S CHILI, KIND OF

1½ cups raw long-grain rice	2 tablespoons ground cumin
1 tablespoon extra virgin olive oil	1 tablespoon ancho chile powder
1 medium onion, chopped	½ teaspoon chipotle chile powder
1 garlic clove, chopped	1 ounce bittersweet chocolate, chopped
1¼ pounds ground beef	
2 cups canned crushed tomatoes	1 (15-ounce) can small kidney beans, drained
2 tablespoons chili powder	

1. Put the rice on to cook according to the package directions.

2. While the rice cooks, heat the oil in a Lodge 5-quart cast iron Dutch oven
over medium-high heat. Add the onion and garlic, and cook, stirring, until
softened, about 5 minutes. Add the ground beef, and cook until no longer pink,
breaking the meat into small pieces with a wooden spoon.

3. Add the tomatoes, and stir until well mixed. Add the spices and ground
chiles, and stir to combine. Add the chocolate, and let stand for a couple of
minutes to soften and begin melting, then stir into the mixture.

4. Add the beans, and stir to combine. Let the chili start to bubble, then
reduce the heat to low, and let simmer for about 20 minutes. Serve ladled over
the rice. **Serves 6**

The word *wash-tunk-ala* is from the Lakota Sioux and means dried deer or buffalo meat. This game-and-corn stew is one favored by the Plains Indians. There are many versions, this one from Holly Arnold Kinney, second-generation owner of The Fort restaurant just outside of Denver, Colorado. "As a little girl, my father, Sam Arnold, food historian and founder of The Fort, would make this over the campfire in the restaurant's courtyard," remembers Holly.

WASH-TUNK-ALA INDIAN STEW

2   tablespoons olive oil
6   wild onions, green onions, or scallions, cut diagonally into ¾-inch pieces
2   pounds jerked meat (buffalo, beef, deer, elk, or a combination), cut into bite-size pieces
4   large red potatoes, peeled and cut into bite-size pieces
2   medium carrots, cut into bite-size pieces

1   large red bell pepper, seeded and cut into bite-size pieces
3   ears reconstituted dried corn (see kitchen note) or 1 ear corn, shucked and cut into 1-inch-thick discs
Salt to taste
3   tablespoons New Mexican red chile powder
2   quarts beef broth
3   tablespoons cornmeal

1. Heat oil in a Lodge 7-quart cast iron Dutch oven over high heat. Add the onions, and sauté until slightly browned and translucent. Add the meat, and slowly stir until it is seared brown. Add the potatoes, carrots, bell pepper, and corn. Add salt to taste and New Mexican red chile powder. Stir.

2. Add the broth. Add a little cold water to the cornmeal, mix to create a paste, then stir into the soup. Slowly simmer for 2 hours. **Serves 6**

kitchen note:
To reconstitute dried ears of corn, soak them in water to cover overnight, or until tender.

a cooking secret from Holly

You can use fresh meat in the place of dried meat. If you use jerky, be sure to buy pure dried meat and not commercial jerky, which is full of additives. With jerky, you'll end up with a more chewy texture.

MY CAST IRON REDISCOVERY

Sheri Castle

Author of The New Southern Garden Cookbook, *Chapel Hill, North Carolina*

My family always cooked with cast iron, so I have no clear moment of discovery. However, my moment of rediscovery was when I got serious about cooking and started working hard at it. The first dish I prepared in cast iron was eggs. We had a little skillet that was just right for one or two eggs. I started with scrambled, moved on to fried, and eventually tackled omelets. No one in my family had ever even heard of an omelet until I made one for them. Shortly after, I learned that my cast iron pieces delivered more than memories. For some tasks, they outperformed my fancier, shinier, costlier pots and pans. Plus, they were reliable, durable, and tolerant of my ways.

Cast iron skillets were a given in my family's kitchens, as certain and commonplace as knives and bowls and aprons. For something to be considered an heirloom, some sort of sentiment must develop. That happened for me when a beloved aunt died unexpectedly more than 30 years ago. I inherited her engagement ring and some of her cast iron cookware. The ring is in a safe-deposit box, where I rarely see it. But the pans are in my kitchen cabinets, where I use them almost daily. I've accumulated other family cast iron pieces, bought and refurbished old pieces from yard sales and flea markets, and invested in a few new items. My collection has grown to around 60 pieces. My favorite is a 9-inch skillet that was handed down from my great-grandmother. To my knowledge, for upwards of a century, nothing other than cornbread has ever been cooked in that one. It shines like ebony. Someday I will hand it to my daughter. Until then, I use it to make my version of cornbread.

My favorite cast iron recipe is cornbread, which is sugar free, bacon blessed, and skillet born. It is the plain truth that cornbread must be made in a cast iron skillet.

It is challenging to find a crowd-pleasing chili that features vegetables, but this one fits the bill. It's hearty, colorful, and full of flavor, says Sheri Castle.

WINTER VEGETABLE CHILI

3 tablespoons vegetable oil
1 medium onion, chopped
2 medium garlic cloves, very finely chopped
2 large red, yellow, and/or orange bell peppers, seeded and cut into ½-inch pieces
4 small parsnips, peeled and cut into ½-inch pieces
2 large carrots, peeled and cut into ½-inch pieces
1 medium sweet potato or 1 small winter squash, peeled and cut into ½-inch pieces
1 teaspoon kosher salt, plus more to taste

2 tablespoons ground ancho or chipotle chile powder
1 tablespoon ground cumin
1 tablespoon ground coriander
1 teaspoon ground cinnamon
1 tablespoon smoked paprika
1 cup amber ale
1½ cups vegetable juice, such as V8
1 (14-ounce) can fire-roasted diced tomatoes, undrained
1 (15-ounce) can hominy, rinsed and drained
2 (15-ounce) cans black beans, rinsed and drained
Orange wedges, sour cream, and corn chips, for serving

1. Heat the oil in a 3-quart enameled cast iron Dutch oven over medium-high heat. Add the onion, and cook, stirring often, until softened, about 5 minutes. Add the garlic, bell peppers, parsnips, carrots, sweet potato, and salt, and cook, stirring often, until the vegetables begin to soften, about 8 minutes.

2. Add the ground chile, cumin, coriander, cinnamon, and paprika, and cook, stirring constantly, for 3 minutes. Reduce the heat if the spices begin to scorch.

3. Add the ale and vegetable juice. Stir to scrape up the browned glaze from the bottom of the pot. Bring to a boil, reduce the heat, partially cover the pot, and simmer until the vegetables are almost tender, about 8 minutes, stirring occasionally.

4. Stir in the tomatoes, hominy, and beans. Simmer until heated through, about 8 minutes.

5. Season with salt to taste. Serve warm with the oranges, sour cream, and chips on the side. **Serves 8**

a cooking secret from Sheri

For best results, make this chili at least one day ahead. To store, cool, cover, and refrigerate for up to 3 days. Warm over medium heat, and check the seasoning before serving.

SQUASH BISQUE WITH MASCARPONE AND APPLE-CHEESE CROSTINI

This is a great soup served either hot or cold. Danny Mellman makes it with a variety of winter squash, with his favorite garden-fresh choices being butternut and acorn squash. You can also add some pumpkin and celebrate the fall harvest.

Bisque:
1 medium butternut squash, peeled, seeded, and diced
1 medium acorn squash, peeled, seeded, and cut into chunks
1 sweet onion, left unpeeled, cut in half
2 cinnamon sticks
5 allspice berries
2 star anise
Pinch of salt
Pinch of freshly ground black pepper
6 tablespoons (¾ stick) butter, melted
2 cups heavy cream
1 tablespoon chopped peeled fresh ginger

½ vanilla bean
¼ cup orange juice
Grated zest of 1 lime
Crostini:
1 Fuji apple, cored and thinly sliced
4 thin oval slices crusty bread
4 ounces cheese, preferably Asiago or Kashkavalo (an Israeli semihard cheese), thinly sliced
¼ cup mascarpone, softened
Leaves from 5 sprigs fresh mint, chopped
Leaves from 1 sprig fresh thyme, chopped

1. Preheat the oven to 360°.

2. Make the bisque: In a large bowl, toss both squashes, the onion, whole spices, salt, and pepper with the melted butter until well coated. Pour into a Lodge 15-inch cast iron skillet, arrange in a single layer, and bake until tender, about 1 hour and 10 minutes. Discard the whole spices, and let cool.

3. While the vegetables roast, combine the cream and ginger in a small, heavy saucepan. Scrape the seeds of the vanilla bean into the mixture, and add the vanilla bean as well. Bring to boil, then immediately remove from the heat, and let cool; remove the vanilla bean.

4. Peel the cooled onion, and put in a food processor, along with the squash and pan drippings. Process until smooth. Add the cream, orange juice, and lime zest; pulse until the mixture is just smooth and uniform. (Be careful to not overblend or the cream will break.) Refrigerate until ready to serve.

5. Make the crostini: Preheat the broiler. Place a thin layer of sliced apple on each piece of bread, and top with the Asiago cheese. Set on a baking sheet, and place under the broiler until the cheese melts.

6. To serve, pour the bisque into 4 Lodge 1-pint cast iron Country Kettles. Garnish each serving with 1 tablespoon mascarpone, swirled in the center of the bisque, and sprinkle with the mint and thyme. Serve with the crostini.
Serves 4

HARVESTING LOCAL: THE LODGE KETTLE

Danny Mellman

Chef/owner of Harvest on Main in Blue Ridge, Georgia

We bought a vacation home in the mountains of North Georgia 10 years ago and fell in love with the area. Blue Ridge holds this fabulous small-town charm that my wife, Michelle Moran, and I both experienced growing up. So after 25 years cooking along the west coast of Florida with a focus on seafood and fresh, local ingredients, we decided to make the leap to the quiet foothills of the Blue Ridge Mountains. When we planned out the space, we wanted to really showcase the area's Appalachian agricultural roots and spotlight local artisans.

Along with farmers and ingredients, I wanted to focus on the cookware that Lodge offers. I use cast iron in many of my recipes, and I've always trusted Lodge. So when we began building this space and found our-selves in driving distance to the Tennessee foundry, it just made sense to include them in our local mission. That's how the Lodge Kettle on our menu was born.

Little did we know The Kettle would become a staple—a local favorite at Harvest on Main. The daily lunch comes served up in the cast iron kettle, filled to the brim with a soup or stew dreamed up by the chef each day. (See our recipe for Squash Bisque with Mascarpone and Apple-Cheese Crostini at left.)

We serve it with a simple green salad with a house-made dressing and topped with our pickled dilly green beans. It's simple but really fresh. Our guests look forward to seeing what we come up with each day. It's also great to explain to them the origin of the kettle, that it was made 100 miles from our restaurant in the oldest remaining working foundry in the United States. I feel good about what we're serving and how we're serving it.

We've continued to grow from our original from-scratch mission, opening a marketplace next door to the restaurant. The new Blue Ridge Grocery gives our team a chance to shift gears, baking fresh breads, crafting ice creams, curing hams, canning, pickling—and teaching guests how to cook in cast iron.

What more can you say about a product that's not only American made, local, and sustainably crafted, but one that's simply great to use?

MAYA DAILEY'S CHILE VERDE
Green Chile Stew

aya Dailey is the founder and owner of Maya's Farm, located in the urban setting of Phoenix, Arizona. Maya supplies certified organic vegetables, herbs, flowers, and eggs to local markets, restaurants, and schools.

Chile verde is one of Maya's favorite comfort foods, which, not surprisingly, she makes with her own tomatillos and peppers, topping each bowl with a generous shower of torn fresh cilantro leaves.

¼ cup good-quality cold-pressed extra virgin olive oil
½ cup all-purpose flour
Salt and freshly ground black pepper
2 pounds boneless pork shoulder, trimmed of excess fat (leave some on for good flavor) and cut into ½-inch cubes
2 tablespoons ground cumin
1 tablespoon ground Chimayo green chile powder (see kitchen note)
1 dried pasilla chile, seeded and chopped
½ cup chopped green onions
12 tomatillos, husked, rinsed, and finely chopped

2 medium yellow onions, finely chopped
2 serrano chiles, seeded and finely chopped
2 Anaheim chiles, seeded and finely chopped
1 green bell pepper, seeded and finely chopped
2 cups chicken stock (store-bought is fine)
1 (15-ounce) can or 2 cups green chiles (Maya uses Bueno brand, which is sold frozen and comes mild, hot, or extra hot)
1 bunch fresh cilantro

1. Heat the oil in a Lodge 5-quart cast iron Dutch oven over medium heat until sizzling.

2. While the oil heats, season the flour generously with salt and pepper. Toss the pork cubes with the seasoned flour until well coated; shake off any excess. Add the floured cubes to the hot oil in batches, and cook until nicely browned on all sides, 5 to 10 minutes. Remove the pork to a plate as it browns.

3. Add the cumin, chile powder, and pasilla chile to the oil left in the pot, and stir to combine well; cook over low heat, stirring constantly, until you can smell their fragrance, about 1 minute. Add the green onions, tomatillos, yellow onions, fresh chiles, and bell pepper, and cook over medium heat, stirring a few times, until the onions are caramelized, about 30 minutes. Add the meat back to the pot, along with the stock and green chiles, and let simmer until the flavors come together and the pork is tender, about 45 minutes, although Maya says, "It can simmer forever—the longer you simmer, the better it gets!" Adjust the heat as needed to prevent any scorching on the bottom.

4. To serve, ladle into bowls, and tear the cilantro leaves right over the stew.
Serves 4 to 6

kitchen note:
Shop for ground Chimayo chile and dried pasilla chiles online.

This dish is a marriage between two iconic Southern flavors, living in permanent honeymoon mode together. "I've seen some versions where the chicken is fried ahead of time and then pulled from the bones and stirred into the gumbo, crispy skin and all, which is delicious but causes the skin to get soggy in the broth," says Steven Satterfield, chef and co-owner of Miller Union in Atlanta. This version preserves the crunch of the fried chicken by using boneless, skin-on chicken and adding it at the last minute, cut into bite-size pieces and set atop the gumbo.

FRIED CHICKEN GUMBO

Fried chicken:
- 1 (3- to 3½-pound) whole chicken
- 6 quarts cold water
- 1½ cups kosher salt
- 4 cups buttermilk
- 3 cups bleached cake flour
- 1 cup cornstarch
- 1 tablespoon fine sea salt
- 1 tablespoon freshly ground black pepper
- 1 tablespoon dry mustard
- 1 teaspoon Hungarian paprika
- 1 teaspoon cayenne pepper
- 8 to 10 cups frying oil (canola, peanut, or vegetable oil)

Gumbo:
- 1 cup canola or peanut oil
- 2 cups bleached cake flour
- 2 cups diced onions
- 2 cups diced celery
- 2 cups diced green bell peppers
- 2 cups thinly sliced okra
- Kosher salt
- 1 tablespoon chopped garlic
- 2 tablespoons gumbo filé
- 1 teaspoon cayenne pepper
- 1 teaspoon freshly ground black pepper
- ½ teaspoon dried thyme
- 2 bay leaves
- 1 (28-ounce) can peeled whole tomatoes, drained and chopped
- 2 quarts chicken stock (store-bought is fine), heated
- 1 pound smoked sausage, such as andouille or kielbasa (optional), cut into ¼-inch-thick pieces

Rice:
- 2 tablespoons unsalted butter
- 1 cup long-grain rice (Steven likes to use Carolina Gold)
- 2 cups water or chicken stock (store-bought is fine)
- ½ teaspoon kosher salt
- Thinly sliced green onions for garnish

1. Prepare the chicken for frying: Remove the breast and dark meat from the bone (or ask your butcher to do this for you). (The wings are left on the bone and fried with the rest of the chicken as a chef's snack.) In a large container with a lid, combine the water and kosher salt, and whisk until the salt is dissolved. Carefully add the chicken pieces to the brine, cover, and refrigerate 8 to 12 hours (no longer than 12). Remove the chicken from the brine.

2. Rinse the container you used, and pour in the buttermilk. Add the chicken, turning to coat the pieces. Cover and refrigerate for 8 to 12 hours (no longer than 12).

3. Make the gumbo: (You can prepare the gumbo the day before and refrigerate; reheat before frying the chicken.) Make sure you have everything chopped and sliced before you start. Combine the oil and flour in a Lodge 15-inch cast iron skillet over high heat, and cook until the roux is the color of caramel or milk chocolate. Whisk or stir it constantly (this is always important to do when making a roux, but particularly so here, with it being cooked over high heat); Steven switches between a whisk and spatula because a whisk can't reach the edge of the pan and a spatula can—the goal is to agitate all the parts of the roux and to keep it moving. When the color is right, remove the skillet from the heat, and stir in the onions, celery, bell peppers, okra, and a few tablespoons of kosher salt. Return the skillet to medium-high heat, and cook 3 to 5 minutes, whisking constantly. Add the garlic, gumbo filé, cayenne, black pepper, thyme, and bay leaves, and cook 2 more minutes, whisking all the while. Stir in the tomatoes and stock, and simmer for 45 minutes, stirring frequently. Add the sausage, if using, during the last 10 minutes of cooking. Taste for seasoning. Remove bay leaves before serving.

4. Make the rice: Melt the butter in a small, heavy saucepan over medium heat. Add the rice, and cook, stirring, until it turns opaque. Add the water and kosher salt, and stir to combine. When the liquid begins to simmer, turn the heat down to its lowest setting, and cover. Check after 15 minutes for doneness. Fluff with a fork, then allow to cool.

5. Fry the chicken: Combine the flour, cornstarch, sea salt, black pepper, mustard, paprika, and cayenne, and whisk until combined. When ready to fry, heat 2 inches of oil in a Lodge 15-inch cast iron skillet over high heat to 325°, checking the temperature with an oil thermometer. As you are frying, adjust the heat under the skillet to keep it at a steady 325°.

6. Squeeze off as much buttermilk as you can from the chicken pieces (but don't pat them dry; they need to be slightly wet going into the flour), then dredge them in the flour mixture. Without crowding the skillet, slowly lower each piece into the hot oil. Fry off the pieces until they are golden brown on all sides and cooked through, 10 to 12 minutes, depending on their size; the dark meat might take a little longer than the white. Drain on a wire rack or paper towels. Serve the chicken within two hours of frying.

7. For each serving, place a mound of rice in a deep bowl using an ice cream scoop to form a round mold. Ladle the hot gumbo over the rice, then slice the boneless fried chicken pieces, and place on top. Garnish with green onions, if desired. Serve the wings on the side as an extra snack, or eat them while you are simmering your gumbo. **Serves 12**

CHICKEN AND MUSHROOM STEW WITH WILD RICE

his soothing, rustic dish gets its deep flavors from the old-school chicken and wild rice casserole and its technique from a country-style French braise," says Hunter Lewis, executive editor at *Southern Living* magazine, who makes his in a battered Lodge Logic 6-quart enameled cast iron Dutch oven. Hunter recommends using real wild rice rather than quick-cooking. "You want that nutty flavor and slightly chewy texture from the grain to help sop up all of the good chicken and gravy."

3 tablespoons extra virgin olive oil
1 (2-ounce) slice country ham or 2 slices bacon, finely chopped
6 skinless, boneless chicken thighs, cut into 2-inch pieces
Kosher salt and freshly ground black pepper
4 cups button mushrooms, quartered
¼ cup white wine vinegar
1 carrot, finely chopped
1 medium onion, finely chopped
3 garlic cloves, finely chopped
1 bay leaf
3 tablespoons salted butter
¼ cup all-purpose flour
1 cup whole or skim milk
2½ cups chicken broth
½ teaspoon freshly grated nutmeg
½ teaspoon dry mustard
1 (4-ounce) box wild rice, cooked according to package directions
2 tablespoons chopped fresh flat-leaf parsley

1. Preheat the oven to 325°.

2. Heat 1 tablespoon of the oil in a Lodge 5-quart cast iron Dutch oven over medium-high heat. Add the ham, and cook, stirring occasionally, until browned, about 6 minutes. Transfer to a plate with a slotted spoon.

3. Add 1 tablespoon oil to the pot. Season the chicken with salt and pepper. Working in 2 batches, sear the chicken until browned on both sides, about 6 minutes for each batch. Transfer the chicken to the plate with the ham.

4. Add the remaining 1 tablespoon oil and the mushrooms to the pot, and cook, stirring occasionally, until just softened, about 4 minutes. Transfer to the plate with the chicken and ham. Add the vinegar to deglaze, and cook until reduced by half, loosening any browned bits from the bottom of the pot with a wooden spoon. Stir in the carrot, onion, garlic, and bay leaf, and cook, stirring occasionally, until the onion is softened, about 6 minutes. Remove from the heat, and return the ham, chicken, mushrooms, and any juices accumulated on the plate to the pot.

5. Melt the butter in a medium saucepan over medium-low heat until bubbling. Add the flour, and cook, whisking constantly, 1 minute. Whisk in the milk, and cook, whisking often, until the sauce thickens and coats the back of a spoon, about 4 minutes. Whisk in the broth, nutmeg, and mustard, and cook until the sauce thickens again. Season with salt and pepper to taste.

6. Pour the gravy over the chicken mixture. Stir to combine. Cover the Dutch oven, and bake until the chicken is very tender, about 45 minutes. Serve the stew ladled over the rice and sprinkled with the parsley. Remove the bay leaf before serving. **Serves 6**

ROAST BEEF, BLUE CHEESE, AND ONION JAM PANINI

This panini tastes like a good steak dinner nestled between two slices of bread. It's even better when toasted on a cast iron grill pan. Sheri Castle advises that you keep a jar of the Onion Jam stashed in the fridge at all times. "It's habit forming, and you never know when a craving might strike."

½ cup crumbled blue cheese
1 tablespoon mayonnaise
1½ teaspoons prepared horseradish, or to taste
12 large ½-inch-thick slices country-style white bread
6 ounces thinly sliced high-quality roast beef
1 Granny Smith apple, unpeeled, cored, and sliced paper thin
¾ cup Onion Jam (recipe follows)
3 tablespoons salted butter, softened

1. In a small bowl, stir the blue cheese, mayonnaise, and horseradish together, mashing the cheese with a fork until the mixture is almost smooth. Store in the refrigerator, covered, for up to 3 days, if desired. Return to room temperature before using.

2. Place 6 slices of the bread on a work surface, and spread each with 1 heaping tablespoon of the blue cheese spread. Divide the roast beef and apple among the bread slices, covering each evenly. Spread about 1 tablespoon of the Onion Jam over the top of each. Set the remaining bread slices on top. Generously butter the tops and bottoms of the panini.

3. Heat a Lodge 12-inch cast iron grill pan over high heat. Working in batches, arrange the panini on the hot surface, and weigh down the top with a cast iron grill press or skillet or by pressing with a metal spatula. Toast, turning once, until the bread is browned, about 5 minutes per side. Serve warm with the remaining Onion Jam on the side. **Serves 6**

how Sheri makes a panini

1. Use a spread or some other type of condiment on the bread slices to help the sandwich hold together during cooking.

2. Use a heavy pan, like another cast iron skillet, to press down the sandwich when it's cooking on the grill pan.

3. You can use a metal spatula to press the sandwich, if desired.

4. Wait until the bread is nice and browned before turning—this will take about 5 minutes per side.

ONION JAM

6 tablespoons (¾ stick) salted
   butter
2 pounds yellow onions, halved
   lengthwise and thinly sliced
¼ cup firmly packed light brown
   sugar

¼ cup red wine
1 tablespoon balsamic vinegar
2 teaspoons finely chopped fresh
   rosemary
Kosher salt and freshly ground
   black pepper

1. Melt the butter in a Lodge 12-inch cast iron skillet over medium heat. Add the onions, and stir to coat. Cover the skillet, and cook, stirring occasionally, until the onions are completely limp, about 15 minutes.

2. Uncover the skillet, and reduce the heat to medium-low. Cook, stirring often to scrape up the brown glaze that forms on the bottom of the skillet, until the onions are very soft and golden brown, about 25 minutes more.

3. Add the brown sugar, wine, and vinegar. Stir until the sugar dissolves and the liquid cooks away, about 5 minutes.

4. Remove from the heat. Stir in the rosemary, and season with salt and pepper to taste. Set aside to cool to room temperature. Store in the refrigerator, covered, for up to 1 week. **Makes about 2 cups**

TOASTED CHILE-CUMIN MARINATED SKIRT STEAK TACOS

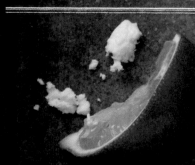

I love to create marinades using toasted whole chiles and spices because they allow you to create richness and depth of flavor quickly," enthuses Norman King, *Southern Living* Test Kitchen professional. In this recipe the marinade plays a dual role: imparting flavor and tenderness to the meat. Plus, cooking it without wiping off the excess marinade gives the steak its own sauce. After the steak stands, simply slice and serve. "No hot sauce required," says Norman.

3 dried guajillo chiles (see kitchen note)
1 cup boiling water
2 tablespoons olive oil
½ cup chopped sweet onion
2 garlic cloves, peeled
½ teaspoon cumin seeds
½ teaspoon dried oregano
2½ teaspoons kosher salt

1 tablespoon cider vinegar
1½ pounds skirt steak, trimmed of fat
Radish-Tomatillo Salad (recipe follows)
8 to 10 (6-inch) fajita-size corn tortillas
1 tablespoon vegetable oil
Crumbled queso fresco

1. Heat a Lodge 12-inch cast iron skillet over medium heat until hot, about 5 minutes. Add the chiles, and toast, turning often, until they puff and become fragrant, 1 to 2 minutes. (Chiles burn quickly, so keep a watchful eye.) Cut the chiles open with kitchen shears; remove the seeds. Cut off the stems. Place the chiles in a heatproof medium bowl, and cover with the boiling water. Let stand 10 minutes.

2. Meanwhile, heat the olive oil in the same skillet over medium heat. Add the onion, garlic, cumin seeds, and oregano, and cook, stirring, until the onion is just tender, 2 to 3 minutes. Let cool 5 minutes. Add the onion mixture, salt, and vinegar to the chiles and their soaking water, and process in a blender or food processor until smooth. Cover and chill 30 minutes. Wash and dry the skillet.

3. Pour the chile mixture over the steak in a shallow dish, cover, and chill 2 to 4 hours.

4. Make the Radish-Tomatillo Salad.

5. Lightly brush the tortillas with the vegetable oil on both sides. Heat the same cast iron skillet over medium heat. Once hot, cook the tortillas one at time until slightly charred, 1 to 2 minutes per side. Wrap in aluminum foil, and keep warm.

6. Heat the same skillet over medium heat. Remove the steak from the marinade, discarding the marinade; don't wipe off any of the clinging marinade. Cook the steak in the hot skillet to your desired degree of doneness, 7 to 8 minutes per side for medium.

7. Remove the steak to a cutting board. Let stand 5 to 10 minutes before slicing against the grain into thin strips. Serve in the charred tortillas with Radish-Tomatillo Salad and queso fresco. **Serves 4**

kitchen note:

Dried chiles are easily found in the ethnic or Latin sections of local supermarkets. They are commonly sold in small cellophane bags and are nestled next to dried herbs and spices in similar packaging. If guajillo chiles are not available, feel free to substitute the same amount of New Mexico chiles.

RADISH·TOMATILLO SALAD

1	cup radishes, cut into thin strips	1½	teaspoons kosher salt
1	medium tomatillo, husked and diced, or green tomato, diced	¼	teaspoon sugar
1	small Kirby cucumber, halved lengthwise and thinly sliced	½	cup chopped fresh cilantro
		¼	cup chopped fresh mint
		1	tablespoon fresh lime juice

1. In a medium bowl, toss together the radishes, tomatillo, cucumber, salt, and sugar. Transfer the mixture to a colander, and let stand 30 minutes.

2. Transfer the mixture back to the bowl, and stir in the cilantro, mint, and lime juice just before serving. **Makes about 2 cups**

hef Jaime Marin blends the rich flavors of his native Mexico with the long tradition of Mexican cuisine in Los Angeles in this recipe. Carnitas, literally "little meats," is a type of braised or roasted pork traditionally made using the richly marbled Boston butt or picnic ham. It is seasoned heavily and slow cooked until it is so tender it can be pulled apart by hand or forks, then fried until crispy.

Carnitas:
¼ cup lard or ¾ cup vegetable oil
3½ pounds boneless pork shoulder, trimmed of fat and cut into large chunks
1 onion, chopped
5 garlic cloves, chopped
1½ cups water
½ cup orange juice
1 tablespoon finely shredded orange zest
5 sprigs fresh thyme
2 tablespoons salt
1 tablespoon dried Mexican oregano (see kitchen note)
1½ teaspoons cayenne pepper
4 bay leaves
Taco topping:
½ onion, chopped
1 large bunch fresh cilantro, chopped
Small corn tortillas
Salsa verde or roja

1. Melt 2 tablespoons of the lard or heat ½ cup of the oil in a Lodge 7-quart cast iron Dutch oven over medium heat until hot. Brown the pork chunks evenly in the hot oil on all sides, moving the pieces frequently so they don't stick. (You'll likely have to brown the meat in batches.)

2. When all the meat is browned, return it to the pot, add the onion and garlic, and cook, stirring frequently, until the onion is a little browned and has softened, 3 to 5 minutes. Add the water, orange juice and zest, thyme, salt, oregano, cayenne, and bay leaves; mix well, and bring to a boil. Reduce the heat to a gentle simmer, cover, and cook for 2 hours.

3. Remove the lid, increase the heat so the mixture is at a gentle boil, and cook until nearly all the liquid has evaporated, about 40 minutes, stirring occasionally.

4. Melt the remaining 2 tablespoons lard or heat the remaining ¼ cup oil in a Lodge 12-inch cast iron skillet over medium-high heat until hot. Working in small batches, remove the pork from the Dutch oven, and fry it in the hot oil until crisp, 4 to 6 minutes. As they finish cooking, transfer the crispy carnitas to a cutting board. When all the pork has been fried, chop the carnitas into bite-size pieces.

5. Make the taco topping: In a small bowl, mix the onion and cilantro together.

6. To serve, place some of the carnitas on a heated tortilla, top with the cilantro and onion mix, add your favorite salsa, and enjoy. **Serves 4**

kitchen note:

Mediterranean and Mexican oregano are two different plants, but because they have a somewhat similar flavor, they are both called oregano. Mediterranean oregano has a sweet, strong flavor and is an essential ingredient in many of the dishes from the region. Mexican oregano is stronger and less sweet, well suited to the spicy, hot, cumin-flavored dishes of Mexico and Central America—perfect for chili and salsa. Both types should be added in the beginning of cooking, so they have time to meld with the other flavors of the dish.

GRILLED SWORDFISH SANDWICHES

2 swordfish steaks (¾ to 1 inch thick)
Extra virgin olive oil
Sea salt and freshly ground black pepper
⅓ cup mixed greens
2 small ciabattas, cut open
4 slices ripe tomatoes
2 teaspoons capers
Balsamic vinegar for sprinkling

1. Wash and pat dry the swordfish steaks. Coat both sides with oil, and season with salt and pepper to taste.

2. Heat a Lodge 12-inch cast iron grill pan over high heat until hot. Add the swordfish steaks to the pan, and grill just until cooked through, 3 to 4 minutes per side.

3. To assemble each sandwich, layer half the greens on the bottom half of a ciabatta, set a swordfish steak on top of 2 tomato slices, sprinkle with 1 teaspoon of the capers and a little vinegar, and finish with a drizzle of olive oil. Top with the other half of the ciabatta, cut the sandwich in half with a serrated knife, and serve. **Serves 2**

This simple yet elegant swordfish sandwich is from Chuck Aflitto, TV personality and owner of Chef Chuck's Cucina, an importer of fine Italian food and wine based in Arizona. "Using a Lodge pan to cook this quick and healthy recipe will ensure a juicy and perfectly crusted swordfish steak," says Chef Chuck. "Enjoy!"

SOUPS & SANDWICHES

My Mother's Chicken and
Potatoes, page 116

POULTRY

NEW ENGLAND CHICKEN POTPIE WITH BISCUIT CRUST

All-American chicken potpie most likely came to us via an early New England stew made with a sturdy biscuit crust and baked in a heavy cast iron pot or casserole. The original pie probably contained neither peas nor mushrooms, but few would argue that this later innovation isn't at least partly responsible for the dish's popular and long-lasting appeal all over the country. This version is from cookbook author Jim Villas.

Filling:
2 tablespoons butter
2 medium onions, diced
1 celery rib, diced
1 large carrot, diced
3 cups cubed (1-inch) cooked
   chicken
1½ cups fresh or frozen green peas
1 cup diced fresh mushrooms
Salt and freshly ground black pepper

¼ cup vegetable shortening
¼ cup all-purpose flour
1½ cups chicken broth
1 cup half-and-half
Biscuit Crust:
2 cups all-purpose flour
1 tablespoon baking powder
½ teaspoon salt
¼ cup chilled vegetable shortening
1 cup whole milk

1. Grease a Lodge 2-quart cast iron casserole.

2. Make the filling: Melt the butter in the casserole over medium heat, add the onions, celery, and carrot, and stir until the vegetables soften, about 5 minutes. Stir in the chicken, peas, and mushrooms, season to taste with salt and pepper, and set aside.

3. In a heavy medium saucepan, melt the shortening over medium heat, sprinkle the flour over the top, and stir constantly for 3 minutes; don't let the roux color. Remove from the heat, and gradually add the broth and half-and-half, stirring constantly until well blended. Return the mixture to the heat, and cook, stirring constantly, until the sauce thickens. Pour over the chicken and vegetables in the casserole.

4. Preheat the oven to 425°.

5. Make the biscuit crust: In a medium bowl, whisk the flour, baking powder, and salt together. Add the shortening, and cut it in with a pastry cutter or rub it into the flour with your fingertips until the mixture is mealy. Add the milk, and stir just until the dough forms a ball. Transfer to a lightly floured work surface, knead about 8 times, then pat the dough out about ⅓ inch thick. Cut the dough to fit the top of the casserole, drape it over the filling, and secure the edges by crimping them. Cut a few vents in the top with a sharp knife, and bake until the crust is nicely browned and juices are bubbling up through the vents, about 25 minutes. **Serves 6**

SKILLET ROAST CHICKEN

1	(3½- to 4-pound) roasting chicken		Salt and freshly ground black pepper
3	tablespoons cold butter, divided	2	tablespoons softened butter
1	lemon	½	teaspoon smoked Spanish paprika
1	or 2 garlic cloves, peeled		Wine, chicken broth, or water
2	or 3 sprigs fresh rosemary		(optional)

John Schenck, publisher of *Edible Rhody* magazine, always roasts his chicken in a cast iron skillet. "I know roast chicken recipes are a dime a dozen, but this one provides guaranteed moist breast meat and great pan juices," he maintains. A key to the recipe's success is that your chicken just fits in the pan. The heat radiating from the raised rim of the skillet helps ensure that the legs cook as fast as the breast and that the skin browns uniformly. A 9- or 10-inch pan should work for a 4-pound chicken.

1. Preheat the oven to 450°. Pull the liver, gizzard, and other innards from the cavity, and save for another use or discard. Dry the chicken inside and out with paper towels. Remove the flaps of fat from the cavity opening—there should be one on each side. (If your butcher has removed the fat, you can use cold butter for this step. Figure on 1 tablespoon for each breast.) Cut each piece of fat in half. Work your fingers under the skin of each breast, being careful not to tear it, going as far back as you can. Put two pieces of the cavity fat under the skin on each breast, one in back, toward the wing, the other farther forward near the leg. Position them fairly high up so that, as the chicken cooks, they melt down over and into the breast meat, keeping it moist.

2. Poke the lemon with a poultry needle to make about 12 holes. Insert the lemon in the cavity. Now put the garlic, rosemary, and a little salt and pepper in there, and close up the cavity with the needle.

3. Rub the chicken all over with about half the softened butter, then sprinkle it with the paprika and salt and pepper.

4. Put the rest of the softened butter in a Lodge cast iron skillet, and turn the burner to high. Once the butter has melted and is sizzling, put the chicken in the pan, breast side up. It should fit snugly, with the legs almost touching the wall of the pan. If they do touch, that's fine. Let the chicken sizzle in the pan for a minute or two, then put it in the oven. Roast the chicken for 30 minutes, then turn off the oven, and leave the bird in it for another 30 minutes. Do not open the oven.

5. Take the pan out of the oven, and let the chicken rest in it for at least 20 minutes. With an instant-read thermometer, check the internal temperature at the thigh; it should be 165°. Transfer the chicken to a serving platter. Carve it, and cover with aluminum foil to keep it warm while you heat up the pan juices—you can add a little wine, chicken broth, or water to it if you like. Let it boil for a couple of minutes, then, off the heat, stir in remaining 1 tablespoon cold butter, whisking or stirring until it melts into the juices. Serve the chicken pieces with the pan juices poured over. **Serves 4 to 6**

how John roasts a chicken

 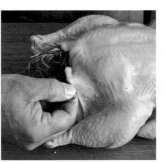  

1. Use kitchen shears to remove the flaps of fat from both sides of the cavity opening—there should be one on each side—and to cut each piece in half.

2. Gently use your fingers to push the pieces of fat under the skin without tearing it. If the skin tears, the fat will melt into the pan instead of directly into the meat.

3. Stuff the cavity with ingredients such as rosemary, garlic, and lemon. Use a poultry needle to close the cavity so that the flavors will be trapped in the cavity and infuse into the meat while baking.

4. Place the chicken in a heated skillet with melted butter. The skillet needs to be small enough so that the legs almost touch the sides of the skillet.

HAY-ROASTED CHICKEN

3 ounces country white bread, cut into 1-inch cubes
⅓ cup buttermilk (Tyler likes to use Cruze Farm Dairy buttermilk from Knoxville, Tennessee)
3 garlic cloves, crushed
3 golden shallots, coarsely chopped
2½ tablespoons extra virgin olive oil
5 tablespoons rendered duck fat or unsalted butter
3 tablespoons chopped fresh flat-leaf parsley
1 tablespoon coarsely chopped fresh rosemary
1 ounce sprigs fresh thyme
2 tablespoons whole-grain mustard
Kosher salt and freshly ground black pepper
1 (2½-pound) roasting chicken
2 handfuls unsprayed wheat straw
Finely grated zest of 2 lemons
Finely grated zest of 2 oranges
10 star anise
2 tablespoons fennel seeds
2 tablespoons coriander seeds
1 tablespoon canola oil

1. Preheat the oven to 350°.

2. In a medium bowl, combine the bread and buttermilk; let stand until the bread softens, about 5 minutes. Drain, then squeeze the excess buttermilk from the bread.

3. In a covered Lodge 10-inch cast iron skillet over low heat, sweat the garlic and shallots in 1½ tablespoons of the olive oil, stirring occasionally, until tender, about 10 minutes. Let cool, then transfer the mixture to a food processor or blender. Add the bread, duck fat, 1 tablespoon of the parsley, the rosemary, and thyme, and process into a paste. Stir in the remaining 1 tablespoon olive oil and 2 tablespoons parsley and the mustard, and season to taste with salt and pepper.

4. Gently separate the skin from the chicken breasts with your fingers, being careful not to tear it. Spoon in a little of the stuffing, and spread it evenly across each breast by gently running your hand over the skin to smooth it out. Spoon the remaining stuffing into the cavity of the bird. Truss the cavity closed with kitchen twine. Season the chicken with salt and pepper to taste, and set aside.

5. Combine the hay, citrus zest, star anise, and fennel and coriander seeds in a Lodge 7-quart cast iron Dutch oven.

6. Heat the canola oil in a Lodge 12-inch cast iron skillet over high heat, then brown the chicken well on all sides. Place the browned chicken on top of the hay mixture, cover, and roast until the juices run clear at the thigh when pierced, about 1½ hours. Let stand for 10 minutes before carving into serving pieces. **Serves 4**

This is a recipe from Tyler Brown, executive chef of the Capitol Grille at the Hermitage Hotel in Nashville, Tennessee.

POULTRY

a cooking secret from Tyler

Roasting the chicken in wheat straw allows it to retain its moisture and develop a very earthy flavor. Purchase unsprayed wheat straw from a local farmers' market or feed store.

"I n my family, favorite dishes are always being altered according to what is available and what is best—especially when I'm cooking," says Lidia Bastianich, restaurateur, best-selling cookbook author, and one of the best-loved chefs on television. "Here's a perfect example: Chicken and potatoes, fried together in a big skillet so they're crisp and moist at the same time, is my mother's specialty. Growing up, my brother and I demanded it every week; our kids, Tanya, Joe, Eric, Paul, and Estelle, clamored for it too. And now the next generation of little ones is asking their great-grandmother to make chicken and potatoes for them."

MY MOTHER'S CHICKEN AND POTATOES
(WITH MY SPECIAL TOUCHES)

Basic Chicken and Potatoes:
- 2½ pounds skin-on, bone-in chicken legs or assorted pieces
- ½ cup canola oil
- ½ teaspoon kosher salt, or more to taste
- 1 pound Red Bliss potatoes, preferably no bigger than 2 inches across
- 2 tablespoons extra virgin olive oil, or more as needed
- 2 medium-small onions, quartered lengthwise
- 2 short branches fresh rosemary with plenty of needles

Lidia's Special Touches (try either or both):
- 1 or 2 pickled cherry peppers, sweet or hot (or none, or more!), cut in half and seeded
- 4 to 6 ounces sliced bacon (5 or 6 slices)

1. Rinse the chicken pieces, and pat dry with paper towels. Trim off excess skin and all visible fat. Cut the drumsticks from the thighs. If using breast halves, cut each into 2 smaller pieces.

2. If using the bacon, make roll-ups: Cut the bacon slices in half crosswise, and roll each half into a neat, tight cylinder. Stick a toothpick through the roll to secure it; cut or break the toothpick so only a tiny bit sticks out.

3. Pour the canola oil into a Lodge 15-inch cast iron skillet, and set over high heat. Sprinkle the chicken on all sides with ¼ teaspoon of the salt. When the oil is very hot, lay the pieces, skin side down, an inch or so apart—watch out for oil spatters. Don't crowd the chicken: if necessary, fry it in batches, similar pieces (like drumsticks) together. Drop the bacon rolls into the oil around the chicken, turning and shifting them often. Let the chicken fry in place for several minutes to brown on the underside, then turn and continue frying until it's golden brown on all sides, 7 to 10 minutes or more for dark meat pieces. Fry breast pieces only for 5 minutes or so, taking them out of the oil as soon as they are golden. Let the bacon rolls cook and get lightly crisp, but not dark. Adjust the heat to maintain steady sizzling and coloring; remove the crisped chicken pieces and bacon rolls with tongs to a bowl.

4. Meanwhile, rinse and dry the potatoes; slice each one through the middle on the axis that gives the largest cut surface, then toss them in a bowl with the olive oil and remaining ¼ teaspoon salt.

5. When the chicken and bacon are cooked and out of the skillet, pour off the frying oil. Return the skillet to medium heat, and put all the potatoes, cut side down, in a single layer in the hot pan. With a rubber spatula, scrape all the olive oil out of the bowl back into the skillet; drizzle over a bit more oil if the pan seems dry. Fry and crisp the potatoes for about 4 minutes to form a crust, then move them around the pan, still cut side down, until they're all brown and crisp, 7 minutes or more. Turn them over, and fry another 2 minutes to cook and crisp on their rounded skin sides.

6. Still over medium heat, toss the onion wedges and rosemary branches around the pan with the potatoes. If using the cherry peppers, cut the seeded halves into ½-inch-wide pieces, and scatter them in the pan too. Return the chicken pieces—except the breast pieces—to the pan, along with the bacon rolls; pour in any chicken juices that have accumulated in the bowl. Raise the heat slightly, and carefully turn and tumble the chicken, potatoes, onions, bacon, and pepper pieces, so they're heating up and getting coated with pan juices—but take care not to break the potato pieces. Spread everything out in the pan—the potatoes on the bottom as much as possible so they can keep crisping up—and put on the cover.

7. Lower the heat to medium, and cook for about 7 minutes, shaking the pan occasionally, then uncover and tumble everything again. Cover and cook another 7 minutes or so, then add the breast pieces and give everything another tumble. Cover and cook for 10 minutes more.

8. Remove the cover, turn the pieces again, and cook in the open skillet for about 10 minutes to evaporate the moisture and caramelize everything. Taste a bit of potato (or chicken) for salt, and sprinkle on more as needed. Turn the pieces now and then. When everything is all glistening and golden and the potatoes and chicken are cooked through, remove the skillet from the stove and—as Lidia does at home—bring it right to the table. Serve portions of chicken and potatoes, or let people help themselves. **Serves 4 to 6**

a cooking secret from Lidia

Sticking a toothpick through each bacon roll to secure it will allow the bacon to roll around in the pan and cook evenly.

BUTTERMILK-BRINED FRIED CHICKEN WITH HOT PEPPER HONEY

Elizabeth Karmel, North Carolina native and executive chef of Hill Country Barbecue and Hill Country Chicken in New York City, serves her fried chicken with spicy honey. "The hot pepper honey is a variation on the theme of one of my Southern staples, hot pepper jelly. It elevates the chicken, adding a fiery sweetness that captures the best of Southern fried chicken in one bite!" says Elizabeth. You can also melt down hot pepper jelly for the same effect.

Hot Pepper Honey (recipe follows)
Southern Buttermilk Brine (recipe follows)
1 (4-pound) whole chicken, cut into 8 pieces
Seasoned flour:
2½ cups all-purpose flour
1 tablespoon kosher salt
2 teaspoons coarsely ground black pepper
2 teaspoons granulated garlic
2 teaspoons onion powder
2 teaspoons smoked Spanish paprika
1 quart peanut oil

1. Make the Hot Pepper Honey (preferably several days in advance to let the flavors develop) and Southern Buttermilk Brine.

2. Pat the chicken pieces dry, and remove excess fat. Place the chicken in a heavy-duty brining bag or a nonreactive food-safe container with a lid. Pour the brine on the chicken, cover, and refrigerate for 2 to 3 hours. The smaller pieces will take less time and the larger pieces will take more time. DO NOT OVER-BRINE or the chicken will be too salty.

3. In a medium bowl, whisk the seasoned flour ingredients together.

4. Remove the chicken from the brine; drain off the excess liquid. Coat evenly in the seasoned flour, shaking off any excess. Let stand for 5 minutes, then coat again with the seasoned flour, and let stand another 5 minutes before frying.

5. Pour enough oil in a Lodge 5-quart cast iron chicken fryer to reach ½ inch up the side. Heat the oil to 325°. You may have to adjust the heat level under the pot to maintain a steady temperature.

6. Immediately place the chicken, skin side down, in the hot oil, and cover the pot. Once you see that the bottoms of the chicken pieces are golden brown and the tops are beginning to cook, about 10 minutes, turn the chicken over. Place the lid back on the pot, and fry for another 5 minutes or so. You can remove the lid when the chicken is almost done to crisp up the skin. Cook a total of 20 to 25 minutes, depending on the size of the chicken pieces. Remember, turn only once, and larger pieces may take longer. The chicken should be cooked all the way to the bone. Note: It may help to place the thighs in the middle of the skillet where the oil is the hottest and surround them with the breasts, legs, and wings.

7. Drain the chicken on a wire rack set on a baking sheet, and place in a low oven (250° to 300°) until ready to serve. Serve with the Hot Pepper Honey on the side. **Serves 6**

HOT PEPPER HONEY

¼ cup favorite fruity hot sauce, preferably habañero

1 to 2 generous teaspoons red pepper flakes, to your taste

Pinch of fine sea salt

1 cup best-quality honey

1. In a small bowl, mix all the ingredients together well. Taste and adjust the level of heat to your liking. Store in a glass jar in the refrigerator. This gets better after it stands for a couple of days. It will keep for up to a week. Stir before using. **Makes about 1¼ cups**

SOUTHERN BUTTERMILK BRINE

3 cups hot water

1 cup kosher salt

1 cup firmly packed dark brown sugar

2 tablespoons dried rosemary or 3 large sprigs fresh rosemary

1 generous teaspoon cracked black peppercorns

2 generous cups ice cubes

4 cups cold buttermilk

1 teaspoon cayenne pepper

1. In a large saucepan over high heat, bring the water, salt, sugar, rosemary, and peppercorns to a boil, stirring to dissolve the sugar and salt. Stir and let steep and cool for 15 minutes.

2. Add the ice cubes, buttermilk, and cayenne. Whisk well. **Makes about 2 quarts**

how Elizabeth fries chicken

1. For an extra crispy crust, coat the chicken pieces twice in the seasoned flour. After each coat, let the chicken stand for 5 minutes.

2. Be sure the oil reaches 325° before frying the chicken. To see if the oil has reached the right temperature, drop a cube of bread in the oil. If it floats and immediately starts to bubble and brown on the edges, then the oil is ready.

3. Carefully place the chicken in the hot oil. Keep the pot covered while frying and only remove it once the chicken is almost done. This final step will ensure the skin gets crisp.

4. Remove the chicken from the oil, and drain on a wire rack set on a baking sheet; place in an oven heated at 250° to 300° until ready to serve.

This is one of those back-pocket recipes that I share with my friends and family who want to know more about the merits of cast iron cooking," says Hunter Lewis. It will serve you well on a busy Wednesday night or a lazy Sunday afternoon. This recipe will deliver super juicy meat with potato chip-crisp skin. "I usually squeeze lemon into the pan juices and serve them with the chicken, slices of a rustic French or Italian bread, a green salad, and a glass of wine," says Hunter.

6   skin-on, bone-in chicken thighs
Kosher salt and freshly ground black
    pepper

2   teaspoons vegetable oil

1. Preheat the oven to 425°.

2. Season the chicken thighs with salt and pepper to taste. Heat the oil in a Lodge 12-inch cast iron skillet over medium-high heat until it shimmers. Nestle the chicken thighs in the skillet, skin side down, reduce the heat to medium, and cook, rotating the skillet every 2 minutes to promote even cooking, until the skin is golden brown, about 12 minutes.

3. Transfer the skillet to the oven, and roast the chicken until just cooked through, about 12 minutes more. Using tongs, flip the chicken, skin side up, and cook 2 more minutes to air-dry the skin. Transfer the chicken to a plate, and let stand 5 minutes before serving. **Serves 4**

a cooking secret from Hunter

The key to this dish is the technique: Sear the chicken thighs, skin side down, in a skillet. Then pop the skillet in the oven and continue cooking the chicken through. Once the skin is deep golden, flip the chicken thighs to air-dry the skin.

According to Honolulu-based culinary product specialist Ann Hall Every, this is one of the most popular foods in Hawai'i when ordering a "plate lunch," which is not just for lunchtime eating. Drive-ins are a classic place to experience a plate lunch, as well as many other casual restaurants. A plate lunch comes with two scoops of rice (medium-grain white rice scooped with an ice cream scoop) and a scoop of macaroni salad, which in Hawai'i sometimes includes cooked cubed potatoes.

SHOYU CHICKEN

- 1 cup shoyu (see kitchen note)
- 1 cup water
- ¼ cup mirin (sweet cooking wine)
- ⅓ cup firmly packed dark brown sugar
- ⅓ cup granulated sugar
- 6 garlic cloves, finely minced
- 1 tablespoon minced fresh ginger (no need to peel)
- 1 teaspoon freshly ground black pepper
- 1 teaspoon red pepper flakes
- 12 skin-on, bone-in chicken thighs (preferably organic)

1. In a glass or ceramic dish large enough to hold the chicken in a single layer, mix together the shoyu, water, mirin, both sugars, garlic, ginger, and black and red pepper; stir to dissolve the sugars.

2. Place the chicken thighs in the marinade, turning to coat them, then cover with plastic wrap, and refrigerate for up to 12 hours. Remove from the refrigerator 1 hour before grilling.

3. Heat a Lodge 12-inch cast iron grill pan over medium-high heat for 5 minutes. Lightly pat dry the chicken, and place in the hot grill pan, skin side down. Lower the heat to medium-low, and grill until the chicken is cooked through, about 15 minutes per side. **Serves 4 to 6, depending on size of chicken thighs**

kitchen note:

Shoyu is the Japanese name for soy sauce; you can use a reduced-sodium version, if desired.

Cast Iron Memories

I bought a 12-inch skillet back in the 1970s when I first learned that fried chicken was best when cooked in cast iron! I bought it at my local hardware store in Manhattan—when neighborhood hardware stores still existed—brought it home, and proceeded to "season" the pan by cooking a batch of French fries in vegetable oil. I do not remember when or how this pan got lost, but I have since replaced it with the preseasoned cast iron that Lodge now manufactures. After all these years, my favorite cast iron recipe is still Southern fried chicken!

—*Ann Hall Every*

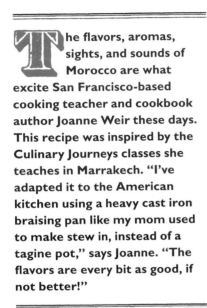

he flavors, aromas, sights, and sounds of Morocco are what excite San Francisco-based cooking teacher and cookbook author Joanne Weir these days. This recipe was inspired by the Culinary Journeys classes she teaches in Marrakech. "I've adapted it to the American kitchen using a heavy cast iron braising pan like my mom used to make stew in, instead of a tagine pot," says Joanne. "The flavors are every bit as good, if not better!"

BRAISED CHICKEN
WITH DRIED APRICOTS,
ALMONDS, AND HONEY

2 tablespoons olive oil	1 teaspoon turmeric
12 bone-in chicken thighs, skinned (3 to 3½ pounds)	¼ teaspoon ground cinnamon
2 teaspoons ground ginger	1 teaspoon kosher salt
2 teaspoons ras el hanout	1 small red onion, diced
1½ teaspoons freshly ground black pepper	1½ cups low-sodium chicken broth
Large pinch of saffron threads	24 dried pitted apricots
	½ cup whole natural almonds
	2 tablespoons honey

1. Warm the oil in a Lodge 7-quart cast iron Dutch oven over medium-high heat. Add the chicken in batches, and cook until light golden on both sides, about 5 minutes per batch.

2. Add the ginger, ras el hanout, pepper, saffron, turmeric, cinnamon, salt, onion, and broth to the pot. Bring to a boil, reduce the heat, cover, and simmer slowly for 20 minutes.

3. Add the apricots and almonds, and continue to cook, covered, until the chicken is tender and the meat is falling off the bone, another 10 to 15 minutes.

4. Remove the pan from the heat, spoon the chicken, apricots, and almonds into a serving bowl, and drizzle with the honey. Serve immediately. **Serves 6**

a cooking secret from Joanne

Ras el hanout is a spice blend that's commonly used in Moroccan cuisine. It can be purchased at specialty food stores or online. You can also prepare the blend yourself using a combination of spices such as cardamom, cloves, paprika, coriander, cumin, and nutmeg.

On busy weeknights, Nashville-based Matt Moore, author of *Have Her Over for Dinner: A Gentleman's Guide to Classic, Simple Meals,* still finds time to put together a wholesome, healthy meal. The versatility of cast iron allows Matt to create a perfect sear on skin-on, bone-in chicken breasts on the stove-top—then he finishes the dish off with the remaining ingredients by roasting everything in the oven. This meld of flavors tastes like it took hours of preparation when, truth be told, the meal can be prepped, cooked, and served in about a half hour.

PAN-ROASTED CHICKEN BREASTS WITH ROASTED TOMATOES AND WHITE BEANS

2   tablespoons extra virgin olive oil
2   (8-ounce) skin-on, bone-in chicken breasts
1   cup cherry tomatoes
4   garlic cloves, peeled
Kosher salt and freshly cracked pepper

½   tablespoon dried rosemary
1   cup canned **Great Northern**, navy, or other white beans, rinsed and drained

1. Preheat the oven to 425°.

2. Heat a Lodge 12-inch cast iron skillet over medium-high heat for 1 minute. Add the oil—it should shimmer in the pan and just begin to smoke. Add the chicken breasts, skin side down, and sear for 3 minutes (leave them totally alone, no fussing or poking). After 3 minutes, flip the chicken breasts; add the tomatoes and garlic so they make contact with the pan. Season everything lightly with salt and pepper, and sprinkle with the rosemary.

3. Place the skillet in the oven, and roast until the chicken is just cooked through at its thickest point, 18 to 22 minutes. Add the beans for the last 5 minutes of cooking, stirring them together with the tomatoes and garlic.

4. Remove the skillet from the oven, and serve, discarding the garlic cloves.

Serves 2

The real star of this dish is the grilled fruit salsa. It can be made and served with almost any protein. Chef Elizabeth Karmel serves it most with grilled chicken thighs, but it is equally good with grilled fish, pork chops, pork tenderloin, and shrimp. The salsa can be made hotter with the addition of minced habanero or jalapeño chiles, but make sure to taste your roasted poblano before adding any more heat. The heat quotient of the poblano varies widely and can be just as hot as a jalapeño.

GRILLED MANGO, PEACH, PASSIONFRUIT, AND POBLANO PEPPER SALSA WITH CHICKEN

Salsa:

1 to 2 green poblano peppers, depending on size

2 large ripe (but not mushy) mangoes

Peanut or hazelnut oil

Kosher salt

2 large ripe (but not mushy) peaches, preferably white

½ cup chopped red onion

¼ to 1 jalapeño or habanero chile (optional, depending on heat level you want), seeded and finely chopped

3 tablespoons chopped fresh mint

1 teaspoon finely grated lime zest (use a Microplane®)

2 tablespoons fresh lime juice

2 tablespoons passionfruit pulp (from about 1 passionfruit) or puree (see kitchen note)

Freshly ground black pepper

Chicken:

8 skin-on, bone-in chicken thighs or other favorite protein

Extra virgin olive oil

Kosher salt and freshly ground black pepper

1. Make the salsa: Roast the poblano(s). Turn all the burners of a gas grill on high. Rinse and dry the poblano(s). Place directly on the cooking grate. Turn occasionally until the skin blackens and blisters all over. (You can do the same thing using your oven's broiler.) Remove from the heat, immediately put in a paper bag or plastic container, close or seal, and let stand until cool to the touch. Remove and discard the skin and seeds (the skin will slip off easily). Cut into strips, then chop into a rough dice. Reserve for salsa.

2. Grill the fruit: Preheat the oven to 350°. Place a mango on a cutting board, resting it on one of its narrow edges, and, using a sharp knife, cut lengthwise slightly off center, cutting off all the flesh from one side of the pit. Repeat on the other side. Brush the cut side of the mango with peanut or hazelnut oil. Sprinkle lightly with salt. Repeat with the other mango. Pit the peaches, and cut them into quarters. Brush the cut sides with peanut or hazelnut oil, and sprinkle lightly with salt. Place the fruit, cut side down, on the grill side of a very clean Lodge Double Play Reversible Grill Griddle that's been preheated over medium-low heat. Grill until the fruit is nicely marked and beginning to warm, about 2 minutes. Remove from the grill, and place the fruit, skin side down, on a wire rack set on a baking sheet. Bake until the skin of the peach begins to pull away from the flesh, 5 to 7 minutes. Remove the grilled fruit to a clean platter.

3. Place one of the mango slices, flesh side up, on a cutting board, and score the flesh lengthwise and then crosswise, forming ½-inch cubes and taking care not to cut through the peel. Press against the center of the peel to force the cubes upward; some of the cubes will come off at this point, others may need to be sliced along the peel to release all the cubes into a bowl. Repeat with the other slices. Remove the skin from the peaches, and chop into ¼-inch pieces.

4. In a medium bowl, combine the roasted poblano, grilled mangoes and peaches, onion, chile if using, mint, lime zest and juice, and passionfruit pulp. Toss gently to mix. Season with salt and pepper to taste. Let stand at room temperature for at least 20 minutes before serving with grilled chicken or other grilled protein. If you make it more than 20 minutes in advance, cover and refrigerate.

5. Grill the chicken: Remove and discard excess fat from the chicken. Pat dry. Brush lightly with olive oil. Season with salt and pepper to taste.

6. Preheat the oven to 350°. Clean the reversible grill griddle, then preheat over medium heat. Place the chicken, skin side down, on the hot grill. Let the chicken cook, untouched, until the pieces lift off easily, about 5 minutes. The chicken should be well marked. (You do not need to grill the chicken on both sides since you are finishing the cooking time in the oven.) Remove the chicken from the grill, and place it, bone side down, on a wire rack set on a baking sheet. Bake until an instant-read thermometer inserted at the thickest point registers 170°, 15 to 20 minutes. If you don't have an instant-read thermometer, cook the chicken until no longer pink and the juices run clear. Remove the grilled chicken to a clean platter, and let stand 10 minutes before serving with the salsa on the side. **Serves 4 to 8, with 3 cups salsa**

kitchen note:
You can substitute tropical-flavored orange juice for the passionfruit.

a cooking secret from Elizabeth

When you are grilling indoors, you need to sear the food until you have great grill marks, and then move it to an oven, where the roasting heat approximates the indirect heat of a grill. This way you have the best of both worlds—caramelization from the grill marks and tender doneness from the heat of the oven.

CHICKEN-FRIED CHICKEN WITH CREAM GRAVY AND MASHED POTATOES

Tools matter, even for simple recipes, says Elaine Corn, the food and lifestyle reporter for Capital Public Radio in Sacramento, California. For her chicken-fried chicken, a cast iron skillet is a must, as well as paper towels, wax paper or plastic wrap, a meat mallet or rolling pin, a sheet of aluminum foil, and a reliable thermometer to measure the temperature of the frying oil.

Chicken:
1 cup buttermilk
4 to 6 drops hot sauce
4 skinless, boneless chicken breast halves
1 cup all-purpose flour
1 teaspoon salt, or to taste
1 teaspoon freshly ground black pepper, or more to taste
Mashed Potatoes (recipe follows)

Vegetable oil, for frying
Cream Gravy:
¼ cup all-purpose flour
1 cup whole milk
Salt
Generous amount freshly ground black pepper (it should be peppery)

1. Make the chicken: In a medium bowl, combine the buttermilk and hot sauce.

2. Rinse the chicken breasts, and pat dry with paper towels. One at a time, sandwich a breast between two sheets of wax paper or plastic wrap. Pound until thin and of even thickness. If you don't have a meat mallet, pound the breasts with a rolling pin. Add the pounded breasts to the buttermilk, turning to coat them if necessary. Let stand 20 to 60 minutes at room temperature.

3. Meanwhile, line a dinner plate or baking sheet with wax paper. To a paper bag, add the flour, salt, and pepper. Shake to mix well. Place the breasts, one at a time, in the paper bag, and shake until coated with the seasoned flour. Place the breasts in a single layer on the lined dinner plate. Let the coating set about 20 minutes. Meanwhile, start the mashed potatoes. Warm a serving platter in a preheated 150° oven. Line another plate with two thicknesses of paper towels, and have it convenient to the stove.

4. Heat a Lodge 12-inch cast iron skillet over medium-high heat. When hot, pour in oil to a depth of 1 inch. Heat to 350° to 375°. Slip the breasts into the hot oil. Don't crowd, or they will stick. Adjust the heat to keep it at an even temperature. Fry the chicken until golden brown, crusty, and crisp on both sides, turning with tongs, about 5 minutes per side. Drain on the paper towels. Transfer the breasts to the warm platter, cover loosely with aluminum foil, and keep warm in the oven while you make the gravy.

5. Make the gravy: Pour off all but 3 tablespoons of oil from the skillet. Return the skillet to medium-high heat. Add the flour, and whisk well until the roux is completely smooth, about 1 minute; don't let it take on any color! Be sure to loosen and scrape up any crusty bits that may be stuck to the bottom of the pan. Slowly add the milk, whisking constantly until there are no lumps. Season with salt and pepper to taste. Reduce the heat to low, and simmer, stirring, until slightly thickened, about 5 minutes.

6. To serve, arrange the chicken and a serving of mashed potatoes on 4 dinner plates. Ladle on cream gravy until smothered. **Serves 4**

MASHED POTATOES

4 russet potatoes, peeled and cut
   into chunks
2 tablespoons unsalted butter

½ cup milk or heavy cream
   Salt and freshly ground black
   pepper

1. Bring a pot of salted water to a boil, drop in the potato chunks, cover, reduce the heat to medium, and cook until a knife easily glides into a potato chunk, 12 to 15 minutes.

2. Pour off the water, and return the pot to low heat to dry out the potatoes a bit. Add the butter, milk, salt to taste, and lots of pepper. Whisk by hand or with a handheld electric mixer until smooth. Keep warm until ready to serve.
Serves 4

Cast Iron Memories

How many years had it taken me to fully season my first cast iron skillet? As long as I'd owned it—about 32 years. I'd carefully seasoned it with oil in an oven to get it going, I'd rendered bacon bits in it every chance I got to keep the seasoning maintained, and I'd given the bacon to my dog for the next half year. I carefully washed my skillet and set it over modest heat to dry for a few minutes or so. About 15 years in, by now I kissed it every time I hung it on its own hook on the pegboard. One day, after three decades of use, I dropped it. It broke into three sections. The crack looked like a Mercedes Benz logo or, from a different perspective, a peace sign. But I was feeling no peace. Short of looking for a new skillet in a store with old pans, I bought a new Lodge. The seasoning process began anew. I'm 10 years into it, and now I've concluded this: One is ALWAYS seasoning a cast iron skillet. With love.

—*Elaine Corn*

ET'S HEALTHY GLUTEN-FREE FRIED CHICKEN STRIPS

I   pound skinless, boneless
    chicken breasts
Buttermilk marinade:
I   cup buttermilk
I   large garlic clove, minced
I   teaspoon garlic powder
½   teaspoon Cajun-style seasoned
    salt
⅛   teaspoon freshly ground black
    pepper
½   teaspoon Mrs. Dash or Spike
    Salt Free Seasoning (optional)

Rice flour dredge:
¾   cup brown rice flour
¼   cup cornstarch
I   tablespoon sweet paprika
½   teaspoon dried thyme
¼   teaspoon black pepper
½   teaspoon garlic powder
½   teaspoon onion powder
½   teaspoon Cajun-style seasoned
    salt
About ¼ cup grapeseed oil, for
    frying

1. Wash and pat dry the chicken breasts with paper towels. Place the breasts between two sheets of parchment or wax paper, and pound with a meat mallet or rolling pin to ¼- to ⅓-inch thickness. Cut across chicken into finger-like strips; set aside.

2. In a medium bowl, combine the buttermilk marinade ingredients, and blend well. Add the chicken strips; blend to coat them well. Cover and refrigerate for at least I hour or overnight.

3. When ready to fry, combine the rice flour dredge ingredients in another medium bowl.

4. Heat a Lodge 10- or 12-inch cast iron skillet for I to 2 minutes over medium heat. Add just enough oil to coat the bottom by about ¼ inch. When the oil is hot (test by tossing a pinch of flour into the hot oil to see if it creates bubbles), commence with the next step.

5. Place one piece of chicken in the dredge, and coat it lightly and evenly; shake off any excess, and place it in the hot oil. You should see a line of bubbles form along the edges of the chicken. If you do, the oil is the proper temperature and you are ready to fry the rest of the chicken.

6. Quickly dredge the remaining chicken strips in the flour mixture in the same way. Add them to the hot oil, leaving about ½ inch of space between each strip; do not crowd the pan (you may need to fry them in batches). Fry until the bottoms are lightly browned and crisp to the touch, 4 to 5 minutes. Turn the strips over, and fry until the other side is golden brown, another 4 to 5 minutes.

7. Transfer the chicken to a paper towel-lined plate to drain. Test the strips to be sure the center is cooked through; it should be white, not pink. If the meat is still pink, finish cooking in a 400° oven for 10 minutes. **Serves 6**

According to private chef June Pagan, Elizabeth Taylor had a great sense of humor and was very generous with the people who worked for her.

"When I first introduced my healthier version of fried chicken to ET," remembers June, "I explained that I would serve it in boneless finger-shaped strips. She asked me—quite quizzically— 'How many fingers are you planning to serve me?'" I advised her that 4 to 5 'fingers' would be a 4-ounce portion (the recommended serving under the Pritikin guidelines that I was utilizing to optimize her weight-loss initiative). She laughed as she replied, 'OK, as long as you don't serve me just one.'"

This is one of Whendi Rose Grad's favorite ways to enjoy the honey she and her husband, Garnett Puett (a fourth-generation beekeeper), produce at Big Island Bees on the island of Kealakekua in Hawai'i. Big Island Bees offers three single-floral varietals, made from the raw honey harvested by bees feasting off 'ohi'a lehua, macadamia nut, or Christmasberry blossoms. Whendi likes to prepare this dish using their Organic Wilelaiki Blossom Honey, from the Christmasberry, but it's delicious prepared with any good-quality honey.

HONEY-ROASTED CHICKEN BREASTS
WITH PRESERVED LEMON AND GARLIC

2 large skin-on, bone-in chicken breasts (about 2½ pounds)
1½ teaspoons fine sea salt
Freshly ground black pepper to taste
¾ teaspoon ground cumin
1 preserved lemon, cut into quarters, flesh cut away from the rind and discarded (use only the rind)

¼ cup good-quality honey
2 tablespoons extra virgin olive oil
1 tablespoon unsalted butter
10 garlic cloves, crushed and halved

1. Preheat the oven to 375°.

2. Season the chicken with the salt and pepper, and sprinkle the cumin both under and on the skin. Carefully tuck 2 quarters of preserved lemon rind under the skin of each breast. Pour the honey under and over the top of the skin of each.

3. Heat a Lodge 10-inch cast iron skillet over medium-high heat for a few minutes (you want to get the skin really crunchy and brown). Add the oil and butter to the skillet; when the oil is hot and the butter melted, add the chicken, skin side down. Arrange the garlic in the pan so the cloves all make contact with the bottom. Cook for 7 minutes, then turn the chicken, skin side up, and transfer the skillet to the oven. Roast until the chicken is cooked through and the juices run clear, about 25 minutes.

4. Remove the skillet from the oven, and let the chicken cool in the pan for 5 minutes. Serve the chicken cut off the bone with all of the caramelized garlic pieces and the thick sauce underneath it. **Serves 6**

At her restaurant Scrimshaw in Greenport, New York, on the North Fork of Long Island, chef Rosa Ross offers duck breast served with a classic cherry sauce made with reduced duck stock—far too much work for the home cook. At home, Rosa will sauté ripe cherries or raspberries in a little duck fat, then sprinkle them with vinegar, the acidity bringing the perfect balance to the rich duck. "This is such a delicious and quick meal. Served with asparagus and parsleyed new potatoes, it makes a lovely spring dinner," says Rosa.

PAN-SEARED DUCK BREASTS WITH FRESH RASPBERRIES

2 whole (4 halves) skin-on, boneless duck breasts (about ½ pound each)
Salt and freshly ground black pepper
1 pint fresh raspberries or pitted sweet or sour cherries, depending on what's in season

2 tablespoons raspberry vinegar
½ teaspoon sugar
Fresh rosemary leaves

1. Preheat the oven to 350°.

2. Score the duck skin in a diamond pattern, and sprinkle the breasts with salt and pepper. Place the breasts, skin side down, in a Lodge 12-inch cast iron skillet. Set the skillet over medium heat, and cook until the skin is golden brown. Carefully pour off as much of the fat as possible, and refrigerate in a tightly covered container for a future use (like browning potatoes).

3. Turn the breasts over, skin side up, and place the skillet in the oven. Cook the duck to your desired degree of doneness, 8 to 10 minutes for medium-rare. Transfer the duck breasts to a warm platter to stand at least 5 minutes. The breasts may then be sliced or left whole to serve.

4. Meanwhile, return the skillet to medium heat, add the raspberries, and cook just until they are beginning to burst, about 1 minute or less, depending on their ripeness. Sprinkle them with the vinegar and sugar, and toss to blend. Add a little water to deglaze the pan, scraping up the tasty browned bits from the bottom of the skillet. Pour over the duck breasts to serve. Sprinkle with rosemary. **Serves 4**

Cast Iron Memories

In my everyday kitchen, my cast iron skillet is the first pan I reach for—for eggs, burgers, steaks, potatoes, and almost everything I want to sauté.

I "inherited" a set of skillets from a neighbor when we bought our house on the North Fork of Long Island. Until then, I had a 9-inch cast iron skillet that I had been working on for years to get just the right temper, but it was still a little "young." The pans I inherited were at least two generations old, and they were truly black and absolutely nonstick.

Years before, I had taken a class with James Beard, and he showed us how to cook hamburgers in a cast iron skillet: Heat the skillet to smoking, sprinkle a layer of salt in the bottom, and put in the patties, then cook the burgers till they release, and flip over. Cook to your desired degree of doneness, preferably rare to medium-rare. Needless to say, my patties have never stuck, and I've only gotten juicy, delicious results. An old black pan is essential to the perfect hamburger!

—*Rosa Ross*

QUAIL AND DUMPLINGS

William Dissen, chef-owner of The Market Place Restaurant in Asheville, North Carolina, uses wild game like quail on his menus. Preparing the velouté sauce in a cast iron Dutch oven allows for the development of rich, deep flavor when cooking the roux, as does pan searing the quail breasts in a cast iron skillet. French Perigord black truffles are now available in western North Carolina and add an earthy flavor to this unique interpretation of chicken and dumplings.

Velouté sauce:
3   tablespoons unsalted butter
1   tablespoon olive oil
¼   cup diced (¼-inch) red onion
¼   cup diced (¼-inch) celery
¼   cup diced (¼-inch) carrot
¼   cup diced (¼-inch) fennel bulb
1½ tablespoons minced garlic
½   cup white wine
¼   cup all-purpose flour
1   quart chicken stock
¼   cup heavy cream
1   tablespoon hot sauce
Kosher salt and freshly ground black
   pepper
1½ tablespoons finely chopped fresh
   flat-leaf parsley

Dumplings:
1½ quarts chicken stock
1   cup plus 2 tablespoons self-rising
   flour

1   tablespoon sliced fresh chives
½   teaspoon kosher salt
¼   teaspoon freshly ground black
   pepper
¼   cup buttermilk
1   large egg, beaten
2   tablespoons unsalted butter,
   melted and cooled

Quail:
6   quail, cut into breasts and legs
2   tablespoons olive oil
Kosher salt and freshly ground black
   pepper
¼   cup (½ stick) unsalted butter
4   sprigs fresh thyme
2   garlic cloves, peeled

Garnish:
2   tablespoons thinly sliced fresh
   chives
Aleppo pepper
1½ ounces black truffles (optional)

1. Make the sauce: Heat the butter and oil together in a Lodge 5-quart cast iron Dutch oven over medium-high heat. When the butter begins to foam, add the onion, celery, carrot, and fennel, and cook, stirring, until translucent, 2 to 3 minutes. Stir in the garlic, and cook until aromatic. Add the wine, and scrape up any browned bits from the bottom of the pot. Continue to stir, and reduce the wine to a glaze, then sprinkle in the flour, and cook for about a minute, stirring, to create a roux. Whisk in the stock, and bring to a simmer over medium-high heat. Let cook for 15 to 20 minutes, then reduce the heat to medium, stir in the cream, and cook for another 5 minutes. Stir in the hot sauce, season with salt and pepper to taste, and stir in the parsley. Taste and season as necessary. Keep warm.

2. Make the dumplings: Bring the stock to a light simmer in a large saucepan.

3. In a medium bowl, mix the flour, chives, salt, and pepper together. Form a well in the center, and add the buttermilk, beaten egg, and melted butter. Mix the flour into the wet ingredients. Add more buttermilk as necessary to yield a wet but stiff dough.

4. Working with 2 teaspoons, form the batter into oval dumplings the size of the teaspoon, adding them to the simmering stock as they are formed (you need 24 dumplings). Lightly poach the dumplings until they are firm, 6 to 8 minutes. Using a slotted spoon, remove the dumplings to a bowl, and cover with aluminum foil to keep warm.

5. Prepare the quail: Place the quail legs in the still-simmering liquid used to poach the dumplings, and poach until cooked through, about 5 minutes. Remove from the liquid with a slotted spoon. When cool enough to handle, shred the meat from the bones. Reserve the meat, and discard the bones.

6. Heat the oil in a Lodge 15-inch cast iron skillet over medium-high heat until it begins to shimmer. Season the quail breasts with salt and pepper to taste, and place, breast side down, in the hot pan. Cook the quail until golden, then turn over, reduce the heat to medium, and cook for 4 to 5 minutes.

7. Spoon the oil out of the skillet, then add the butter, thyme, and garlic. When the butter begins to foam, tilt the pan, and baste the quail with the butter until they are semifirm to the touch or an instant-read thermometer inserted into the thickest part of the breast registers 140°.

8. For each serving, place a Lodge 5-inch square Wonder Skillet on a folded white napkin on a serving plate. Place 4 dumplings in each skillet, and spoon about ½ cup of the Velouté Sauce over the dumplings. Sprinkle some of the shredded quail leg meat, sliced chives, and Aleppo pepper to taste over the sauce. Place a cooked quail breast in the center of the pan. If you like, shave 3 or 4 slices of black truffle over the quail, and serve immediately.

Serves 6

Marty Nation's Short Ribs,
page 144

MEATS

DELTA-STYLE TAMALES

5 pounds ground beef
¼ cup vegetable oil
1 medium onion, minced
¼ cup chili powder
2 tablespoons kosher salt
1 tablespoon onion powder
1 tablespoon garlic powder
2 teaspoons black pepper
1 teaspoon cayenne pepper
1 teaspoon ground cumin
8 cups self-rising white corn meal mix
2 teaspoons kosher salt
1¾ cups lard

48 coffee filters
2 (32-ounce) cans tomato sauce
Hot sauce
1 medium onion, minced
3 jalapeño chiles, seeded and minced
2 tablespoons kosher salt
1 tablespoon onion powder
1 tablespoon garlic powder
2 teaspoons black pepper
1 teaspoon cayenne pepper
1 teaspoon ground cumin

Mostly known for dishes like cornbread, greens, and fried catfish, the Mississippi Delta also has a rich history of serving up tamales. This regional staple gained its popularity when Latin immigrants moved to the area in the early 1900s. In this version from Chef Tyler Brown, he prepares his tamales with pasture-raised beef and uses coffee filters to wrap them instead of the traditional dried corn husks, a trick he picked up down South. Serve them with saltine crackers and hot sauce or with limes, salsa and sour cream.

1. Place the ground beef in a large, heavy stockpot. Cover with cold water. Bring to a boil over high heat. Cover the pot, reduce the heat to medium-low, and simmer until the meat is very tender, 2 to 2½ hours. Reserving the cooking water, drain the meat into a colander. Heat the oil in a Lodge 7-quart cast iron Dutch oven over medium heat. Stir in the onion, chili powder, salt, onion and garlic powders, black pepper, cayenne, and cumin until the onion is well coated with the spices. Add the meat, and stir to coat. Cook, stirring often, until the meat is hot, 7 to 10 minutes. Remove from the heat.

2. Combine the corn meal mix, salt, and lard in a Lodge 5-quart cast iron Dutch oven, and mix well. Cook the dough over low heat for 10 minutes. Remove from the heat.

3. Lay a coffee filter on a clean work surface. Spread ¼ to ½ cup of the dough in an even layer across the center of the filter. Pat it out to your desired thickness in the form of a rectangle. Spoon 1 to 2 tablespoons of the filling in a line down the center of the dough. Holding opposite sides of the filter, roll the tamale so that the dough surrounds the filling and forms a narrow cylinder or package. Fold the top and bottom of the filter under to enclose the tamale. Tie the package closed crosswise with kitchen twine. Place the completed tamales in a single layer on a baking sheet. Repeat until all the dough and filling are used. Wash and dry the 7-quart Dutch oven. Arrange the tamale bundles in a single layer on the bottom of the Dutch oven.

4. In a large saucepan, combine the tomato sauce, 6 cups of the reserved meat broth, hot sauce to taste, onion, jalapeños, and next 6 ingredients. Bring to a boil, then carefully pour over the tamales. Cover the pot, and cook the tamales at a slow simmer for 3 to 4 hours. An instant-read thermometer inserted in the center of a tamale should register 180°. To serve, remove the tamales from their coffee-filter jackets, and top with their simmering sauce. **Makes 48 tamales**

PERFECT FILETS

4   filet mignons, 1¼ inches thick
Kosher salt and freshly ground black
    pepper

1   tablespoon olive oil

1. Preheat the oven to 395°.

2. Pat the beef dry with paper towels. Generously season the filets on both sides with salt and pepper.

3. Heat the oil in a Lodge 12-inch cast iron skillet over medium-high heat until a few droplets of water sizzle when carefully sprinkled in the pan. Sear the steaks until well browned on both sides, about 3 minutes per side.

4. Place the steaks in the oven to finish cooking, about 8 minutes for medium-rare. **Serves 4**

A uthor of coobooks *Simply Salads, Simply Suppers,* and *Simply Grilling,* Jennifer Chandler thinks the best way to prepare a filet, or any steak for that matter, is to sear it in a cast iron skillet on the stovetop and then allow it to finish cooking in the oven. "The results are a more tender and juicy steak than any I have ever had off a grill."

Ken and Patti Fisher, of the website datenightdoins.com, based in Hemet, California, love grilled sirloin steak—straight from the fire, but also used later in the week as part of another dish. So when Ken throws a sirloin on the grill, he makes sure it's a big one.

GRILLED SIRLOIN ALFREDO ELEGANT AND EASY

1 tablespoon extra virgin olive oil	¼ cup dried garlic
½ pound baby bella mushrooms, thickly sliced	2 tablespoons seasoning sauce or steak sauce
2 cups sliced (¼-inch-thick) green onions	1 (16-ounce) jar alfredo sauce, heated
1 cup sun-dried tomatoes, cut into strips	1 pound fettuccine, cooked al dente according to package directions
2 pounds leftover grilled sirloin, thinly sliced (see kitchen note)	1 cup grated Parmesan cheese

1. Heat the oil in a Lodge 12-inch cast iron skillet over medium-high heat. Add the mushrooms, green onions, and tomatoes, and cook, stirring, until the onions soften, about 5 minutes. Add the steak, garlic, and seasoning sauce, reduce the heat to medium, and cook just until heated through.

2. Add the alfredo sauce to the hot drained fettuccine, and toss until coated. Arrange the noodles on a warm serving platter, and top with the steak mixture. Sprinkle with the Parmesan, and serve. **Serves 4**

kitchen note:

The easiest way to thinly slice leftover steak is to freeze it for an hour.

GARLIC-TOPPED FLANK STEAK ROULADE

This elegant yet easy recipe comes from Tammy Credicott, best-selling author of *The Healthy Gluten-Free Life* and *Paleo Indulgences*. **And while this tasty flank steak may look challenging, the steps are quite simple and will leave your guests thinking you're a culinary rock star! You can find more delicious recipes on her website at thehealthygflife.com.**

2   pounds grass-fed flank steak
Sea salt and freshly ground black pepper
4   strips pork bacon, cooked (but not crispy) and chopped
2   cups loosely packed organic spinach leaves, chopped

⅓   cup chopped organic sun-dried tomatoes
1   cup chopped organic button mushrooms (7 or 8 whole mushrooms)
2   tablespoons coconut oil
5   organic garlic cloves, minced

1. Preheat the oven to 425°.

2. With a meat mallet or rolling pin, pound the flank steak to an even ⅓-inch thickness. This will give you more surface area to work with when stuffing it.

3. Season the steak with salt and pepper on both sides, then lay it out flat in front of you. Sprinkle the chopped bacon over it in a single layer, then evenly layer on the spinach, tomatoes, and mushrooms, in that order. Roll the steak up lengthwise tightly into a log (roulade), then tie it with kitchen twine in 2 or 3 places to hold it together. (At this point, you can wrap the roulade in plastic wrap and refrigerate overnight, if you like. Bring to room temperature before cooking.)

4. Heat the oil in a Lodge 12-inch cast iron skillet over medium-high heat. When the pan is really hot, sear the roulade until browned on all sides, 2 to 3 minutes total.

5. Remove the pan from the heat, and sprinkle the garlic all over the roulade. Place the skillet in the oven until the stuffing is hot but the meat is still pink in the center, 10 to 15 minutes.

6. Remove from the oven, and let the roulade stand for 10 minutes. Remove the twine, slice into pinwheels, and serve! **Serves 4 to 6**

how Tammy makes a roulade

1. Pounding the steak to an even ⅓ inch guarantees the steak will cook evenly. This step also tenderizes the steak to prevent it from being chewy.

2. Sprinkle the stuffing ingredients over the meat; leave a ½-inch border around the edge to keep the stuffing from spilling out when the steak is rolled up.

3. Roll the steak up lengthwise tightly into a log, then tie it with kitchen twine in 2 or 3 places to hold it together.

4. Make sure the pan is very hot before you place the roulade into the pan for searing so that each side gets nice and brown.

Jane Handel's bond with her brother, Marty, extends to a mutual love of good food prepared in cast iron pans, like his succulent recipe for short ribs—a favorite on cold nights.

MARTY NATION'S SHORT RIBS

5 pounds beef short ribs, cut into 2½-inch lengths	1 cup hearty red wine
Salt and freshly ground black pepper	1½ cups beef stock
2 tablespoons canola or other vegetable oil that can withstand high temperature	6 medium russet or Yukon Gold potatoes, peeled and halved
1 cup chopped yellow onions	3 to 4 medium yellow onions, quartered
½ cup chopped carrots	4 large carrots, cut into 1½-inch pieces
¾ cup chopped celery	½ pound green beans, trimmed and cut into 2-inch lengths, and/or 1 cup green peas
2 tablespoons tomato paste	
2 tablespoons unbleached all-purpose flour	

1. Preheat the oven to 375° (or 400° if you want the short ribs to cook faster).

2. Season the short ribs with salt and pepper on both sides. Heat the oil in a Lodge 7-quart cast iron Dutch oven over high heat until very hot. In batches, add the short ribs in a single layer, and sear until golden brown on both sides. Remove the ribs from the pan, and pour off and discard all but 2 tablespoons of fat.

3. Add the chopped onions, carrots, and celery to the Dutch oven, and cook over low heat, stirring occasionally until tender and translucent, 15 to 20 minutes. Add the tomato paste, stir, and cook until reduced and darkened, about 4 minutes. Add the flour, and stir until fully combined with the vegetable mixture; cook another 3 to 4 minutes, stirring continuously.

4. Add the wine, scraping up any browned bits on the bottom of the pot. Reduce the wine over medium heat by three-quarters, then add the short ribs, pour the stock over the ribs, and simmer over low heat until the liquid is reduced again by three-quarters, about another 15 minutes. Place in the oven, and roast, uncovered, until the short ribs seem to be about 80 percent done, 1 to 1½ hours. Add the potatoes, quartered onions, and carrot pieces to the pot. Return to the oven, uncovered, and cook until the vegetables and short ribs are tender. Add the green beans and/or peas, and cook until they are tender, another 5 to 10 minutes.

5. Remove the pot from the oven. Transfer the meat (which should be so tender that it is falling off the bone) to the center of a large platter, and surround it with the vegetables. If the sauce seems too thin, reduce it over high heat on top of the stove. Another way to thicken it would be to puree the chopped vegetables in it using an immersion blender. Pour some of the reduced sauce over the meat on the platter, and serve the remainder in a pitcher at the table for anyone who desires extra sauce. **Serves 4 to 6**

THE LIFE AND TIMES OF AN IRON PAN

Jane Handel

Writer, artist, editor, and co-publisher of Edible Ojai

In 2006, my brother, Marty Nation, competed in the First Annual BBQ'n at the Autry Barbecue Championship and Festival in Los Angeles. He brought along a family heirloom and special talisman—our late mother's oversized cast iron frying pan. This pan was her primary and favorite cooking equipment for many decades. It had cooked a lifetime of family meals, from Southern fried chicken to spaghetti sauce and just about everything else. It was the one thing of hers that Marty requested when she died, and it soon became a favorite cooking tool in his own kitchen.

Marty cooked with that big iron skillet throughout the Championship weekend. He even won first prize in the "Anything But Barbecue" category and credits our mother's pan with helping him to win against seasoned competitors from all over the country. Of course the pan played a significant role. But the fact that he's a graduate of the French Culinary Institute in New York and has cooked at some of New York City's top restaurants might also have contributed a soupçon to Chef Marty's success.

Sadly, when he returned home after the competition, Marty discovered that his lucky pan had, rather mysteriously, developed a crack across the bottom. But instead of being thrown out, it soon became the namesake—Iron Pan—of a restaurant he opened in Ojai, California. Prominently displayed during the lifespan of the restaurant, the now-retired pan shared a place of honor next to his trophy from the contest. And when he wasn't behind the stove cooking, Marty would regale one and all with stories about his mother's now-legendary iron pan.

Over the years, Marty became a zealous collector of cast iron pans of every description, obsessively scouring flea markets and antiques stores for them on road trips far and wide. I, too, have my own trusty assortment that are used on a daily basis—whether I'm making pancakes on the iron griddle, a frittata in the iron skillet, or of course, spaghetti sauce adapted from our mother's recipe in the iron Dutch oven. I can't imagine cooking in anything else.

What worked for our mother continues to work for us. Like her, I've now had some of my iron pans for more than 40 years and suspect that my children and niece, Marty's daughter, will continue to cook with them when we're gone. For that matter, all of those trace elements of iron in our systems could mean that the iron pan legacy will continue well into the future as part of our family's DNA.

Marty Nation

eef chuck roast is a classic braising cut—and no cookware does it better than cast iron, says Wendy Taggart, who, with her husband, Jon, operates Burgundy Pasture Beef, their ranch and butcher market store located just south of Dallas/Fort Worth in Texas. Typically, cuts that are not naturally tender (but very flavorful, with their complexity of fat, connective tissue, and muscle) are the best braising cuts. It is the braising process that "tenderizes" the meat.

S-L-O-W BRAISED BEEF CHUCK ROAST

1 (3- to 4-pound) boneless or bone-in chuck roast
1 tablespoon dried herbes de Provence (or your favorite combination of dried herbs)
1 teaspoon coarse kosher or sea salt
½ teaspoon cracked black pepper
1 tablespoon olive, peanut, or grapeseed oil, or more as needed

1 cup chopped onion
2 garlic cloves, chopped
¾ cup chopped celery
1 bay leaf
2 to 3 leafy celery tops (optional)
½ cup red wine (optional)
2 tablespoons cold butter (optional)

1. Pat the roast dry with paper towels. In a small bowl, combine the herbes de Provence, salt, and pepper, then liberally apply the mixture to the roast—top, sides, and bottom—rubbing it in so it adheres. Preheat the oven to 200°.

2. Heat a Lodge cast iron Dutch oven or skillet just big enough to fit the roast over medium-high heat. When the pan is hot, add the oil, and swirl to coat the bottom. Place the roast in the pan to brown. The heat should be high enough that the roast gives off a peppy "sizzle," but not so hot that the herb rub burns. Sear the roast until it has a rich brown crust on all sides, 5 to 8 minutes per side. Remove the roast to a platter.

3. If necessary, add a little more oil, then add the onion, garlic, and celery. Cook, stirring a few times, until the vegetables are softened, about 5 minutes. Spread the vegetables evenly over the bottom of the pan, and set the chuck roast over them. Add the bay leaf and celery tops, if using. Place a tight-fitting lid over the pot (using parchment paper between the lid and pot, if desired, to prevent moisture from escaping), and braise in the oven until the roast is fork-tender, about 4 hours. The real test of doneness is that it tears apart easily with a fork. Transfer the roast to a serving platter, and cover with foil to keep it warm.

4. The finished roast will yield a wonderfully rich au jus in its purest form since no additional liquid was added. The key is the oven temperature—200°—which allows the roast to produce its own juices during the slow braising process. You may serve the jus as is by pouring it back over the roast or serving it on the side with a ladle (discard the bay leaf and celery tops). Or you can reduce it over medium heat to strengthen the flavor; be sure to use a whisk to incorporate any tasty browned bits hanging onto the pan. Or you can make a red wine sauce from the jus—add the red wine, and boil over medium heat until reduced by about a third or more (taste test it for where you want it to be). Remove from the heat, and swirl in the cold butter (melting as you mix it), if using. Season with salt and/or pepper to taste. **Serves 6 to 8**

how Wendy braises beef

1. Season the beef before searing. Rub the seasoning mixture with your hands so the seasonings will adhere, covering all sides of the roast evenly.

2. Select a pan with a lid that is closest in size to the cut you will braise. The lid needs to be heavy to prevent moisture from escaping during cooking.

3. Sear the roast until a rich brown crust forms on all sides, and then cook at a very low temperature.

4. If there is a lot of airspace in the pot, place a piece of parchment paper over the top of the pan, and push it down so it hangs about 1 to 2 inches above the meat. Set the lid on top of the parchment.

Chef Nora Pouillon, co-owner of Restaurant Nora in Washington, D.C., the first certified organic restaurant in America, came to this country from Vienna, Austria. Says Nora, "My mother always fried her Wiener Schnitzel until they were crispy and delicious in a cast iron pan that had sides two inches high." Her mother used peanut oil, but Nora prefers sunflower oil.

WIENER SCHNITZEL

4 (4- to 5-ounce) veal cutlets
Salt and freshly ground black pepper
¼ cup unbleached all-purpose flour
1 large egg beaten with
   1 tablespoon milk

1½ cups fine, dry breadcrumbs, or
   more, if needed
Sunflower oil
1 lemon, cut into 4 wedges
4 sprigs fresh flat-leaf parsley

1. Make tiny incisions along the outside rim of the cutlets to prevent curling. Pound the cutlets to ¼-inch thickness between two sheets of wax paper, and season with salt and pepper. Dredge the cutlets completely in the flour, and shake off any excess. Dip the cutlets in the egg mixture, and dredge them in the breadcrumbs. Be sure to coat them completely, patting on the crumbs so they adhere. Set aside.

2. Heat 1 inch of oil in a Lodge 10-inch cast iron skillet over medium heat until a small piece of bread tossed in it sizzles and turns golden brown. Fry the cutlets in the hot oil without crowding them (you might need to cook them in batches) until each side is golden brown, 2 to 3 minutes per side. Drain on paper towels.

3. Serve the cutlets hot with a wedge of lemon and topped with a sprig of parsley (which you can fry if you wish). **Serves 4**

The Publican is one of Tim Burton's favorite places to eat in Chicago—or anywhere, for that matter. "The trio of chef/partner Paul Kahan and chefs Brian Huston and Kim Leali really know how to make a swine lover swoon," says Tim, owner of Burton's Maplewood Farm in Medora, Indiana. Tim and his wife, Angie, regularly host overnight stays on their farm for chefs across the nation, and this is the dish Tim cooks when the Publican pros come to visit.

ROAST PORK LOIN WITH BARREL-AGED MAPLE-BOURBON-MUSTARD SAUCE

Barrel-Aged Maple-Bourbon-Mustard Sauce:
- ½ cup Burton's Bourbon Barrel Aged Maple Syrup
- ¼ cup mayonnaise (preferably Hellmann's Real Mayonnaise)
- 1 tablespoon Dijon mustard
- ½ teaspoon freshly ground white or black pepper
- ¼ teaspoon salt

Pork roast:
- 1 teaspoon salt
- 1 teaspoon freshly ground black pepper
- 1 (4- to 5-pound) boneless center-cut loin pork roast

1. Preheat the oven to 325°.

2. Make the mustard sauce: In a small bowl, whisk the ingredients together until well blended. Set aside.

3. Make the pork roast: Mix together the salt and pepper, and rub it into the roast on all sides. Heat a Lodge 7-quart cast iron Dutch oven over medium-high heat, then sear the roast on all sides until golden brown.

4. Cover the Dutch oven, transfer to the oven, and roast for 30 to 40 minutes.

5. Baste the roast with about half the sauce, cover, and continue to roast until an instant-read thermometer inserted in the thickest part reads 140°, another 30 to 40 minutes.

6. Remove from the oven, and let the roast stand for 10 to 15 minutes. Its temperature should continue to rise and finish around 145°. Slice the roast, and arrange on a serving platter. Pour the remaining sauce over the roast just before serving. **Serves at least 6 to 8**

CENTER-CUT BONE-IN PORK CHOPS WITH APPLES AND CHESTNUT SAUCE

The secret to these chops is the searing they get on a cast iron griddle," declares Karen Cassady, coordinator of the Central Market Cooking Schools in Texas. The rich, deep flavors of the chestnut puree and the bright, spicy notes of the ichimi togarashi complement the classic combination of apples and pork. "I was introduced to this Japanese powdered red pepper by Tre Wilcox, a chef and *Top Chef* contender from Dallas who teaches in our cooking schools," says Karen.

2 slices apple-smoked bacon, finely chopped
1 tablespoon finely chopped shallot
1 medium Rome apple, peeled, cored, and chopped medium fine
2 bone-in center-cut pork chops (about 1 inch thick)
Fine sea salt to taste (about 1 teaspoon)
Ichimi togarashi (red pepper) to taste (about ¼ teaspoon; see kitchen note)
3 fresh sage leaves, finely chopped
2 tablespoons canned chestnut puree
4 tablespoons heavy cream
1 teaspoon chestnut honey or other full-flavored honey

1. Preheat the oven to 350°.

2. Heat a Lodge 10½-inch cast iron griddle over medium heat until the pan is hot. Add the bacon; cook, stirring occasionally, until it has rendered some fat and begins to crisp. Add the shallot and apple, and cook, stirring occasionally, until the apple begins to soften, about 3 minutes.

3. While the apples cook, dust the chops with the sea salt, red pepper, and half the sage.

4. Using a slotted spoon, transfer the apple mixture to a heatproof bowl, leaving as much liquid behind on the griddle as possible (there won't be much). Toss the remaining sage with the mixture in the bowl.

5. Over medium heat, sear the chops on the griddle in the liquid until browned, 1 to 2 minutes per side. Return the apple mixture to the griddle, surrounding the chops with it. Place the griddle in the oven, and bake until the chops register 160° when an instant-read thermometer is inserted at the thickest point.

6. While the chops are in the oven, place the chestnut puree, 2 tablespoons of the cream, and the honey in a small bowl. Using a fork, mix to combine thoroughly.

7. When the chops are ready, remove the griddle from the oven, and transfer the chops and apple mixture to a tray. Place the griddle over medium heat, and scrape up any browned bits from the surface. Add the remaining 2 tablespoons cream, and stir with a whisk to incorporate the pan scrapings into the cream. Add the chestnut mixture and, stirring quickly, incorporate the cream with the pan scrapings into that mixture. This will form a thin sauce.

8. Pour a pool of the sauce on two warm dinner plates. Arrange the chops on the sauce, and top with the apple mixture. Enjoy! **Serves 2**

kitchen note:

Ichimi togarashi is a Japanese powdered red pepper available in specialty grocery stores and Asian markets. You can substitute freshly ground red pepper flakes.

You can order this "Pad-kee-mow" everywhere in Thailand, says St. Louis, Missouri-based cookbook author and cooking school teacher Naam Pruitt, as well as in most Thai restaurants in the U.S. It's part of the Thai lunch repertoire. "'Kee-mow' translates into 'drunken' in English, but there is no alcohol in this dish," explains Naam. "Instead, because of its extreme spiciness, it's supposed to sober you up!"

DRUNKEN RICE NOODLES WITH PORK

½ (14-ounce) package dried medium rice noodles

¼ cup canola oil

4 garlic cloves, chopped

2 Thai chiles (see kitchen note), chopped

2 boneless pork chops (about 1 pound), trimmed of fat, thinly sliced, and marinated in 2 teaspoons soy sauce for 5 minutes

2 tablespoons sweet soy sauce

2 tablespoons soy sauce

1 tablespoon Thai fish sauce

1 tablespoon oyster sauce

2 tablespoons sugar

1 teaspoon ground white pepper

½ cup water, or as needed

1 red bell pepper, seeded and cut into thin strips

1 cup snow peas, trimmed and cut in half on a diagonal

1 cup fresh Thai basil leaves

1. Soak the noodles in warm water to cover for 20 minutes, then drain off the water, and set aside.

2. Heat a Lodge 14-inch cast iron wok over medium-high heat until hot. Add the oil, and wait until it is hot. Add the garlic and chiles; using a wide metal spatula, stir around until the mixture is fragrant and the garlic starts to turn color, about 1 minute.

3. Add the pork, and stir until cooked through. Add the drained noodles, both soy sauces, fish sauce, oyster sauce, sugar, white pepper, and water, and cook until the noodles are almost soft, stirring constantly, 5 to 8 minutes.

4. Stir in the pepper strips and snow peas, and cook until tender-crisp and the noodles are soft, just a few minutes. Turn off the heat. Stir in the basil, and serve. **Serves 2 to 4**

kitchen note:

Thai chiles have a lingering heat. They have an elongated, pointed shape and are 1 to 1½ inches long, with a thin skin and copious seeds. On a heat scale of 1 to 10, they clock in at 8.

a cooking secret from Naam

Soy sauce varies a great deal from brand to brand and country to country. I prefer to use Thai sweet soy sauce, which has a thick consistency and the flavor of molasses, with a subtle hint of soy. It is used to add sweetness and a dark color to a dish.

This is a favorite dish of Jennifer Brush, owner of The Pastry Brush bakery in Chardon, Ohio, and her husband, Andrew. They especially enjoy making it when they go camping, because the meat can be grilled briefly first to develop a crust and then cooked over a low fire or on a grill in a covered pot. It goes well with egg noodles or mashed potatoes, and Jennifer and Andrew like to serve it with homemade biscuits and coleslaw.

SPICED BRAISED PORK SHOULDER

Spice rub:
- 2 tablespoons sugar
- 2 teaspoons kosher salt
- ½ teaspoon ground coriander
- ½ teaspoon ground cumin
- ½ teaspoon freshly ground black pepper
- ½ teaspoon ground cinnamon
- ½ teaspoon ground cardamom

Braised pork:
- 1 (3- to 4-pound) pork shoulder
- 3 tablespoons vegetable oil
- 1 bottle lager beer (avoid using a hoppy beer like an IPA)

Gravy:
- All-purpose flour as needed
- 2 teaspoons cider vinegar
- ¼ cup chopped fresh cilantro

1. Pour all the spice rub ingredients into a 1-gallon zip-top plastic bag, seal, and shake. Dry the pork shoulder with a paper towel, and place it in the bag. Rub the dry ingredients into the meat until they are nearly all adhered to the meat and all of the surfaces of the meat are covered. Squeeze the air out of the bag, seal, and refrigerate for 24 hours.

2. Preheat the oven to 225°. Heat the oil in a Lodge 7-quart cast iron Dutch oven over medium-high heat until it sizzles. Brown all sides and edges of the pork shoulder. Pour in enough beer to cover the bottom of the pot—about ⅜ inch deep—no more! Bring the beer to a boil. Cover the pot, and place in the oven. Cook until the meat shreds easily with a fork, 3 to 4 hours.

3. Remove the meat from the pot, and wrap in aluminum foil. Pour the liquid from the pot into a heatproof measuring cup. Measure 1 tablespoon flour per cup of liquid, and place in the Dutch oven. Over low heat, add the braising liquid very slowly to the pot, whisking thoroughly to eliminate lumps, until all the liquid is added and the gravy is smooth. Turn the heat to high, and bring the gravy to a boil to thicken. Remove from the heat. Whisk in the vinegar and cilantro.

4. Shred the meat using two forks, and discard any fatty pieces. Mix the shredded meat with the sauce in the pot, and serve. **Serves 4 to 6**

COUNTRY HAM AND FIG PIZZA

ountry ham is a mainstay of the Southern table. It is best sliced thin and is frequently served on biscuits—and in grilling expert and cookbook author Elizabeth Karmel's home, with fig jam. If you don't have access to country ham in your area, you can substitute thick-sliced prosciutto for it. This recipe is adapted from *Pizza on the Grill* (Taunton Press), which Elizabeth co-authored with Bob Blumer.

½ cup ricotta cheese
¼ cup mascarpone
1 tablespoon honey
¼ cup uncooked grits or polenta, for rolling the dough
1 ball prepared pizza dough, at room temperature
2 tablespoons extra virgin olive oil
½ cup fig jam
8 fresh figs, sliced, or 6 dried figs, sliced on an angle as thin as possible (try to get 4 slices per fig)
6 ounces country ham, thinly sliced (about 5 biscuit-size slices) and broken into pieces or diced
¼ cup walnut halves, toasted (see kitchen note)
Freshly ground black pepper
Kosher salt

1. In a medium bowl, combine the ricotta, mascarpone, and honey until smooth. Set aside.

2. Preheat a gas grill by setting all burners on high. Close the lid, and leave on high for 10 minutes, then reduce all the burners to medium. Place a Lodge 14-inch cast iron baking pan in the center of the cooking grate. (If you have a charcoal grill, let the coals burn to a gray ash, and spread in an even layer. Place the pan on the cooking grate, and let it preheat for 5 minutes.)

3. Sprinkle a work surface with the grits. Roll out and shape the dough, ideally into a thin, organically shaped piece of dough about ¼ inch thick. Drizzle or brush both sides with the oil. Pick up the dough by the two corners closest to you. In one motion, lay it down flat on the pan from front to back. Grill, with the lid down, until the bottom is nicely browned, about 3 minutes.

4. Using tongs, flip the crust over. Spread the grilled side with the jam. Artfully arrange the fig slices on top, and sprinkle with the ham and walnuts. Spoon small dollops of the ricotta mixture over the top.

5. Return the pan to the cooking grate, and grill, with the lid down, until the bottom of the crust is well browned and the toppings are hot.

6. Remove from the grill, and season with pepper to taste. Since the ham is salty, taste first, then salt only if necessary. Slice and serve immediately.

Serves 4 to 6

kitchen note:

To toast nuts, spread on a baking sheet in a single layer, and bake in a preheated 300° oven until golden brown, 5 to 15 minutes, depending on the type of nut. Turn once during cooking. Let cool before using.

how Elizabeth grills pizza

1. To guarantee a crisp crust, preheat a baking pan in center of the cooking grate on the grill before placing dough on the pan.

2. To transfer the dough to the grill, pick up the dough by the two corners closest to you. Lay the dough on the pan, grits side up.

3. Once the crust is ready to be turned over, use long tongs to flip the crust over.

4. Add the toppings; cook, covered, until the crust is browned and toppings are hot.

SMOKED HAM HOCKS
WITH HOPPIN' JOHN AND CARAMELIZED ONION JUS

Stephen Stryjewski, chef and co-owner of Cochon in New Orleans, has had ham hocks on the menu since the restaurant opened. "It's an underappreciated cut of meat that lacks versatility but packs incredible flavor," says Stephen. Making the multiple components of this dish requires a good bit of time, but it is worth the effort. For the hocks, choose large pork knuckles from the front legs above the first joint. They can have the skin on or off. "I like the texture of the slow-cooked skin, although hocks with the skin still on are hard to come by."

2 cups kosher salt
1 cup sugar
1 teaspoon curing salt (see kitchen note)
2 tablespoons juniper berries
2 tablespoons allspice berries
2 tablespoons fennel seeds
5 star anise
½ cup coriander seeds
10 bay leaves
8 garlic cloves, peeled
5 sprigs fresh thyme
2 sprigs fresh rosemary
½ cup black peppercorns
8 cups (2 quarts) water
1 gallon ice cubes
6 unsmoked ham hocks (2 to 3 pounds each)
Hoppin' John (recipe follows)
Caramelized Onion Jus (recipe follows)

1. Make the brine: Stir the salt, sugar, herbs, and spices together in a large stockpot. Add the water, bring to a boil, and let simmer, stirring, until the salt and sugar are dissolved. Remove from the heat. Pour the ice in to cool.

2. Add the ham hocks to the cooled brine, adding additional water if needed to cover. Cover the stockpot, and refrigerate for 4 days.

3. Remove the hocks from the brine, and pat dry. Place the hocks on a wire rack set on a large baking sheet in the refrigerator, uncovered, for 24 hours to develop a pellicle (a sticky film) to which the smoke can adhere.

4. In a smoker or using a charcoal or gas grill, smoke the hocks over indirect heat at 225° until the meat falls off the bone with light pressure, about 6 hours.

5. While the hocks smoke, make the Hoppin' John and Caramelized Onion Jus.

6. To serve, place a scoop of the Hoppin' John in the center of a Lodge cast iron mini server or a deep dish, and top with a ham hock. Top with ¼ cup of the caramelized onions, and serve. **Serves 6 to 8**

kitchen note:
Curing salt will give the hocks the nice rosy red color. Look for it online at sausagemaker.com; you'll want their Insta Cure #1 for this.

HOPPIN' JOHN

½ pound dried black-eyed peas, rinsed and picked over

⅓ pound tasso or country ham, diced

5½ cups water

1 medium onion, cut in half, one half diced

2 garlic cloves, peeled

1 bay leaf

¼ pound bacon, cut into small dice

½ large green bell pepper, seeded and diced

2 celery ribs, cut into small dice

½ jalapeño chile, seeded and minced

½ teaspoon fresh thyme leaves

¾ cup raw brown jasmine rice

3 green onions, thinly sliced

Leaves from ½ bunch fresh flat-leaf parsley, chopped

1 teaspoon kosher salt

1 teaspoon freshly ground black pepper

1. In a Lodge 7-quart cast iron Dutch oven, combine the black-eyed peas, tasso, and 4 cups of the water. Add the onion half, garlic, and bay leaf. Bring to a boil over high heat, reduce the heat to medium-low, and simmer gently until the peas are tender but not mushy, 2 to 2½ hours. Drain the peas, reserving the cooking liquid. Remove and discard the onion, garlic, and bay leaf from the peas. Transfer the peas to a bowl, and wipe out the Dutch oven.

2. Add the bacon to the pot, and render over medium-high heat until golden, stirring frequently. Add the diced onion, bell pepper, celery, and jalapeño, and cook, stirring a few times, until the onion is translucent, about 10 minutes. Add the thyme and remaining 1½ cups water to the pot, and bring to a boil. Add the rice, cover, reduce the heat to a simmer, and cook until the rice is tender, 17 to 22 minutes.

3. Stir the green onions, parsley, and black-eyed peas gently into the rice (you don't want to break the grains), season with the salt and pepper, and adjust the consistency with a bit of the reserved bean cooking liquid, if you like. Keep warm until ready to serve. **Makes about 4 cups**

CARAMELIZED ONION JUS

2 tablespoons lard

3 quarts thinly sliced onions (3 to 4 large onions)

½ cup thinly sliced garlic (about 12 cloves)

2 tablespoons fresh thyme leaves

½ cup balsamic vinegar

1 quart pork stock, roasted chicken stock, or good-quality reduced-sodium beef stock

Kosher salt

Fresh lemon juice

1. Melt the lard in a Lodge 7-quart cast iron Dutch oven over high heat. Add the onions, reduce the heat to low, and cook, stirring frequently and allowing onions to caramelize slowly and turn golden. This will take about an hour.

2. Add the garlic, and let it become golden brown slowly, about 10 minutes, stirring often. Add the thyme, and deglaze with the vinegar. Reduce the liquid by half, then add the stock. Bring to a simmer, and continue to simmer, uncovered, until the liquid reduces by one-quarter to one-third and the jus is thick without being tacky, about 20 minutes. Season with salt and lemon juice to taste, if necessary. **Makes about 4 cups**

This comforting dish of sausage, potatoes, onions, and red roasted peppers from Chuck Aflitto, TV personality and chef, bakes up in just a half hour. The aromas are intriguing, the taste sweet and spicy all at once, and the potatoes crispy and delicious.

BAKED SAUSAGE AND POTATOES
WITH ROASTED RED PEPPERS

3 tablespoons salted butter
2 tablespoons extra virgin olive oil
2 large onions, thinly sliced
4 russet potatoes, peeled and thinly sliced
2 hot sausage links, casings removed

½ (8-ounce) jar roasted red peppers, drained
¼ cup grated Parmigiano-Reggiano cheese
Sea salt and freshly ground black pepper

1. Preheat the oven to 450°. Grease a Lodge 12-inch cast iron oval server with 1 tablespoon of the butter.

2. Melt the remaining 2 tablespoons butter with 1 tablespoon of the oil in a Lodge 10-inch cast iron skillet over medium heat. Add the onions, and cook, stirring occasionally, until golden brown, about 20 minutes. Remove from the heat.

3. Layer the potato slices evenly over the bottom and up the side of the oval server, overlapping them; reserve enough of the potato slices to cover the top. Crumble the sausage meat over the potatoes. Arrange the sautéed onions evenly over the sausage, then the roasted peppers. Arrange the remaining potatoes over the peppers, drizzle with the remaining 1 tablespoon oil, sprinkle with the cheese, and season with salt and pepper to taste.

4. Bake until the potatoes are browned, the sausage is fully cooked, and you can easily insert a sharp knife through the center, about 25 minutes.
Serves 6 to 8

Cast Iron Memories

There is nothing better than a Sunday afternoon filled with friends and family, hovering around the kitchen, waiting to sit down to dinner. In our family, food is what brings us together. We sit at the table a little longer than most, soaking up extra sauce with our bread and sipping on wine. This passion for food and family was cultivated at an early age in my mother's kitchen. She taught me not only about cooking, but about the craft of adapting old family recipes from Italy for today's American families. The lifeblood that fuels my passion for cooking is the same that courses through the veins of the folks who make Lodge pans—a devotion to quality, perfection, and family tradition. With Lodge pans I can trust that our food will be cooked to perfection.

—*Chuck Aflitto*

ANDOUILLE SAUSAGE, APPLES, AND POTATOES
WITH BRANDIED CIDER

For this recipe, says James Harris, executive chef of the restaurant Zynodoa in Staunton, Virginia, cast iron is essential. No other cooking medium will produce the same results. Also, choose your ingredients wisely. This recipe has a simple flavor profile, so you need to start with top-quality ingredients, and then focus on the execution. Zynodoa uses sausage, potatoes and apples from local farms. James prefers locally sourced food because it generally is fresher and picked closer to perfect ripeness...all of which translates into a tastier meal.

1½ cups Brussels sprouts, trimmed and cut in half

2 potatoes (preferably Kennebec and the size of the apples), peeled and cut across into ¾-inch-thick rounds

5 tablespoons bacon drippings

4 (8-inch) links andouille sausage, cut in half lengthwise and across into ½-inch-thick half moons

4 Granny Smith or other tart apples, peeled, cored, each cut across into 4 rings, and placed in water with a squeeze of lemon juice

Kosher salt and freshly ground black pepper

2 large shallots, cut ¼ inch thick and pulled apart into rings

¼ cup brandy

2 cups fresh unpasteurized apple cider

¼ cup (½ stick) unsalted butter, cut into pieces

1 tablespoon roughly chopped fresh sage

Sugar

Good-quality red wine vinegar or cider vinegar (James uses Virginia Vinegar Works Merlot Vinegar)

1. Preheat the oven to the lowest setting.

2. Bring a large, heavy-bottomed pot of generously salted water to a boil. (The water should taste like the sea, and the pot should be large enough that the Brussels sprouts, when dropped into the water, do not stop the water from boiling—an 8-quart pot or larger.) Cook the Brussels sprouts in batches until tender but not mushy, about 4 minutes. Drain and set aside.

3. While the Brussels sprouts cook, place the potatoes in a 2-quart saucepan. Cover with cold water, and add enough salt to make the water taste of it. Bring to a boil, and simmer until tender but not overcooked, 10 to 12 minutes. Drain and set aside.

4. While the potatoes cook, heat a Lodge 12-inch cast iron skillet over medium heat. Add the bacon drippings, and place the sausage pieces flat side down (cook the sausage in batches so as not to overcrowd the skillet). Don't move the sausage until that side begins to caramelize. Pay attention to what your ears and nose as well as your eyes are telling you—with a little practice you should be able to know when to flip the sausage without looking at it. The sausage is ready to turn when you hear a sizzling, snapping sound and it gives off a nutty, caramel aroma. Flip and repeat on the other side. Remove to a baking sheet, and keep warm in the oven while you finish cooking the remaining sausage.

5. Place the potatoes in the sausage-seasoned skillet, and cook over medium heat until crispy and golden brown, 3 to 4 minutes per side, working in batches so as not to overcrowd the skillet. Continue to rely on your senses of smell and sound. Add the browned potatoes to the baking sheet with the sausage.

6. Increase the heat under the skillet to high, add the Brussels sprouts, cut side down, and cook until caramelized on that side, about 2 minutes. Be sure not to overcrowd the skillet. Transfer the browned Brussels sprouts to the baking

sheet. Reduce the heat a bit to medium-high, place the apple rings in the skillet, and brown on both sides, seasoning them with salt and pepper to taste as they cook. Transfer the rings to the baking sheet.

7. Reduce the heat to low, and add the shallots. Cook until translucent, stirring frequently. Add the brandy, and carefully ignite with a long match (watch out for dangling hair or long sleeves). Let the flames die out on their own. Add the cider, and reduce the liquid by half. Remove the skillet from the heat, and swirl in the butter until fully incorporated. Season with salt to taste. Stir in the sage. Taste for salt again, and season with pepper, sugar, and vinegar to taste.

8. Divide the potatoes and apples among 4 dinner plates, setting an apple ring on top of a portion of potatoes and placing the sausage pieces over that. Spoon the Brussels sprouts around the plates, as if they fell from heaven. Spoon sauce over each component, and serve. **Serves 4**

This recipe works great in a 9-quart Dutch oven. It isn't just the horseradish that contributes to the tangy flavor but also the watercress. Abundant in many small Nevada streams, watercress is often available in specialty markets. This all-in-one meal has been converted by master Dutch oven chef, cowboy poet, and Reno, Nevada, resident, Dennis Golden, for indoor cooking from one originally buried and cooked all day in camp.

TANGY DUTCH OVEN HORSERADISH VENISON ROAST

4   to 6 tablespoons olive oil
1   (4-pound) venison shoulder roast, cut to fit Dutch oven
2   cups solid-pack peeled whole tomatoes, undrained
½   cup dry sherry
1   cup beef broth
1   tablespoon celery seeds
3   tablespoons onion salt

3   tablespoons garlic pepper
6   tablespoons prepared horseradish
1   cup fresh watercress sprigs, chopped
6   small red potatoes, quartered
6   small yellow onions, quartered
4   medium carrots, cut into 1-inch lengths
4   celery ribs, cut into 1-inch lengths

1. Preheat the oven to 300°.

2. Heat the oil in a Lodge 9-quart cast iron Dutch oven until a sprinkle of water sizzles when added. Add the roast, and brown on all sides.

3. While the roast browns, combine the remaining ingredients in a medium bowl. When the roast is browned, pour the mixture all around it in the Dutch oven. Cover and bake on the middle rack in the oven until the roast is fork-tender, 3 to 4 hours. Check on it occasionally, and increase or reduce the oven temperature to maintain a simmer.

4. Slice the meat, and serve with the vegetables from the Dutch oven.

Serves 6 to 8

PORK AND SAUSAGE JAMBALAYA

½ pound bacon, diced
1 medium onion, diced
½ green bell pepper, seeded and diced
1 celery rib, diced
1 pound smoked pork sausage, sliced ½ inch thick
3 cups raw converted or parboiled Louisiana white rice
1 teaspoon smoked paprika

1 teaspoon dried thyme
1 teaspoon red pepper flakes
5 cups chicken broth
1 cup tomato sauce or canned chopped tomatoes
2 cups diced cooked pork
3 green onions, chopped
Salt
Hot sauce

Jambalaya is a special dish to Chef John Besh, a New Orleans-based chef, author, and restaurateur, as it is a meal he has been eating since he was a child.

1. In a Lodge 7-quart cast iron Dutch oven, cook the bacon over medium-high heat until the fat is rendered, about 3 minutes. Add the onion, and cook, stirring often, until browned. Add the bell pepper, celery, and sausage, and cook, stirring, for 3 minutes. Add the rice, paprika, thyme, and red pepper, and stir until the rice is coated with bacon fat and the ingredients are well mixed.

2. Increase the heat to high, and add the broth and tomato sauce, then the diced pork and green onions. Stir well, and bring to a boil. Cover, reduce the heat to low, and simmer until the rice is cooked, about 18 minutes. Remember, the pork and sausage are already cooked, you're only making the rice at this point. Remove the pot from the heat, and it's ready to serve! Season with salt and hot sauce to taste. **Serves 10 to 12**

a cooking secret from John

This recipe calls for converted rice, but any type of rice with personality and flavor will work, such as jasmine, pecan, or Carolina Gold. Using these types of rice adds another level of flavor.

A well-kept secret of California wine country is the outstanding and abundant lamb produced there. Mint is a classic pairing with lamb, but this recipe also includes garlic. For those who find classic mint jelly overwhelming, the combination of fresh mint and garlic provides a welcome and light alternative. Completing his twist on the traditional dish, Al Hernandez, the food and wine editor for *The Vine Times*, also uses cauliflower as an alternative to mashed potatoes.

LAMB CHOPS WITH GARLIC-MINT SAUCE AND CAULIFLOWER "MASHED POTATOES"

12 (1- to 1½-inch-thick) lamb loin chops
Kosher salt
½ cup tightly packed fresh mint leaves, finely chopped
1 tablespoon finely chopped garlic
¼ cup balsamic vinegar
¼ cup plus 1 tablespoon olive oil
1 head cauliflower, cut into small florets
1 tablespoon unsalted butter
½ cup heavy cream
Freshly ground black pepper

1. Season the lamb chops on both sides with salt; set aside.

2. In small bowl, mix the mint, garlic, vinegar, and ½ teaspoon salt together. Add ¼ cup of the oil in a slow, steady stream, whisking constantly, until it thickens into an emulsion. Taste for salt. Set aside.

3. Bring ¼ to ½ inch water to a boil in a covered medium saucepan over medium heat. Place the florets in a steamer basket, set in the saucepan, cover, and steam until the cauliflower is tender, 8 to 10 minutes.

4. While the cauliflower steams, heat the remaining 1 tablespoon oil in a Lodge 15-inch cast iron skillet over medium-high heat about 1 minute. Add the lamb chops (you may need to cook them in batches), and cook 2 to 5 minutes per side, depending on their thickness and your desired degree of doneness (2 to 3 minutes per side for rare and 5 minutes plus for medium to medium-well). Remove to a plate, cover with aluminum foil, and let stand while you finish the cauliflower.

5. Remove the steamer basket from the saucepan, and discard the steaming water. Melt the butter in the pan, add the florets, and mash as you would for mashed potatoes. (For a smoother consistency, do this in a blender or food processor.) Add the cream, and heat through over low heat, 2 to 3 minutes. Season with salt and pepper to taste.

6. To serve, spoon cauliflower mash in the center of each plate, surround with 3 lamb chops, and spoon a little of the sauce over each chop. **Serves 4**

Cast Iron Memories

I was either 3 or 4 years old, living in Spain, when I learned about cast iron. My grandmother's house had a wood-burning oven and stove, so every dish she made was cooked in cast iron. She owned everything from cast iron skillets to teakettles and even a cast iron clothes iron. Those pieces are now family heirlooms and are with various relatives who still use them.

Today, I have my own assortment of cast iron cookware, and I don't think I will ever be able to select one favorite piece because cast iron is so versatile. Plus, you can always tell when something has been cooked in cast iron. Everyone always mentions cast iron's durability and flexibility, but for me, it is the character that cast iron gives to a dish that cannot be duplicated. You can have identical ingredients and measurements, but only cast iron cookware can impart the development and layers of flavor that make a dish memorable.

— *Al Hernandez*

This recipe from chef Jimmy Kennedy may seem a little long and complicated, but it's mostly just cooking time and well worth the effort.

DUTCH OVEN RABBIT AND SAUCE OVER CHEDDAR-BUTTERMILK BISCUITS

Cheddar-Buttermilk Biscuits:
6 tablespoons (¾ stick) unsalted butter, plus 1 or 2 teaspoons for greasing
2½ cups unbleached all-purpose flour (Jimmy uses King Arthur)
1¼ teaspoons baking powder
¾ teaspoon baking soda
½ teaspoon salt
¼ cup buttermilk
1 cup (4 ounces) grated sharp cheddar cheese (Jimmy uses Cabot)

Rabbit:
1 rabbit (about 2½ pounds), dressed and cut into 8 pieces
Salt and freshly ground black pepper
⅓ cup canola oil
1 cup diced onion
½ cup diced celery
½ cup diced carrot
3 or 4 garlic cloves, minced

3 cups chicken stock (store-bought is fine)
1 cup white wine
1 teaspoon dried rosemary or leaves from 2 fresh sprigs
½ teaspoon dried thyme or leaves from 5 fresh sprigs
½ teaspoon dried oregano

Sauce:
¼ cup canola oil or butter
½ cup diced onion
¼ cup diced carrot
¼ cup diced celery
1 garlic clove, minced
2 tablespoons tomato paste
2 tablespoons all-purpose flour
¼ teaspoon dried thyme or leaves from 3 fresh sprigs
½ teaspoon dried rosemary or leaves from 1 fresh sprig
Salt and freshly ground black pepper to taste

1. Make the biscuits: Preheat the oven to 400°. Grease a baking sheet with the extra butter.

2. In a large bowl, stir together the flour, baking powder, baking soda, and salt. Using a small knife, cut the 6 tablespoons butter into small pieces, and distribute throughout the flour. Using a pastry blender or your fingertips, mash the butter into the flour until the mixture has the consistency of coarse cornmeal. Add the buttermilk, and mix briefly, just until all the dry ingredients are incorporated into a dough. Add the cheese, and mix lightly (overmixing will make the biscuits tough).

3. Turn the dough onto a well-floured work surface, and knead it briefly, working in more flour, if necessary, so that it is not completely sticky. Pat it out to a thickness of 1½ to 2 inches. Cut with a 3½-inch round cookie cutter or the

floured rim of a drinking glass or any shape you desire. Pat the scraps together and cut out more biscuits.

4. Place the first biscuit at the center of the prepared baking sheet. Nestle the other biscuits around the first one so the sides are touching. Bake until golden brown, 20 to 25 minutes. Set aside.

5. While the biscuits bake, start the rabbit. Season the rabbit pieces generously with salt and pepper. In a Lodge 7-quart cast iron Dutch oven, heat the oil over medium-high heat until it is hot but not smoking. Add the rabbit, and brown well on all sides. Do not crowd the pot; if you need to, work in batches. Transfer the rabbit to a plate as it browns.

6. Add the onion, celery, carrot, and garlic to the pot, and cook for a couple of minutes, stirring. Add the stock, wine, rosemary, thyme, and oregano, and bring to a low boil. Turn off the heat, add the rabbit back to the pot, and cover.

7. When the biscuits come out of the oven, reduce the oven temperature to 375°. Put the Dutch oven in the oven. After 30 minutes, remove the lid, rotate the rabbit pieces, re-cover, and place back in the oven for another 30 to 45 minutes. After 1 to 1½ hours of braising, the rabbit should be fork tender; if it isn't, cook a little longer. When the rabbit is good and tender, remove the pieces to a baking dish, and cover with aluminum foil.

8. Make the sauce: Place the Dutch oven over low heat.

9. In a Lodge 10-inch cast iron skillet, heat the oil over medium heat until hot but not smoking. Add the onion, carrot, celery, and garlic, and cook, stirring a few times, until the onion starts to soften. Add the tomato paste and cook, stirring, for 3 to 4 minutes. Add the flour, and stir well, scraping the bottom of the pan to make a thick roux. Jimmy likes to use a wooden spoon for this. Continue stirring and scraping for a couple of minutes, then turn off the heat, and stir in the herbs.

10. Turn the heat to medium-high on the Dutch oven. When the braising liquid just starts to come to a boil, reduce the heat back to low, and slowly add the roux while constantly stirring or whisking. When it has all been added and the sauce is nice and smooth, season to taste with salt and pepper. Reduce the heat to barely a simmer.

11. Reheat the rabbit and biscuits in the oven for 10 or 15 minutes (it's a good idea to do this when you start making the roux). When the rabbit and biscuits are nice and hot, remove from the oven, open up the biscuits, place a piece of the braised rabbit on top, ladle the hot sauce over the rabbit, and serve.

Serves 12

Trout Almondine,
page 178

FISH & SHELLFISH

TEXAS FRIED CATFISH

atfish is one of the few things openly accepted by ranchers and cattlemen as an alternative to beef," states Tom Perini, owner of Perini Ranch Steakhouse in Buffalo Gap, Texas. "Catfish can be found in most every river, lake, and pond in Texas, and we all grew up fishing for them." Now you can find farm-raised catfish in most every supermarket across the country, but for the best quality, buy fish raised in the U.S.

6 (5- to 7-ounce) U.S. farm-raised catfish fillets

Egg dip:
¾ cup whole milk
1 large egg, beaten
2 teaspoons seasoning salt
½ teaspoon ground white pepper

Seasoned cornmeal:
2 cups yellow cornmeal
¼ cup all-purpose flour
1 teaspoon salt
1 teaspoon cayenne pepper
½ teaspoon freshly ground black pepper
¼ teaspoon onion powder
¼ teaspoon garlic powder
Vegetable oil (enough so that the fish can be fully submerged in the oil)

1. Slice each fillet in half lengthwise. In a shallow bowl, combine the egg dip ingredients, and mix well. On a large plate, combine the ingredients for the seasoned cornmeal.

2. Heat enough oil over medium-high heat to 350° so that the fish fillets will be submerged in a Lodge 7-quart cast iron Dutch oven.

3. While the oil heats, dip the catfish fillets, one at a time, in the egg dip, coating each piece fully and letting any excess drip off. Dredge each piece in the seasoned cornmeal, coating it completely. Shake off any excess.

4. When the oil is hot, carefully slip the fillets into the oil without crowding them (you may have to fry them in batches). Fry until the fillets float to the top of the oil, about 6 minutes. When the fish is ready, the meat will be flaky. Transfer them to a wire rack to drain. **Serves 6**

This recipe from Sean Brock, chef-partner of the restaurants Husk in Charleston, South Carolina, and Nashville, Tennessee, showcases one of his passions, seed preservation. Working with various farmers and seedsmen, Sean raises heirloom varieties of beans, corn, grains, and benne (sesame seeds) that date back to before the Civil War and were once at risk of becoming extinct before his timely intervention.

CORNMEAL-CRUSTED CATFISH WITH HEIRLOOM BEANS, CHOW CHOW, AND TOMATO GRAVY

Chow Chow:

Kosher salt

¾ pound butterbeans, shelled

1½ quarts cider vinegar with an acidity of at least 5%

2 cups firmly packed light brown sugar

1 tablespoon yellow mustard seeds

1 tablespoon ground turmeric

1½ teaspoons celery seeds

1½ teaspoons red pepper flakes

1 medium sweet onion (about 1 pound), cut into small dice

2 red bell peppers (about ¾ pound), seeded and cut into small dice

1 jalapeño chile, seeded and minced

1 small head cabbage (about 1½ pounds), cored, thinly sliced, and cut into small pieces

3 medium green tomatoes (about 1½ pounds), cored and cut into small dice

½ cup prepared yellow mustard

Heirloom Beans:

1 cup dried heirloom beans (Sea Island red peas, Reverend Taylor butterbeans, rice peas, or other heirloom beans of your choice), soaked in water to cover in the refrigerator overnight

2 quarts stock (preferably pork, but chicken will work; homemade is preferred but store-bought is fine)

1 medium onion, cut into ½-inch dice

1 large carrot, cut into ½-inch dice

2 celery ribs, cut into ½-inch dice

2 garlic cloves, thinly sliced

½ jalapeño chile, seeded and chopped

1 bay leaf

Several sprigs fresh thyme

Kosher salt

Tomato Gravy:

2 tablespoons bacon drippings

2 tablespoons fine white cornmeal (Sean uses Anson Mills)

3 cups home-canned tomatoes or canned peeled whole San Marzano tomatoes (don't substitute fresh)

1 tablespoon kosher salt

1 tablespoon cracked black peppercorns

Catfish:

Canola oil

4 (6-ounce) skinless catfish fillets

Kosher salt

Cayenne pepper

1 cup fine white cornmeal

1. Make the chow chow: Bring a large Lodge cast iron Dutch oven of heavily salted water to a boil over high heat. Add the butterbeans, and cook for 4 minutes. Drain and spread the butterbeans out on a baking sheet to cool at room temperature.

2. Combine the vinegar and brown sugar in a Lodge 6-quart enameled cast iron Dutch oven over high heat, and bring to a boil, stirring well to dissolve the sugar. Reduce the heat to medium-high, and cook until it has reduced by half, about 20 minutes. Add the mustard seeds, turmeric, celery seeds, and red pepper, and stir to combine well. Add the onion, bell peppers, jalapeño, cabbage, and tomatoes, and cook over medium-high heat, stirring occasionally, until the vegetables are tender, about 15 minutes. Stir in the butterbeans and yellow mustard.

3. Remove from the heat, transfer the mixture to a sterilized glass or stainless steel container, and let cool to room temperature. Cover tightly, and refrigerate. It will keep for 3 to 4 weeks.

4. Make the heirloom beans: Drain the soaked beans, and set aside. In a large stockpot, bring the stock to a simmer, then add the beans, onion, carrot, celery, garlic, jalapeño, bay leaf, and thyme. Reduce the heat to low, partially cover the pot, and simmer until the beans are tender, about 1 hour. Season with salt to taste.

5. Make the tomato gravy: Heat the bacon drippings in a Lodge 4-quart cast iron Dutch oven over high heat. Stir in the cornmeal with a wooden spoon. Reduce the heat to low, and cook, constantly stirring, until the cornmeal turns a light brown color, about 5 minutes. Using your hands, crush the tomatoes into small bite-sized pieces. Add them to the pot, and stir to combine. Increase the heat to medium, bring the gravy to a simmer, and cook, stirring occasionally, until it is slightly thickened and the cornmeal is softened, about 10 minutes. Be careful that it doesn't stick or scorch. Stir in the salt and black pepper. Keep warm (it will hold over low heat for up to 1 hour). Any leftover gravy can be frozen.

6. Fry the catfish: Heat a Lodge 15-inch cast iron skillet over high heat. When the pan is hot, pour in ¼ inch of oil. Season the fish with salt and cayenne. Dredge the fish in the cornmeal, shaking off any excess. When the oil shimmers, add the fillets, with what would have been the skin side up. Do not shake the pan or touch the fish for 1 minute. Reduce the heat to medium-high. Every couple of minutes, using a metal spatula, peek under the fish. When it is golden brown, after 3 to 4 minutes, turn it over, and cook the other side until golden brown. Remove from the pan, and blot on a paper towel.

7. For each serving, ladle a large spoonful of tomato gravy in the middle of a plate, top with a fish fillet, and place a spoonful of chow chow and beans off to the side. **Serves 4**

Because U.S. farm-raised catfish is grown in highly controlled inland ponds and fed a diet of vegetarian feed, it is not only sustainable but also clean and mild tasting. This is chef and food writer Tamie Cook's favorite version of blackening. "Feel free to adapt it to your liking," advises Tamie, "as it is not for the faint of heart!" You may decrease or leave out the cayenne if you prefer.

BLACKENED CATFISH

2 teaspoons smoked paprika
2 teaspoons light brown sugar
1 teaspoon garlic powder
1 teaspoon sea salt
½ teaspoon cayenne pepper
½ teaspoon onion powder
½ teaspoon dried oregano

½ teaspoon ground cumin
¼ teaspoon freshly ground black pepper
4 (6-ounce) U.S. farm-raised catfish fillets
1 tablespoon olive oil
Lemon wedges

1. In a small bowl, combine the first 9 ingredients (through black pepper). Sprinkle the seasoning mix evenly on both sides of each fillet.

2. Heat the oil in a Lodge 10-inch cast iron skillet over medium-high heat. When it shimmers, add two of the fillets, and cook for 2½ to 3 minutes. Turn and cook until the fish is just cooked through and flakes when tested with a fork, another 2½ to 3 minutes. Remove to a plate, and cover with aluminum foil to keep warm. Repeat with remaining fillets. Serve with lemon wedges. **Serves 4**

how Tamie blackens catfish

1. Start by combining all of the spices in a small bowl. This will ensure that they are evenly dispersed on the fillets.

2. Start with cool fish right from the fridge. Don't let the fish warm up to room temperature. The oil will stick better to the cool fish, which is important for even blackening.

3. Preheat your pan and get it really, really hot. Cook the fillets for 2½ to 3 minutes on each side. The spices will begin to smoke (so be sure to open a window), but don't let them burn.

Julia Rutland, senior food editor of *Coastal Living* magazine in Birmingham, Alabama, adapted this from a recipe developed by Alfred Portale of Gotham Bar and Grill in New York City that ran in the magazine. Her version bumps up the amount of garlic and uses her favorite fish, Alaskan halibut. It's scaled down to serve 2, but easily doubles.

OVEN-ROASTED HALIBUT WITH LEMON-GARLIC BUTTER

2 tablespoons butter, softened	1 tablespoon chopped cooked bacon
1 tablespoon chopped fresh flat-leaf parsley	2 teaspoons all-purpose flour
2 garlic cloves, minced	1 tablespoon fresh lemon juice
1 small shallot, minced	1 tablespoon canola oil
½ teaspoon Dijon mustard	2 (6-ounce) Alaskan halibut fillets
	Salt and freshly ground black pepper

1. Preheat the oven to 450°.

2. In a small bowl, combine the first 8 ingredients (through lemon juice); set aside.

3. Heat the oil in a Lodge 10-inch cast iron skillet over medium-high heat. Sprinkle the fish with salt and pepper; cook 3 minutes. Turn the fillets over; cook 1 minute.

4. Spoon half the butter mixture over the tops of the fillets; transfer to the oven, and bake until the fish is cooked through and opaque in the center, about 5 minutes. Add the remaining butter mixture to the skillet. Let melt, then stir into the juices in the pan, and serve. **Serves 2**

a cooking secret from Julia

This is the perfect method for cooking thick fish fillets. Searing the fish first gives you a delicious crust while finishing it in the oven prevents overcooking and guarantees a juicy interior.

his recipe is from George B. Stevenson, chef de cuisine at Pearl's Foggy Mountain Café in Sewanee, Tennessee. It's a classic French preparation, combining the freshness of locally caught rainbow trout, the decadence of butter-browned almonds, and the brightness of freshly squeezed lemon juice.

TROUT ALMONDINE

4   (4-ounce) skin-on, boneless rainbow trout fillets (from 2 fish)
Kosher salt and freshly ground black pepper
2   tablespoons canola oil
5   tablespoons unsalted butter

½   cup sliced natural almonds
2   teaspoons minced shallot
1   teaspoon chopped fresh flat-leaf parsley
1   teaspoon chopped fresh thyme
1½ tablespoons fresh lemon juice

1. Pat the fish dry with a paper towel, then lightly sprinkle both sides with salt and pepper.

2. Place two Lodge 8-inch cast iron skillets over high heat. Add 1 tablespoon of the oil and ½ tablespoon of the butter to each skillet. When the butter is melted, add 2 fillets, flesh side down, to each skillet, and cook over high heat for about 4 minutes. (Note: After 2 minutes, carefully slide a metal spatula under the fish to ensure it is not sticking.) Turn the fillets over (the fish should be nicely browned but not dark), and cook for another 2 to 3 minutes. Carefully remove the trout to warm serving plates. Remove one skillet from the heat.

3. Add the remaining 4 tablespoons butter to the other skillet, and melt over high heat. Add the almonds, and swirl the pan to coat them with the butter. Cook for a minute or so. Add the shallot, parsley, thyme, and salt and pepper (a nice pinch of each should do). Toss the almonds constantly over the heat until they become uniformly light brown. Turn off the heat, add the lemon juice, and toss. The mixture will sizzle and foam. Top each fillet with the almond mixture. **Serves 4**

WHEN FARM TO TABLE
WAS A WAY OF LIFE

Linda Carman

Director of Martha White Test Kitchen

I love fresh summer vegetables and cornbread so much that I almost wish I had been raised on a farm. I was not, but my mother was, and we lived in a rural Alabama town, so I know that farm life is not for the faint of heart. Nevertheless, as the last of five children, I spent many hours in the kitchen with my mother and learned a lot about Southern farm cooking. She cooked with the seasons, respected food, and used it wisely. She peeled vegetables and fruits very thinly and capped strawberries by removing only the green tops and none of the red berry. She stretched a chicken by adding dumplings or pastry and took advantage of leftover pot roast by making delectable roast beef hash or vegetable beef soup with it. It was much later, after learning more about the history of regional cooking, that I began to understand the origin of her wonderful cooking style.

The real charm of Southern cooking did not come from plantations or fancy chefs. Iconic Southern recipes originated from poor farm families when "farm to table" was not a slogan, but a way of life. I think Mark Sohn, author of *Appalachian Home Cooking*, captures farm life at its most resourceful when he describes a farmer living on a small Appalachian farm with little room for crops. But he could raise corn and plant beans that climbed up the cornstalks, and the pig could root around in the woods for food. With these limited resources, the family would have fresh food in summer and cornmeal, cured pork, and dried beans in the winter.

In this world of culinary celebrities, I have the greatest admiration for the people who lived on the land and their legacy of recipes created to stretch the food they had to feed hungry families. Blessed with fertile soil, temperate climate, fish, game, and people from many ethnic backgrounds, the South nurtured an amazingly rich variety of food cultures. Low Country, Cajun, deep inland South, mountain cooking, and others were all born of the necessity to use only local ingredients.

So I give my thanks to those farm families who created Southern cooking, and to the brave young chefs who have made it stylish to eat collards and grits again, but especially to my mother for giving me a love of good, honest home cooking, and an appreciation of her gift of wisely using the foods available to us from farm to table.

CAST IRON TROUT
WITH SMOKED GRITS, POACHED FARM EGGS, AND POTLIKKER JUS

This is an award-winning recipe from William Dissen, chef-owner of The Market Place Restaurant in Asheville, North Carolina. Chef Dissen won the 2013 Cast Iron Cook-Off with it at The Greenbrier Resort in West Virginia. This dish showcased local rainbow trout from Sunburst Trout Farms out of Canton, North Carolina. It is a tribute to Southern ingredients with a creative presentation.

Smoked Grits:
2 tablespoons blended olive oil
¼ cup diced (¼ inch) red onion
1 tablespoon minced garlic
8 cups water
2 cups coarsely ground yellow corn grits
1½ cups heavy cream
½ cup chèvre
2 tablespoons hot sauce
Kosher salt and freshly ground black pepper

Potlikker Jus:
1½ quarts potlikker (see kitchen note)
1 tablespoon unsalted butter
Kosher salt and freshly ground black pepper

Trout:
6 trout, cleaned, boned, heads and tails cut off, and each cut into 2 fillets
Kosher salt and freshly ground black pepper
1½ tablespoons blended olive oil

Farm Eggs:
1 tablespoon distilled white vinegar
6 farm-fresh eggs

Garnish:
12 Pickled Ramps (recipe follows) or green onions, thinly sliced lengthwise on the bias
2 tablespoons finely chopped fresh flat-leaf parsley
Aleppo pepper

1. Make the grits: Heat the oil in a Lodge 5-quart cast iron Dutch oven over medium-high heat. Add the onion, and cook, stirring, until translucent, 2 to 3 minutes. Stir in the garlic, cook for 30 seconds, and pour in the water; bring to a boil over high heat. As the water comes to a boil, whisk in the grits, constantly stirring until they come together and begin to bubble, 3 to 4 minutes. As the grits begin to bubble, remove the pot from the heat; immediately cover with aluminum foil and the lid. Set in a warm place, and let steam for 45 to 50 minutes.

2. After the grits have steamed, place the pot back on the stove over medium heat. Stir in the cream, chèvre, hot sauce, and salt and pepper to taste, and bring to a simmer. Taste and season as necessary. Remove from the heat, and keep warm.

3. While the grits steam, make the potlikker jus: In a small saucepan, bring the potlikker to a simmer, and stir in the butter. Season with salt and pepper to taste. Keep warm.

4. Cook the trout: Season the skin side of the trout fillets with salt and pepper. Heat the oil in a Lodge 15-inch cast iron skillet over medium-high heat. As the oil begins to shimmer, place the trout into the pan, skin side down (you may need to cook the trout in batches). Cook until the trout skin becomes crispy, 2 to 3 minutes. Gently turn the trout over, and reduce the heat to medium. Cook until the trout is cooked through, another 3 minutes. Keep the trout warm.

5. While the trout cooks, bring a medium pot of water to a light simmer, and add the vinegar. Gently crack the eggs into the pot, and poach for about 1½ minutes.

6. For each serving, place a Lodge 5-inch cast iron mini skillet on a folded napkin on a small plate. Place a 3-inch ring mold in the center of the round skillet. Place a teaspoon of the grits in the center of the ring mold. Using a slotted spoon, place a poached egg directly on the grits. Gently mound about 1 cup grits over the poached egg. Place a trout fillet, skin side up, on the grits. Pour about ¼ cup potlikker jus around the outside of the ring mold, and garnish the trout with sliced Pickled Ramps. Garnish the plate with some of the parsley and a sprinkling of Aleppo pepper. **Serves 6**

kitchen note:
Potlikker is what Southerners call the water used to cook collards or other greens. Because the greens are usually simmered for a long time, this cooking liquid takes on its own beloved flavor. If there is any leftover from serving the greens, it is saved and can be used in other dishes, as it is here.

PICKLED RAMPS

Kosher salt
1 tablespoon black peppercorns
1 teaspoon mustard seeds
½ teaspoon caraway seeds
½ teaspoon fennel seeds
½ teaspoon cumin seeds

2 pounds ramps, cleaned, green leaves cut 1 inch above red stem (see kitchen note)
1 cup white wine vinegar
1 cup sugar
2 bay leaves

1. Bring a medium pot of water to a boil. Add enough salt so that it tastes like the ocean.

2. While the water comes to a boil, toast the peppercorns, mustard seeds, caraway seeds, fennel seeds, and cumin seeds in a small sauté pan over medium heat until fragrant, shaking the pan frequently. Pour into a bowl.

3. Add the ramps to the boiling water, and cook until tenderized but still crisp, about 30 seconds. Using a slotted spoon, transfer the ramps to a bowl of ice water to cool. Drain and place the ramps into a sterilized 1-quart canning jar with a lid.

4. Combine the vinegar, sugar, 1 tablespoon salt, the toasted spices, and bay leaves in a small saucepan, and bring to a boil over high heat, stirring to dissolve the salt and sugar. Let boil for about 2 minutes. Immediately pour the mixture over the ramps, and seal the jar.

5. Let the ramps cool to room temperature, then refrigerate. They will keep for 2 to 3 weeks. **Makes 1 quart**

kitchen note:
Ramps are a wild cousin to leeks and garlic and grow prolifically throughout Appalachia in the spring. They add a unique mountain flavor to the dish.

The Sacramento River is California's largest river and boasts runs of king, steelhead, and other types of salmon. The flavor and color of freshly caught wild salmon make for a luxurious and healthy meal. This fish is perfectly paired with another local favorite, asparagus. Areas around Sacramento are known for their asparagus production, and California is one of the nation's leading producers. This recipe is from Al Hernandez, the food and wine editor of *The Vine Times*.

PAN-SEARED SALMON WITH DILL SAUCE AND SAUTÉED ASPARAGUS

4   (4- to 6-ounce) skin-on
    salmon fillets
Kosher salt
2   pounds asparagus (preferably
    thin or medium-thick)
1   tablespoon plus 2 teaspoons olive
    or grapeseed oil

½   cup crème fraîche or sour cream
2   tablespoons finely chopped
    fresh dill
1   teaspoon granulated garlic
Freshly ground black pepper

1. Season the salmon fillets liberally with salt; set aside.

2. Take one spear of asparagus and, using both hands, one at each end of the spear, break it in two. It will naturally break at the right spot. Then cut the rest of the spears using the broken one as a guide. Discard the woody ends.

3. Heat 1 tablespoon of the oil in a Lodge 12-inch cast iron skillet over high heat until hot. Place the salmon, skin side down, in the pan. After about 1 minute, reduce the heat to medium. Cook the fillets another 5 to 8 minutes, depending on their thickness.

4. While the salmon cooks, whisk together the crème fraîche, dill, and granulated garlic in a small bowl until smooth. Season with salt and pepper to taste. Set aside.

5. Turn the fillets over, and cook to medium or medium-well doneness, whichever you prefer, another 3 to 5 minutes. Transfer to a plate, cover with aluminum foil, and let stand for 10 minutes.

6. To the same skillet, still over medium heat, add the remaining 2 teaspoons oil and the asparagus spears, season with salt, and cook, stirring occasionally, until the asparagus spears are tender, 7 to 10 minutes.

7. To serve, arrange asparagus in the center of each plate, set a salmon fillet, skin side down, on top, and spoon dill sauce over the salmon. **Serves 4**

TASSO-SPICED SHRIMP
WITH GRITS, COLLARDS, AND GRAVY

Located in downtown Pensacola, Jackson's Steakhouse is named after General Andrew Jackson, and the re-creation of his signature serves as the restaurant's logo. Overlooking Plaza Ferdinand—where Jackson accepted the transfer of Florida from Spain to the United States in July 1821 and raised the American flag in Pensacola for the first time—executive chef Irv Miller oversees the kitchen. Selected as a Pensacola Celebrity Chef, Irv Miller has represented Northwest Florida cuisine at the James Beard House for the past three years.

Ham hock stock:
- 1 gallon water
- 2 smoked ham hocks
- 2 medium yellow onions, roughly cut
- 1 celery rib, roughly cut
- 2 carrots, roughly cut
- 2 tablespoons kosher salt
- 3 dried bay leaves
- ½ teaspoon black peppercorns

Pork debris gravy:
- 2 tablespoons unsalted butter
- 1 small onion, diced
- 1 small carrot, diced
- 3 tablespoons all-purpose flour
- 1 piece skinless pork belly (¾ pound), very thinly sliced
- 1 cup reserved ham hock stock
- 1 cup chicken stock (store-bought is fine)
- 1 cup water
- 2 garlic cloves, thinly sliced
- 2 tablespoons Worcestershire sauce
- 1 tablespoon hot sauce
- 2 sprigs fresh thyme
- 1 fresh bay leaf
- Kosher salt and freshly ground black pepper to taste

Cheddar grits:
- 1 cup yellow grits
- 2 cups water

- 2 cups whole milk
- 1 teaspoon kosher salt
- 4 cups (1 pound) shredded sharp cheddar cheese
- 6 tablespoons (¾ stick) unsalted butter
- 1 teaspoon cracked black peppercorns

Collard greens:
- 2 quarts reserved ham hock stock
- 2 (16-ounce) bags cut collard greens or 1 (2-pound) bunch fresh collard greens
- Meat picked from ham hocks for ham hock stock
- Pinch of sugar, if needed
- Hot sauce (optional)
- Worcestershire sauce (optional)
- 2 tablespoons unsalted butter

Tasso shrimp:
- 2 teaspoons kosher salt
- 1½ teaspoons smoked sweet paprika
- 1 teaspoon cayenne pepper
- 1 teaspoon finely ground black pepper
- 1 teaspoon granulated garlic
- 1 teaspoon granulated onion
- 15 (21/25 count) Gulf white shrimp, peeled and deveined
- 2 tablespoons canola oil

1. To make the ham hock stock: Combine the first 8 ingredients in a Lodge 7-quart cast iron Dutch oven. Bring to a boil, then reduce the heat, and simmer for 2 hours. Strain the stock in a colander set over a large bowl; reserve the liquid and ham hocks. When the hocks are cool enough to handle, remove the meat, and discard the bones and fat. Reserve the meat to add to the collard greens. Reserve 1 cup of the stock for the pork debris gravy and 2 quarts of the stock for the collard greens. If not using the stock immediately, let cool, then refrigerate, tightly covered, up to 3 days. You can also freeze it 3 to 4 months. It makes 4 quarts.

2. To make pork debris gravy: Melt the butter in a Lodge 9-inch cast iron skillet over medium heat. Add the onion and carrot, and cook, stirring a few times, until the onion just starts to soften, 3 to 4 minutes. Add the flour, and cook, stirring, for 1 minute. Place the sliced meat in the skillet, and add both stocks. Add as much of the water as is needed so the cooking liquid comes three-quarters of the way up the sliced meat. Add the remaining gravy ingredients, bring to a boil, reduce the heat to a simmer, cover, and cook until the meat falls apart, about 2½ hours. Remove the lid, and continue to simmer until the gravy thickens slightly. Keep warm. Remove the bay leaf before serving.

3. To make cheddar grits: Combine the grits, water, milk, and salt in the top of a double boiler. Fill the bottom of the boiler with water so that it will not touch the top of the boiler. Bring the water in the bottom to a boil, and reduce the heat to a simmer. Cover and cook 45 minutes to 1 hour, stirring the grits mixture frequently with a whisk or heavy-duty wooden spoon to avoid lumps. (If the water level gets low in the bottom of the boiler, replenish it.) When the grits are tender, add the cheese, and stir until smooth. Stir in the butter until completely melted. Stir in the pepper. Keep warm.

4. To make collard greens: Bring the stock to a simmer in a Lodge 5-quart cast iron Dutch oven. If using bagged cut collard greens, rinse and use immediately. If using fresh collard greens, rinse well to remove any grit, and cut away the hard stems. Stack a few leaves at a time on top of one another, roll up, then cut across into 1-inch-wide strips. Add the collards to the simmering stock, pushing them down until submerged. Cover and cook until tender, 30 to 45 minutes. Chop the meat from the ham hocks, and add to the greens. Taste. If the greens are slightly bitter, add the sugar. If you like, add hot sauce and/or Worcestershire to taste. Keep the collards warm. Drain before using.

5. Preheat the oven to 450°.

6. For an individual presentation, use Lodge 5-inch cast iron skillets. Grease the skillets with 2 tablespoons butter. Divide the grits evenly between the servers, then top with the drained collards. Ladle pork debris gravy over the collards. Bake until bubbling on the sides, 12 to 15 minutes.

7. Meanwhile, prepare the tasso shrimp.

8. To make tasso shrimp: Combine all the seasonings in a small dish. Coat the shrimp with generous pinches of the spice mix. Heat a Lodge 9-inch cast iron skillet over medium heat 1 to 2 minutes; add the oil, then the shrimp, and cook until they just turn pink, about 3 minutes total.

9. Divide the shrimp evenly among the servers, arranging them attractively on top. Place the hot skillet on a napkin on top of a plate for presentation.

Serves 4 to 6

LEMONGRASS SHRIMP

Cooking school teacher and cookbook author Naam Pruitt's hometown, Prachuabkirikhan, is located on the Gulf of Thailand, so she and seafood are no strangers to one another. And even though she now lives in St. Louis, Missouri, she still prepares seafood for her family every day.

¼ cup canola oil
2 lemongrass stalks (see kitchen note), bruised and cut into 2-inch lengths
1 pound large (26/30 count) shrimp, peeled, deveined, and patted dry
3 tablespoons Thai fish sauce
3 tablespoons fresh lime juice
1 ½ tablespoons sugar

1 shallot, thinly sliced
2 tablespoons thinly sliced lemongrass (from skinny section at top of stalk)
1 or 2 Thai chiles, finely chopped
¼ cup chopped fresh cilantro
¼ cup fresh mint leaves
2 cups raw jasmine rice, cooked according to package directions

1. Heat a Lodge 12-inch cast iron skillet over high heat. Add the oil, and wait until it is hot. Add the bruised lemongrass pieces, and cook until lightly browned, about 5 minutes, stirring occasionally. Add the shrimp, and cook until pink, turning them several times, 3 to 4 minutes. Turn off the heat. Transfer the shrimp to a large bowl. Discard the lemongrass pieces.

2. Add the next 8 ingredients (through mint) to the shrimp, mixing well. Serve with jasmine rice. **Serves 2 to 4**

kitchen note:

Fresh lemongrass is crucial for this recipe, its lemony essence infusing the shrimp as it cooks. When buying lemongrass, size matters; the thicker the stalks, the stronger the flavor. A good rule of thumb is to use thick stalks for cooking and skinnier ones in salads and other preparations where it will be used raw.

how Naam slices lemongrass

1. Trim off the very end of the stalk before using.

2. Use a meat mallet or heavy pestle to bruise the lemongrass, pounding the entire stalk. Doing this will release the essential oil for its distinctive aroma.

3. To slice lemongrass, you need to use the more tender part of the stalk at the top; the lower part of the stalk is much too fibrous to eat.

SEASONED WITH LOVE

MATT MOORE

Author of Have Her Over for Dinner: A Gentleman's Guide to Classic, Simple Meals, *Nashville, Tennessee*

Speaking of pride, ma'ams and sirs, and what I was raised to do or not do, I'll say that my father, a Southern gentleman himself, taught me, with an ear-to-ear grin, to open doors for women right alongside the ways and means of sipping a dark drink. Momma, on the other hand, taught me how to charm and cook. But it was her mother, my grandmother Sitty, as she was known, who schooled me on the ins and outs of cooking with Lodge cast iron. On Sundays, my grandfather Giddy, who by trade was a butcher, would bring home cuts of meat carefully trimmed and preserved by his skilled hands. Sitty would cook and stew all morning long—stopping only to put on her face and attend Sunday services. When we returned to their Valdosta, Georgia, home afterward, family, friends, preacher men, and strangers would all gather to enjoy her Southern splendor at the family table.

The spread, just like the conversation, seemed to stretch for miles…skillet fried chicken, collards, mac 'n' cheese, cornbread, fried okra, biscuits—the Southern staples—were all served right alongside the Middle Eastern favorites from my grandparents' youth: hummus, tabbouleh, kibbeh, and stuffed grape leaves. Together, we lived, ate, cooked, and learned.

Though my grandparents have since passed, those memories and lessons of family and food continue to impact my own life. Their passing did not bequeath me a wealth of monetary goods; rather it was my grandmother's Lodge cast iron skillets that made their way into my hands to cherish forever.

Nowadays, I do most of the work in the kitchen, entertaining family, friends, and strangers just as those who came before me did. Yet I know that I am never alone. As ingredients sizzle and pop in my inherited cast iron pans, I know that my guests will soon savor and enjoy another great meal. For me, I find comfort in knowing that my recipes always taste a bit better coming out of my grandmother's skillets, as they are all seasoned with the very best ingredient in any kitchen—love.

This recipe is the height of simplicity, says Matt Moore. When that's the case, it means the ingredients used need to be of top quality. Matt buys his bacon from Benton's Smoky Mountain Country Hams in Madisonville, Tennessee, where it's smoked over an old-fashioned hickory wood-stoked stove. If you can find a Meyer lemon, please use it—a cross between a lemon and mandarin orange, it supplies great lemon flavor without the tart bite.

PAN-SEARED SEA SCALLOPS

¼ pound hickory-smoked bacon, finely diced

1 tablespoon unsalted butter

1 tablespoon extra virgin olive oil

1 pound sea scallops, patted dry

½ lemon, preferably Meyer

Finely chopped fresh flat-leaf parsley for garnish

1. Heat a Lodge 12-inch cast iron skillet over medium heat for 1 minute. Add the bacon, and cook, stirring a few times, until it is crisp and the fat has rendered. Using a slotted spoon, transfer the bacon to a paper towel-lined plate to drain.

2. Add the butter and oil to the bacon drippings, and heat over medium-high heat until the butter melts. Add the scallops, and cook for 60 seconds on one side—do not touch. Flip the scallops, squeeze the lemon juice over them, and cook for another 60 to 90 seconds, until the scallops are just firm to the touch.

3. Remove the skillet from the heat, plate, and pour the pan drippings over the tops of the scallops. Sprinkle with the bacon and parsley as desired, and serve.

Serves 2

a cooking secret from Matt

Choose dry-packed sea scallops (no water solution injected) for the best flavor and a good sear.

Jambalaya is traditionally cooked on the stove-top, but in this oven version from Atlanta-based chef and cookbook author Virginia Willis, the rice is perfect every time.

VIRGINIA WILLIS' SEAFOOD AND CHICKEN JAMBALAYA

1 tablespoon canola oil	1 garlic clove, very finely chopped
4 skinless, bone-in chicken thighs (about 1½ pounds)	1½ cups raw long-grain rice
Coarse kosher salt and freshly ground black pepper	1 (8-ounce) can tomato sauce
6 ounces andouille sausage, sliced	2 cups homemade chicken stock, reduced-fat/low-sodium chicken broth, or water
1 tablespoon Cajun or Creole seasoning	1 bay leaf, preferably fresh
1 medium sweet onion, chopped	1 pound large (21/25 count) shrimp, peeled and deveined
1 celery rib, chopped	
½ red bell pepper, seeded and chopped	

1. Preheat the oven to 350°.

2. Heat the oil in a Lodge 12-inch cast iron skillet over medium-high heat until shimmering. Season the chicken with salt and pepper on both sides, and add to the hot oil. Cook until browned on both sides, 3 to 5 minutes total. Remove to a plate.

3. Pour off any rendered fat in the skillet, and discard. Add the andouille, and cook, stirring occasionally, until the meat starts to brown and render fat, about 3 minutes. Add the Cajun seasoning, and stir to combine. Add the onion, celery, and bell pepper; cook, stirring occasionally, until the vegetables start to color, 5 to 7 minutes. Add the garlic, and cook until fragrant, 45 to 60 seconds. Add the rice, and stir to coat. Stir in the tomato sauce and stock, and bring to a boil. Return the seared chicken thighs to the skillet, and nestle them, without crowding, into the rice. Tuck the bay leaf into the rice. Transfer to the oven, and bake, uncovered, for 30 minutes.

4. Add the shrimp, and stir to combine. Continue to bake, uncovered, until the rice is tender, the shrimp are opaque, and the juices of the chicken run clear when pierced with the tip of a knife, signifying the chicken is done, about 10 minutes. Remove the skillet from the oven to a wire rack to cool slightly. Taste and adjust the seasoning with salt and pepper. Remove bay leaf before serving. Spoon the jambalaya into warm serving bowls. Serve immediately.
Serves 4 to 6

a cooking secret from Virginia

Don't cover the jambalaya while it's cooking in the oven. Keeping the pan uncovered allows the excess liquid from the broth and tomatoes to evaporate and the rice to cook evenly.

O ften in Pensacola on assignment, and having a husband who works and resides there as well, Susan Benton, food writer and owner of 30AEATS.com, enjoys frequenting Joe Patti's Seafood. Susan says, "It is an experience! Like our own little version of Seattle's Pike Place Market, yet here on the Gulf Coast!" Pick up a container or two of fresh, succulent jumbo lump Gulf crab, and try your hand at making this decadent recipe using Lodge cast iron individual tabletop servers.

JUMBO LUMP GULF CRABMEAT AU GRATIN

½ cup (1 stick) unsalted butter
1 medium onion, finely chopped
1 celery rib, finely chopped
2 tablespoons chopped green onion (white part only)
1 teaspoon minced garlic
2 large egg yolks, slightly beaten
1 (12-ounce) can evaporated milk
½ cup all-purpose flour
1 teaspoon kosher salt

½ teaspoon cayenne pepper
½ teaspoon freshly ground black pepper
2 cups (8 ounces) finely grated Gruyère cheese
1 pound jumbo lump Gulf crabmeat, picked over for shells and cartilage
1 tablespoon minced fresh parsley

1. Preheat the oven to 350°.

2. Melt the butter in a Lodge 10-inch cast iron skillet over medium-high heat. Add the onion, celery, green onions, and garlic, and cook, stirring, until the vegetables are wilted, 3 to 5 minutes.

3. While the vegetables cook, vigorously whisk the egg yolks and evaporated milk together in a small bowl until well blended; set aside.

4. Add the flour to the skillet, and blend well into the vegetables to create a white roux; don't let the flour brown. Using a wire whisk, add the milk mixture, stirring constantly to blend into the roux mixture. Stir in the salt, cayenne, and black pepper, and continue to stir for another 3 to 5 minutes. Remove from the heat, and fold in half the cheese; blend until it is totally melted and fully incorporated.

5. Gently divide the crabmeat among four Lodge 9-ounce cast iron mini servers; try not to break apart the lumps. Top evenly with the cheese sauce, then sprinkle with the remaining grated cheese. Cover and bake until bubbly, about 15 minutes, then reset the oven for broil, and broil until the cheese begins to brown, about 5 minutes. Remove from the oven, and sprinkle with the parsley before serving. **Serves 4**

This is a delicious **Chesapeake Bay** twist on classic macaroni and cheese from Ellen Kassoff Gray, co-owner of Equinox Restaurant in Washington, D.C. The best part is that you get your own bubbling hot, cheesy pan of mac to savor. If you prefer, you can bake this family style in a 9-inch cast iron skillet or casserole.

INDIVIDUAL EASTERN SHORE-STYLE MAC & CHEESE WITH CRAB

8 ounces shell macaroni
½ cup (1 stick) unsalted butter, cut into pieces
½ cup all-purpose flour
6 cups milk
1 cup (4 ounces) shredded medium-sharp cheddar cheese
1 cup (4 ounces) shredded Monterey Jack cheese
1 cup (4 ounces) grated Parmesan cheese

1¼ teaspoons salt
Pinch of freshly ground black pepper
2 cups jumbo lump crabmeat, picked over for shells and cartilage
1 teaspoon seafood seasoning
1 cup panko or other dry breadcrumbs

1. Preheat the oven to 350°. Lightly oil six Lodge 9-ounce cast iron mini servers. Bring a large pot of salted water to a boil over high heat; stir in the macaroni, and cook according to the package directions until al dente (done but still firm to the bite). Drain the macaroni in a colander, and transfer to a large bowl.

2. Meanwhile, melt the butter in a Lodge 9-inch cast iron skillet with 2-inch-high sides over medium-low heat; slowly add the flour, stirring until it forms a thin paste (this is a roux). Slowly whisk in the milk, cooking until well blended and slightly thickened, 8 to 10 minutes (this is a classic béchamel sauce). Add ½ cup each of the cheddar, Jack, and Parmesan to the sauce, stirring constantly with a wooden spoon until the cheeses are melted and incorporated. Season with the salt and pepper; keep warm if the macaroni is still cooking.

3. Add the cheese sauce to the bowl with the macaroni. In a medium bowl, season the crabmeat with the seafood seasoning. Using a wooden spoon, stir the crabmeat into the pasta mixture, being careful not to break it up too much. Spoon about half the pasta mixture into the prepared servers, spreading it evenly. Sprinkle half the remaining cheddar, Jack, and Parmesan over the top. Repeat with the remaining pasta mixture and cheeses. Sprinkle the panko evenly over the top. Bake until the sauce is bubbly and the topping is golden, 12 to 15 minutes. **Serves 6**

CRAB, ANDOUILLE, AND MANGO BREAD PUDDING WITH HABANERO-KEY LIME ANGLAISE

Before Michelle Moran and Danny Mellman relocated to Blue Ridge, Georgia, and opened the restaurant Harvest on Main, they called the west coast of Florida home. "One of our favorite things about living along the Gulf is the melding of all the flavors from the Caribbean to Louisiana," says Michelle. "This savory pudding makes for a great meal. We'd make it at home with fresh-caught blue crabs and homemade sausage, along with Key limes and mangoes picked from trees that grew in our front yard."

1 tablespoon extra virgin olive oil
1 garlic clove, chopped
½ cup diced red onion
6 ounces andouille sausage, ground
2 green onions, chopped
1 cup diced ripe mango
12 ounces brioche (Michelle and Danny use coconut brioche), cut into pieces
2 large eggs
2 large egg yolks
1 cup heavy cream
¾ cup milk (preferably whole or 2%)
1 teaspoon ground allspice
½ teaspoon Colman's dry mustard
¼ teaspoon salt
Pinch of freshly ground black pepper
1 pound Florida golden crab or other crabmeat, picked over for shells and cartilage
Habanero-Key Lime Anglaise (recipe follows)

1. Heat the oil in a deep Lodge 10-inch cast iron skillet over medium heat. Add the garlic and red onion, and cook, stirring a few times, until softened, about 5 minutes. Add the andouille, and heat through but try not to brown it too much. Transfer the mixture to a large bowl, and let cool for 5 minutes.

2. Add the green onions, mango, and brioche to the bowl, and toss well. In a medium bowl, whisk together the whole eggs and yolks. Whisk in the cream, then the milk, then the allspice, mustard, salt, and pepper. Pour the mixture over the brioche, and toss well to coat the bread completely. Fold in the crabmeat, then store in refrigerator, stirring occasionally, until all the bread is evenly moist, about 1 hour.

3. Preheat the oven to 400°. Generously grease a Lodge 10 x 5 x 3-inch cast iron loaf pan.

4. Gently pack the mixture into the prepared loaf pan. Set it in a larger pan, and add enough water to come halfway up the sides of the loaf pan. Cover with aluminum foil. Place on the middle rack of the oven, and bake for 1¾ hours. Remove the foil, and bake until golden brown, about another 15 minutes. Remove from the oven, and let stand for 10 minutes, then unmold onto a plate.

5. To serve, cut the pudding into 1-inch-thick slices. Drizzle each serving plate attractively with the anglaise, then place one slice of the pudding atop it. Drizzle with additional anglaise. **Serves 8**

HABANERO-KEY LIME ANGLAISE

2 large egg yolks
1 tablespoon sugar
⅛ teaspoon kosher salt
1 cup heavy cream
½ habanero chile, ribs and seeds removed
1 vanilla bean, cut in half lengthwise
Grated zest and juice of 1 lime

1. In a small bowl, whisk the egg yolks, sugar, and salt together. Set aside.

2. Put the cream and habanero in a small, heavy saucepan. Scrape the seeds from the vanilla bean into the cream; add the bean. Bring to a boil. Remove from the heat.

3. Add about one-quarter of the hot cream to the egg mixture, whisking to incorporate it. Whisk the remainder of the hot cream into the eggs, then return it to the pan. Cook over low heat, stirring constantly, until the mixture coats the back of a spoon, about 5 minutes. Remove from the heat, and let cool to room temperature. Remove and discard the vanilla bean and habanero.

4. Right before serving, stir in the lime zest and juice. **Makes enough to dress 8 servings of savory bread pudding**

PENN COVE MUSSELS
WITH CHORIZO, GARLIC TOASTS, AND SMOKED PAPRIKA AÏOLI

Smoked Paprika Aïoli:
½ cup mayonnaise
2 teaspoons fresh lemon juice
2 teaspoons smoked Spanish paprika
½ teaspoon grated lemon zest
Kosher salt and freshly ground black pepper

Mussels:
2 tablespoons olive oil
½ cup finely chopped onion
½ cup chopped Spanish chorizo (about 3 ounces)
2 cups canned crushed or chopped tomatoes, undrained

½ cup dry white wine
Kosher salt and freshly ground black pepper
2 pounds mussels, rinsed, scrubbed, and beards removed (discard any that won't close)

Garlic Toasts:
2 or 3 garlic cloves, peeled
4 slices rustic bread, ½ to ¾ inch thick
Olive oil as needed for brushing
Kosher salt and freshly ground black pepper

Garnish:
4 lemon wedges

1. Make the aïoli: In a small bowl, combine the mayonnaise, lemon juice, paprika, and lemon zest. Season with salt and pepper to taste. Cover the aïoli, and refrigerate until ready to use and up to one day.

2. Cook the mussels: Put a Lodge 12-inch cast iron skillet over medium-high heat, and add the oil. When the oil is hot, add the onion, and cook, stirring, until softened, about 3 minutes. Add the chorizo, and sauté for a minute or two. Add the tomatoes and wine, and bring to a simmer; continue to simmer (reducing the heat as needed) until the sauce thickens, 10 to 15 minutes. Season to taste with pepper and a little salt, if needed. Add the mussels to the skillet, increase the heat to medium-high or high, cover the pan, and cook until the mussels open, about 5 minutes (discard any that won't open).

3. While the mussels cook, make the garlic toasts: Preheat the broiler. Smash the garlic cloves with the back of a knife. Rub the slices of bread on one side with the smashed garlic. Brush both sides of the bread with oil, and season with salt and pepper. Toast the bread slices under the broiler, turning once, until golden and toasted, a minute or two per side. Remove the toasts from the broiler.

4. Divide the mussels between 2 shallow soup bowls. Place a dollop of aïoli on each toast, and place a toast on the rim of each soup bowl. Serve immediately, garnished with lemon wedges as desired. **Serves 2 as a main course, 4 as a hearty appetizer**

A mellow, smoky paprika aïoli complements both the spicy sausage and the sweet sea flavor of the mussels in this preparation from Seattle-based chef/restaurateur Tom Douglas. And the crunch of a slice of golden, crusty, toasted bread is mandatory alongside a bowl of mussels!

Tom says to be sure to buy Spanish chorizo, which is different from Mexican chorizo. And if your cast iron skillet doesn't have a lid, use a baking sheet to cover it when steaming the mussels.

MINDFUL EATING: SUPPORTING HOME-RAISED FOODS

TAMIE COOK

Former culinary director of Alton Brown's Food Network show Good Eats, *Atlanta, Georgia*

I started cooking years ago, but it wasn't until after reading *Fast Food Nation* while in culinary school and after living in France that my deep love for food and the appreciation for where it comes from were cultivated. While in France, I purchased ingredients at local farmers' markets and built relationships with the people who grew my food. Not only was I always able to buy the freshest foods, which made the dishes I prepared taste really good—but these dishes became more than just food to eat. They taught me to be more mindful about my food choices and my eating practices. After hearing the farmers' stories and learning about their love for their businesses, I never looked at food the same way again.

Over the years, my passion for mindful eating has grown on both a personal and professional level—my interest has expanded from locally grown produce and artisanal dairy products to sustainably caught seafood. Today, I teach people easy and approachable ways to eat and prepare foods that are better for their health, their neighbors, and our planet.

One way I have helped consumers learn more about sustainable food choices has been by participating in the Tennessee Aquarium's Serve & Protect program. The program partners with some of Chattanooga's top chefs, local restaurants, and seafood suppliers to teach people how wise seafood choices can make a positive impact on the earth's aquaculture. We've created events and educational programming designed to take the intimidation out of selecting and preparing sustainable seafood, making it more accessible for the home cook.

Take trout for example. The South is dotted with trout farm operations that have been around for generations, and U.S farm-raised trout is sustainable due to being produced in a manner that does not harm the environment. Trout is widely available, plus it is delicious and easy to prepare. Whenever I develop trout recipes, first and foremost I don't make them complicated, and I use a cast iron skillet. It's the perfect vessel for a good sear, plus cast iron is also sustainable. There are so many ways to enjoy trout, including burgers or Trout Cakes and Watercress Salad with Basil Viniagrette (opposite). Really, though, nothing's better than pan-seared trout with a fennel-and-grapefruit salad.

When you enjoy fresh-caught seafood that's sustainable, not only are the taste and quality superb, but you support a safe food supply chain for generations to come. For more information about sustainable seafood choices and the Tennessee Aquarium's Serve & Protect program, events, and educational tools, visit www.tnaqua.org/sustainableseafood/ServeandProtect.aspx.

This recipe from chef and food writer Tamie Cook combines fresh basil and lemon zest to make the cakes summery and light. The watercress salad completes it for the perfect lunch or light dinner.

TROUT CAKES AND WATERCRESS SALAD WITH BASIL VINAIGRETTE

1 pound skinless U.S. farm-raised trout fillets, pin bones removed	1 garlic clove, minced
¾ cup panko breadcrumbs	1 large egg, beaten
½ cup red bell pepper, cut into small dice	1 teaspoon fine sea salt
Grated zest of 1 lemon	1 tablespoon olive oil
2 tablespoons chopped fresh basil	8 cups watercress, rinsed and spun dry
	Basil Vinaigrette (recipe follows)

1. Place the trout fillets in the freezer until they begin to firm up but are not frozen, about 30 minutes.

2. While the fillets chill, combine the panko, bell pepper, lemon zest, basil, garlic, egg, and salt in a medium bowl.

3. Coarsely chop the chilled trout, and add to the bowl. Stir to combine. Divide the mixture into 4 equal portions, and shape into cakes about ½ inch thick.

4. Heat the oil in a Lodge 12-inch cast iron skillet over medium heat until it shimmers. Add the trout cakes to the pan, and cook until golden brown, about 4 minutes per side. Remove to a paper towel-lined plate to stand for 5 minutes.

5. To serve, toss the watercress with ¼ cup of the vinaigrette, and serve with the trout cakes, drizzled with additional vinaigrette, if desired. **Serves 4**

BASIL VINAIGRETTE

1 cup packed fresh basil leaves	Freshly ground black pepper to taste
1 garlic clove, peeled	¼ cup olive oil, plus more if needed
Generous pinch of fine sea salt	2 tablespoons Champagne vinegar

1. Place all the ingredients in a small food processor, and process until pureed. Add 1 to 2 tablespoons more oil, if desired, after tasting. Refrigerate in an airtight container for up to 3 days. Remove from the refrigerator 20 to 30 minutes prior to using so the olive oil is not solidified. **Makes ½ cup**

Read *Cast Iron and the Joy of Broiling* for more information on the technique used for preparing this dish from *New York Times* columnist and cookbook author Mark Bittman.

HARD-SHELL CLAMS
WITH PARSLEY PESTO

2 cups fresh parsley leaves (thin
 stems are O.K.), washed
Salt
½ garlic clove, more to taste
½ cup extra virgin olive oil, or more
1 tablespoon sherry vinegar or
 fresh lemon juice

2 dozen hard-shell clams
 (littlenecks or cherrystones),
 scrubbed and rinsed (discard any
 that won't close)

1. Turn on the broiler, and put a Lodge 15-inch cast iron skillet under it while you make the parsley pesto. Combine the parsley with a pinch of salt, the garlic, and about half the oil in a food processor or blender. Process, stopping to scrape down the side of the container, if necessary, and adding the rest of the oil gradually. Add the vinegar, then a little water to thin the mixture slightly. Taste and adjust the seasoning.

2. Carefully remove the skillet from the broiler, add the clams to it, and return to the broiler. They should all open more or less at once, within 10 minutes; remove them as soon as they do to preserve their juices, and put on a plate. (Any clams that do not open are safe to eat; open them with a dull knife, or continue to broil a few minutes longer.) **Serves 4**

GT MUSSELS
WITH TOMATOES
AND GARLIC

1   small Spanish onion, chopped
2   tablespoons blended olive oil
1   tablespoon chopped garlic
1   cup dry white wine
1   (48-ounce) can peeled whole San
    Marzano tomatoes, undrained
Kosher salt
Sugar
Freshly ground black pepper
1   tablespoon finely diced shallot
1   tablespoon finely chopped garlic

1   tablespoon extra virgin olive oil
½   teaspoon unsalted butter
½   teaspoon red pepper flakes
2   pounds Prince Edward Island
    mussels, scrubbed and debearded
    (discard any that won't close)
6   fresh basil leaves, cut across into
    thin chiffonade
12 slices ciabatta bread, grilled or
    toasted and rubbed on each side
    with garlic

1. Sauté the onion in the blended olive oil in a Lodge 5-quart cast iron Dutch oven over medium heat until translucent, about 5 minutes. Add the chopped garlic, and cook for 1 minute. Deglaze with the wine, and stir in the tomatoes. Reduce the heat to low, and simmer, uncovered, until the mixture has reduced to one-third of its original volume, about 45 minutes. Season the sauce with salt and sugar to taste and a small amount of black pepper. Pass the sauce through a food mill or puree it right in the pot with an immersion blender; set aside.

2. Sauté the shallot and finely chopped garlic in the extra virgin olive oil and butter in a Lodge 15-inch cast iron skillet over low heat for 1 minute; do not allow to color. Add the red pepper and mussels. Gently add the hot tomato sauce, and cover the skillet. Let the sauce simmer until the mussels open up. Once the mussels are opened, sprinkle with the basil and a little salt to taste. Serve immediately in shallow bowls with the toasted ciabatta. **Serves 6**

When developing this mussel dish, Giuseppe Tentori, executive chef at GT Fish & Oyster in Chicago, Illinois, meant for it to be rustic, made with garlic and tomatoes, and served with toasted ciabatta and fresh basil. "This is the way I used to eat mussels in Italy," says Giuseppe, who is a native of Lodi, Italy. With this dish, he and his team try to replicate that true Italian experience for their guests.

FISH & SHELLFISH

Southern-Style Creamed Corn,
page 217

SIDES

FARMERS' MARKET RATATOUILLE

This recipe comes from Donita Anderson, executive director of North Union Farmers Market in Cleveland, Ohio. Not surprisingly, she sources almost all the ingredients for this dish from the market: olive oil from Olive Tap, eggplant from Walnut Drive Gardens, onions from Gingerich Farm, fresh garlic from Maximum Garlic Farm, tomatoes from Heritage Lane Farm and Rainbow Farm, red peppers from Weaver's Truck Patch, summer squash from Crooked Creek, zucchini from Don Anna, and fresh herbs from Rainbow Farm and Snake Hill Farm.

1 large round eggplant, peeled and cut into ½-inch dice
Sea salt
2 tablespoons extra virgin olive oil, plus more as needed
1 large white onion, cut into ¼-inch dice
Pinch of red pepper flakes
4 garlic cloves, smashed and finely chopped
3 large tomatoes, cut into ½-inch dice
4 plum tomatoes, cut into ½-inch dice
½ cup water

2 tablespoons good-quality red wine
1 teaspoon good-quality balsamic vinegar
1 teaspoon fresh thyme leaves
½ teaspoon crushed dried rosemary
2 medium red bell peppers, seeded and cut into ½-inch dice
2 medium summer squash, cut into ½-inch dice
2 medium zucchini, cut into ½-inch dice
6 to 8 fresh basil leaves, thinly sliced
Freshly ground black pepper
¾ cup grated Gruyère cheese

1. Place the eggplant dice on paper towels, and lightly salt. Let stand for 30 minutes to sweat. Mop up the moisture on the dice with more paper towels.

2. Heat a Lodge 12-inch cast iron skillet over medium-high heat. Add the oil, and swirl to coat the bottom of the pan. Add the eggplant, and cook, stirring a few times, until browned; remove from the pan, and set aside.

3. Add a little more oil, the onion, red pepper, and salt to taste, and cook over medium heat, stirring a few times, until the onion is softened and very aromatic, 7 to 8 minutes; don't allow the onion to color. Add the garlic, and cook, stirring, for 2 to 3 minutes. Add the tomatoes, water, wine, vinegar, thyme, and rosemary, and season with salt to taste. Simmer, uncovered, until the tomatoes become very pulpy and have broken apart, 15 to 20 minutes.

4. Add the bell peppers, and cook for 5 minutes. Add the summer squash and zucchini, return the eggplant to the pan, season with salt, and cook over low heat, uncovered, until the squash and eggplant are softened, 15 to 20 minutes.

5. Stir in the sliced basil, taste for salt and pepper, then simmer, covered, for 15 minutes.

6. Sprinkle the Gruyère over the ratatouille while it's still warm in the pan. Serve warm or at room temperature over lightly toasted French bread or naan. Leftovers can be wrapped well and frozen. **Serves 6**

ome summer in Tennessee, where cookbook author Jennifer Chandler lives, farmers' markets and home gardens are over-flowing with zucchini, eggplants, and peppers. In an effort to find new ways to serve these bountiful veggies, she came up with this recipe using her new favorite grain, quinoa. High in protein and gluten free, it cooks up like rice and has a texture similar to that of couscous.

GRILLED SUMMER VEGETABLE QUINOA SALAD

1 medium red onion, cut into ½-inch-thick slices	Kosher salt and freshly ground black pepper
1 small eggplant, unpeeled, cut into 1-inch cubes	2 cups quinoa, cooked according to package directions (see kitchen note)
1 medium red bell pepper, seeded and cut into 1-inch squares	1 tablespoon red wine vinegar
1 medium zucchini, cut in half lengthwise and across into ½-inch-thick half moons	1 tablespoon fresh lemon juice
	1 garlic clove, minced
	1 teaspoon red pepper flakes
¼ cup plus 2 tablespoons extra virgin olive oil	¼ cup finely chopped fresh cilantro

1. In a large bowl, toss together the onion, eggplant, bell pepper, zucchini, and ¼ cup of the oil. Season with salt and pepper to taste.

2. Heat a Lodge 12-inch cast iron grill pan or skillet over medium-high heat. Place the vegetables in a single layer in the pan. Cook, turning once or twice, until they are tender and slightly charred, 5 to 7 minutes per side.

3. Place the cooked quinoa in a medium serving bowl. Add the grilled vegetables, and toss to combine.

4. In a small bowl, whisk together the remaining 2 tablespoons oil, the vinegar, lemon juice, garlic, and red pepper. Pour the dressing over the salad, and toss to coat. Season with salt and pepper to taste. Garnish with the cilantro as desired. Serve warm or chilled. **Serves 6**

kitchen note:
The quinoa can be made a day ahead; refrigerate, covered, until ready to use.

Judy Schad, cheesemaker and owner of Capriole Farms in Greenville, Indiana, likes to combine her cheeses with the seasonal produce of local farmers' markets. She feels the intense earthiness of beets and greens contrasts perfectly with the light flavor of fresh goat cheese. She reminds us that the secret to risotto is to add the hot liquid gradually, stirring constantly until the rice has absorbed the liquid before adding more, a process that takes about 20 minutes, until the rice is al dente.

RED BEET RISOTTO WITH MUSTARD GREENS AND FRESH GOAT CHEESE

¼ cup (½ stick) butter

2 (2½- to 3-inch) beets, peeled and cut into ½-inch cubes

1½ cups chopped white onions

1 cup raw Arborio or medium-grain white rice

3 cups low-salt vegetable or chicken broth, brought to a simmer in a saucepan and kept warm

1 tablespoon balsamic vinegar

1 cup dry white wine

Salt and freshly ground black pepper

1½ cups chopped mustard greens

6 ounces Capriole fresh round goat cheese, plain or with herbs, crumbled, plus more for serving

1. Melt the butter in a Lodge 5-quart cast iron Dutch oven over medium heat. Add the beets and onions, cover, and cook, stirring a few times, until the onions are softened, about 8 minutes.

2. Stir in the rice, then add ½ cup of the hot broth and the vinegar. Increase the heat to high; bring to a boil. Reduce the heat to medium-low. When the broth has been absorbed by the rice, add the wine, and cook, stirring, until it is almost completely absorbed. Add more broth, about ½ cup at a time, stirring constantly and allowing the liquid to be absorbed by the rice before adding more. (Run a wooden spoon across the bottom of the pot; when you can create a path through the rice with the spoon, enough broth has been absorbed so that more can be added.) Add the last 2 cups of broth, ½ to 1 cup at a time. Do not allow the rice to stick to the bottom.

3. Season with salt and pepper to taste, and stir in the mustard greens and all but about ½ cup of the cheese. Stir only until the greens have wilted. Serve immediately on individual plates, sprinkled with additional crumbled cheese, if you wish. **Serves 4**

Debbie Moose, a cookbook author and freelance writer in Raleigh, North Carolina, came up with this recipe in response to a friend who doesn't like the flavor of sage, which dominates traditional holiday dressings. "The flavor of this dressing makes it elegant enough to serve year-round," Debbie says.

ROSEMARY-THYME DRESSING

3 tablespoons butter	¾ tablespoon chopped fresh thyme or ¾ teaspoon dried thyme
¾ cup chopped celery	¼ teaspoon salt, or to taste
1 cup chopped onion	¼ teaspoon freshly ground black pepper, or to taste
½ cup chopped green bell pepper	
6 cups cubed (½ inch) French bread	3 cups chicken broth
2½ tablespoons chopped fresh rosemary or 2½ teaspoons dried rosemary	1 large egg, lightly beaten

1. Place a Lodge 9- or 10-inch cast iron skillet in the oven; preheat the oven to 350° while you prepare the stuffing.

2. Place 2 tablespoons of the butter in a small Lodge cast iron skillet over medium heat. Cook the celery, onion, and bell pepper, stirring, until softened but not browned.

3. Put the bread cubes in a large bowl. Stir in the vegetables, then add the rosemary, thyme, salt, and pepper. Stir to combine. Add the broth, and stir well. Let the mixture stand for a few minutes, until the bread absorbs most of the broth. Stir in the egg.

4. Put the remaining 1 tablespoon butter in the heated skillet, and swirl to coat the bottom and sides. Add the stuffing mixture. Bake until browned on top, about 1 hour. **Serves 6 to 8**

Cast Iron Memories

I use a cast iron skillet that my mother received as a wedding gift, which makes the skillet 56 years old. After decades of frying and baking, oiling and buttering, it's as nonstick as any trashy new pan and has lasted a heckuva lot longer. In my mother's time, a cast iron skillet, a deviled egg plate, and a hand-cranked ice cream maker were standard gifts for every bride. Now, couples receive everything from toolboxes to single-serve coffee makers. Some brides might even frown if they receive a cast iron skillet, when they find out they can't throw it in the dishwasher with the travel mugs and microwave plates. But there is no companion in my kitchen like that skillet. Although what I cook in it is very different from my mother's recipes, it reminds me that being in the kitchen and feeding the people I love will always endure.

—*Debbie Moose*

SUN-DRIED TOMATO-RICOTTA GNOCCHI WITH BASIL PESTO AND TOASTED PINE NUTS

⅓ to ½ cup **Basil Pesto** (recipe follows)
2 ounces sun-dried tomatoes
1¼ cups all-purpose flour, plus more for rolling
1 large egg
15 ounces fresh ricotta cheese

1½ teaspoons kosher salt
½ teaspoon plus pinch of freshly ground black pepper
1 tablespoon extra virgin olive oil
1 tablespoon unsalted butter
2 tablespoons pine nuts, toasted in a 350° oven for 5 minutes

1. Make the Basil Pesto.

2. Cover the sun-dried tomatoes with water in a small saucepan, and bring to a boil. Remove from the heat, and let steep for several minutes. Drain, squeeze out any excess water, and chop the tomatoes.

3. Bring a large pot of lightly salted water to a boil.

4. In the bowl of a stand mixer fitted with the paddle attachment, place the chopped tomatoes, flour, egg, ricotta, 1 teaspoon of the salt, and ½ teaspoon of the pepper, and mix on low until combined and the mixture forms a loose dough. Transfer the dough to a lightly floured work surface. Cut in half, then, with lightly floured hands, roll each half into a ¾-inch-diameter log. With a bench scraper or knife, cut the logs on the diagonal into ¾-inch-thick slices.

5. Transfer the gnocchi to the boiling water, and cook until they plump up and float to the surface, 5 to 7 minutes. Using a slotted spoon or skimmer, gently transfer them to a colander to drain.

6. When all the gnocchi have been cooked, heat the oil and butter together in a Lodge 15-inch cast iron skillet over medium-high heat until the butter starts to brown. Add the gnocchi, and sprinkle with the remaining ½ teaspoon salt and pinch of pepper. Allow to brown on all sides, tossing occasionally.

7. Turn off the heat, add the pesto, and toss until the gnocchi are coated. Portion the gnocchi onto plates, and sprinkle with the toasted pine nuts.
Serves 4 to 6 as a side dish

BASIL PESTO

1 cup packed fresh basil leaves
½ tablespoon chopped garlic
2 tablespoons pine nuts
3 tablespoons extra virgin olive oil

Kosher salt and freshly ground black pepper to taste
¼ cup grated Parmigiano-Reggiano cheese

1. Combine the ingredients in a food processor; process until smooth. Will keep, tightly covered, in the refrigerator for 4 to 5 days. **Makes about 1 cup**

how George makes gnocchi

1. If the dough sticks to the work surface when rolling it into logs, sprinkle a small amount of flour onto the surface—too much will make the gnocchi heavy and dense.

2. Be sure to cut the gnocchi into equal sizes (¾ inch thick) so they'll cook evenly.

3. Boil the gnocchi in a large pot of salted water. They'll plump up and bob to the surface when they're ready to serve.

4. Use a slotted spoon or skimmer to remove the gnocchi from the boiling water.

PAN-ROASTED SPRING VEGETABLES

Andrea Kirkland, senior food editor at Oxmoor House in Birmingham, Alabama, makes this simple dish in the spring when thin asparagus spears are abundant. It pairs well with roasted or grilled chicken.

2 tablespoons olive oil
2 carrots, peeled and sliced into 1-inch pieces
1 bunch thin asparagus, trimmed and sliced into 1-inch pieces
3 baby zucchini, sliced
1 garlic clove, minced
1 pint grape tomatoes, halved
½ teaspoon kosher salt
Freshly ground black pepper

1. Heat the oil in a Lodge 15-inch cast iron skillet over medium-high heat for 3 minutes. Add carrots to heated pan; cook, stirring occasionally, about 7 minutes or until tender.

2. Add the asparagus, zucchini, and garlic to pan with carrots. Cook vegetable mixture, stirring occasionally, for 5 minutes or until the vegetables are lightly browned. Stir in tomatoes, and cook for 1 to 2 minutes, or until tomatoes begin to soften. Sprinkle with salt and pepper. **Serves 4 to 6**

CAST IRON-COOKED ASPARAGUS WITH GARLIC

For Chicago-based chef and cookbook author Gale Gand, the saying goes, "less is more." So this simple, straightforward recipe for preparing asparagus in a cast iron pan is her favorite way to do right by this vegetable.

1 bunch asparagus
3 tablespoons extra virgin olive oil
½ teaspoon kosher salt, plus more to taste
2 grinds freshly ground black pepper
1 garlic clove, minced
Grated zest of ½ lemon

1. Cut the ends off the asparagus, and discard them, then rinse the remaining part.

2. Meanwhile, heat a Lodge 15-inch cast iron skillet over medium-high heat for 3 minutes. Add the oil, and let it heat up for a minute, then add the asparagus. Sprinkle in the salt and pepper and, using tongs, toss the asparagus lightly to dress it with the oil. Every 2 minutes, toss the asparagus with the tongs.

3. When the asparagus is still a fairly bright green color but tender, add the garlic and lemon zest, and cook 1 more minute. Transfer to a serving dish, seasoning it with more salt, if needed. **Serves 4**

Greens slow-cooked with bacon are about as Southern as it gets, but when the greens are young and fresh, they don't always need that traditional long, slow simmer to make them tender. When that is the case, historian and cookbook author Damon Lee Fowler likes to braise them instead. This method cuts the cooking time considerably while still infusing the greens with that much-loved rich flavor.

BRAISED KALE
WITH BACON AND ONIONS

2 large bunches fresh young kale (about 2 pounds)

3 or 4 slices extra-thick-cut bacon, cut across into ¼-inch-wide julienne

1 medium yellow onion, split lengthwise and thinly sliced

Kosher or fine sea salt and freshly ground black pepper

1. Wash the greens in several changes of water, until no gritty soil remains on the leaves. Strip away any large, tough stems. Leave small leaves whole, or tear them in half; stack, roll, and cut larger leaves across into 1-inch-wide strips. Set aside in a large bowl.

2. Cook the bacon in a Lodge 10-inch cast iron skillet with a lid or a Dutch oven over medium heat, stirring frequently, until browned and its fat is rendered, 5 to 10 minutes. Add the onion, reduce the heat to medium-low, and cook slowly, stirring occasionally, until golden, about 5 minutes.

3. Raise the heat to medium-high, add a handful of kale, and toss until it is wilted. Continue adding the kale by handfuls, stirring constantly and allowing each addition to wilt before adding more. When all the kale is in the pan, season it with salt and pepper to taste, add a splash of water, cover, and reduce the heat to medium-low. Cook until the greens are nearly tender, 3 to 8 minutes, depending on the youth and freshness of the kale. It should be tender but still retain its lovely green color. **Serves 4**

"There is no better dish than this one to show you the importance of cookware," declares Kelly English, chef-owner of Restaurant Iris in Memphis. "Go ahead . . . I dare you to try to cook this on anything but Lodge cast iron. This is the salad that my entire menu was built around."

"SALAD" OF BRUSSELS SPROUTS, BACON, AND SHERRY

2 pounds Brussels sprouts (Kelly gets his from Woodson Ridge Farms in Oxford, Mississippi)
½ cup olive oil
2 tablespoons sherry vinegar
¼ pound sliced bacon (Kelly likes to use Benton's hickory-smoked country bacon from Madisonville, Tennessee), cut across into strips

2 shallots, minced
4 garlic cloves, minced
2 tablespoons fresh thyme leaves
Kosher salt and freshly ground black pepper

1. Bring a large pot of very salty (salty like the ocean) water to a boil.

2. Trim the stems of the Brussels sprouts, then cut them in half through the stem. Blanch the sprouts in the boiling water until tender but not mushy, about 2 minutes. Drain, then shock the sprouts in ice water to stop the cooking, and drain again.

3. In a small bowl, make a vinaigrette by whisking the oil and vinegar together until thickened (emulsified).

4. In a Lodge 15-inch cast iron skillet over medium heat, cook the bacon; when it begins to crisp and the fat is released, add the sprouts. Cook, stirring a few times, until the sprouts start to take on good color, about 1 minute. Add the shallots, garlic, and thyme, toss to combine, and cook, stirring, until the shallots become translucent.

5. Pour the vinaigrette over the salad (still in the skillet) to coat, and season with salt and pepper to taste. Enjoy! **Serves 4**

Chef Tricia Wheeler, publisher and editor at *Edible Columbus*, thought roasting Brussels sprouts at a high temperature in the oven was the best way to cook them—until she attended the French Culinary Institute. "One day, my chef instructor told me my method made the Brussels sprouts bitter and the best way to cook them was to quickly sauté them in a cast iron skillet. Ever since, I use his method to prepare my Brussels sprouts," says Tricia.

CREAMY BRUSSELS SPROUTS WITH TOASTED PINE NUTS

¼ cup pine nuts

1 pound Brussels sprouts

3 tablespoons extra virgin olive oil, or more as needed

Kosher salt and freshly ground black pepper

¼ cup heavy cream

1. Heat a Lodge 10-inch cast iron skillet over high heat for a few minutes until it is hot. Heat the pan dry, without any oil. Turn off the heat. Toss in the pine nuts, and stir while they lightly brown. This technique helps to ensure you don't burn the nuts. Transfer the pine nuts to a small bowl.

2. Rinse the Brussels sprouts, and trim the bottoms. Cut the sprouts in half through the stems—don't worry if some of the leaves fall off. Gather the prepared Brussels sprouts together in a bowl, and toss with the oil and salt and pepper to season to taste.

3. This time, heat the skillet over medium-high heat. When it's hot, add the Brussels sprouts and a little more oil if needed. Reduce the heat to medium, and cook, stirring occasionally, until they are browned and slightly crispy, 8 to 10 minutes.

4. Add the cream to the pan, and cook until it reduces and the Brussels sprouts are coated, another 5 minutes. Taste for seasoning, and add more salt and pepper, if needed. Toss the creamy Brussels sprouts with the pine nuts. Serve and enjoy! **Serves 6**

During the hot "dog days" of summer, when corn was being harvested out of the gardens, the Newsom family, particularly Colonel Bill and his wife, Jane, would prepare Southern-style creamed corn, his pan-cooked aged country ham, and juicy homegrown tomatoes for an evening meal. Today, Nancy Newsom Mahaffey, owner of Newsom's Old Mill Store, prepares the same meal for her own family when the hot weather hits.

SOUTHERN-STYLE CREAMED CORN

12 ears fresh corn
2½ tablespoons stick margarine or salted butter
1 cup water
1 cup milk
3 heaping tablespoons sugar (optional)

½ teaspoon salt (optional)
Scant ½ teaspoon freshly ground black pepper
3 heaping tablespoons self-rising or all-purpose flour
½ cup warm water

1. Shuck the corn, rinse, and remove the silks from the ears. Stand each ear in the middle of a large low-sided baking dish. Using a sharp serrated knife, shave the tips of each kernel from top to bottom all the way around the ear. Flip the knife over, and scrape the ear with the back, flat side of knife, top to bottom all the way around. This is called "milking the ear." Discard the corn cobs.

2. Slowly melt the margarine in a Lodge 10-inch cast iron skillet over low heat. Add the corn kernels with their milk to the skillet. Increase the heat to medium-high, and add the 1 cup water, milk, sugar and salt, if using, and pepper. Let the mixture bubble in the pan for 3 to 5 minutes, then reduce the heat to medium.

3. Meanwhile, place the flour in a coffee cup, and slowly add the warm water, stirring constantly. Turn the heat under the skillet to low, and add the flour slurry, stirring constantly. Cook, stirring, until the mixture thickens. If you like, you can add more milk or water if the mixture becomes too thick too fast. Serve hot. **Serves 12**

Cast Iron Memories

I first experienced cooking with cast iron with my Grandmother Newsom, "Mawnewsie" (as we called her), and my parents. I remember my Grandmother Newsom using only cast iron to fry her chicken, and also making her chicken 'n' dumplins in a tall-sided cast iron pot, as well as cooking her fresh green beans with, of course, Newsom's Aged Ham in them. She began her cooking with cast iron early in the morning— cooking everything slow and long, while whistling "The Old Rugged Cross." Then, my father and I would arrive for a full dinner at noon, while my mother, Jane, kept the store. I raised my children cooking with cast iron, as my family did before me. I still cook with cast iron. It is my favorite for frying—it provides even heat. I have my parents' cast iron. After all these years, fried chicken, cream-style corn, homemade hash browns, German fried potatoes, beef hash, and French fries cut from raw potatoes are still my favorite cast iron recipes.

— *Nancy Newsom Mahaffey*

This recipe grew out of a small backyard-farming project on the grounds at *Sunset* magazine and was contributed by Margo True, food editor at *Sunset*. For a series of seasonal dinners, Margo and her team cooked only what they could raise or grow. Later the team wrote a book about their adventures, with recipes, called *The One-Block Feast*. Cipollini onions were one of Margo's favorite crops from the project—she loves their dense sweetness—and she still cooks them all the time.

ROASTED CIPOLLINI ONIONS WITH CHILE-ROSEMARY BUTTER

1   pound cipollini onions
1   tablespoon olive oil
2   teaspoons chopped fresh rosemary

Pinch or two of red pepper flakes
Kosher salt
2   tablespoons butter

1. Preheat the oven to 400°. Meanwhile, peel the onions.

2. Pour the oil into a Lodge 10-inch cast iron skillet. Add the onions, sprinkle with the rosemary and red pepper, and season with salt to taste. Turn them over in the oil until thoroughly coated. Roast the onions until they're tender, about 30 minutes, turning them over every 10 minutes so they roast evenly.

3. Set the skillet on the stove-top over medium heat, and add the butter. Cook, stirring every now and then, just until the butter starts to brown, 1 to 2 minutes. Serve with a little of the butter spooned over the top. **Serves 4**

Potato latkes (pancakes) are a holiday tradition in the home of Peter Kaminsky, a food and outdoors writer and cookbook author. His most recent book is *Bacon Nation*.

POTATO "LODGEKES"

12 large Idaho potatoes, peeled and cut into chunks

2 medium Spanish onions, cut into chunks

5 large eggs, beaten

½ cup matzoh meal or cracker meal

Salt (salty is good) and freshly ground black pepper

1½ cups peanut oil (peanut oil has a high smoke point and works best, but you can also use canola oil)

1. In a food processor fitted with the shredding blade, grate the potatoes. As the bowl of the food processor fills up, empty the potatoes into a large colander or sieve placed in the sink.

2. Grate the onions, and set aside in a bowl.

3. Pick up the potatoes, a handful at a time, and squeeze to remove as much liquid as possible. Place the squeezed potatoes in a bowl.

4. When all the potatoes are squeezed, put the chopping blade in the food processor, and process half of the potatoes and all of the onions into a rough puree. Empty the puree into a bowl, and, taking a handful at a time, squeeze as much liquid as possible out of the potato/onion puree. Place in the colander or sieve to continue draining for 15 to 30 minutes. You can also put the puree in cheesecloth and squeeze out the liquid that way. Don't worry if the potatoes turn brown while standing.

5. Transfer the mixture to a large bowl. Add the remaining grated potatoes, the eggs, and matzoh meal. Season with salt and pepper, and mix well with a rubber spatula. Cover with plastic wrap, and set aside.

6. Heat the oil in a Lodge 15-inch cast iron skillet over medium-high heat until it begins to shimmer. The oil should be about ¼ inch deep. Using a large spoon, ladle the batter for two pancakes into the hot oil. Cook until golden brown, about 3 minutes, and flip. Cook 3 minutes more. Remove one and taste. The inside should be cooked through and the outside golden brown on both sides. Keep adjusting the heat and cooking time and adding more oil as you cook the rest of the pancakes, 3 or 4 at a time. Drain on paper towels before serving.

Serves a bunch of people (maybe 15 or so)

Cast Iron Memories

At the Kaminskys' in Brooklyn, New York, the family picks a convenient date in the beginning of December, writes to friends, and invites them to an open house. Says Peter, "I use two big Lodge skillets (usually when you write something like this, it's called product placement, but honest-to-God, I own Lodge skillets and always have)." As a side dish, they often poach a lot of vegetables in white wine and olive oil and arrange them on a big platter. "Also, we put out a quart or two of pickled herring that I fetch from the ladies at Nordic Delicacies in Bay Ridge, Brooklyn (that's the old Scandinavian section of town). Some pals on the West Coast usually send smoked wild salmon from the Pike Place Market, and Nancy Newsom Mahaffey of Princeton, Kentucky, sends one of her amazing country hams, which ain't kosher, but it sure is good [see her recipe for Fried Kentucky Country Ham with Newsom Family Red-eye Gravy on page 76]. For drinks, sparkling wine, sparkling cider, a hearty red wine, or, my favorite, a crisp ale," Peter relates. Top the individual latkes with sour cream, smoked salmon, or applesauce (or nothing).

Peter suggests, "Wear an apron when making these. Or if you are not the apron-wearing type, try overalls…or camo."

— *Peter Kaminsky*

This recipe from James Beard Cookbook Hall-of-Famer Jean Anderson, a North Carolina resident, is an old one adapted from her popular *Family Circle* series, "America's Great Grass Roots Cooks" and subsequent best-selling *Grass Roots Cookbook*. An iron skillet is a must for these potatoes. They're similar to hash browns, but because you begin with raw potatoes instead of leftover cooked ones, they're deliciously crispy.

PENNSYLVANIA DUTCH RAW-FRIED POTATOES

6 medium all-purpose potatoes

2 to 3 tablespoons lard (hog lard, not vegetable shortening) or, for a meatier flavor, a 50-50 mix of lard and bacon drippings

¾ teaspoon salt, or to taste

½ teaspoon freshly ground black pepper, or to taste

1. Peel the potatoes, quarter lengthwise, then cut each quarter into slices ⅛ inch thick.

2. Heat 2 tablespoons lard in a well-seasoned Lodge 12-inch cast iron skillet over medium heat until ripples appear on the pan bottom, about 1½ minutes.

3. Add the potatoes, and fry, scraping browned ones from bottom to top with a pancake turner and adding the additional tablespoon of lard, if needed, until all the potatoes are tender and richly browned, about 25 minutes.

4. Season to taste with salt and pepper, toss well to mix, and serve piping hot with almost any roast or chops. **Serves 4 to 6**

a cooking secret from Jean

The best potatoes to use? All-purpose Maine or Eastern potatoes, not "bakers," which cook down to mush, and not red skins, fingerlings, yellow Finns, or other waxy types, which tend to be "gluey" when cooked this way.

The winter pantry at Rick and Lora Lea Misterly's Quillisascut Farm in Rice, Washington, is filled with colorful squashes. Chef Kären Jurgensen, chef instructor at the farm and at Seattle Culinary Academy, likes to pair the sweetness of the squash with the nuttiness of the Misterly Curado farmstead cheese and Northwest-grown chickpeas (ceci beans). Other varieties of winter squash may be substituted.

ROASTED SQUASH, CECI BEANS, QUILLISASCUT GOAT CHEESE, AND TOASTED PEPITAS

½ acorn squash (about 1 pound), unpeeled, seeded, and cut into medium dice
½ delicata squash (about ½ pound), unpeeled, seeded, and cut into medium dice
2 tablespoons extra virgin olive oil
1 teaspoon red pepper flakes
1 teaspoon freshly grated nutmeg
2 garlic cloves, slivered

Kosher salt and freshly ground black pepper
½ cup cooked ceci beans (chickpeas)
2 tablespoons good-quality sherry vinegar or cider vinegar
2 tablespoons salted toasted pumpkin seeds (pepitas)
3 ounces Quillisascut Curado cheese, grated

1. Preheat the oven to 400°.

2. In a large bowl, toss the cut squash with the oil, red pepper, nutmeg, garlic, and salt and pepper to taste. Arrange in a single layer in a Lodge 12-inch cast iron skillet. Roast for 15 minutes; the squash should be softened and starting to brown.

3. Stir in the ceci beans, and return the skillet to the oven for another 15 minutes. Remove from the oven; the squash should be caramelized and tender.

4. While the squash is still hot, drizzle with the vinegar, then toss with the pumpkin seeds. Allow the squash to cool for 8 minutes; toss with the grated cheese. Adjust the seasonings. Serve warm or at room temperature.

Serves 6 to 8

Cast Iron Memories

It may all sound cliché, but the only frying pan we had growing up was cast iron, so I learned to cook in cast iron, to heat the pan to the right temperature to brown French toast or pancakes, to heat the oil and fry chicken. When I met my husband, Rick, he had a 10-inch cast iron skillet that he used for everything.

My mom used to say if Martha Washington were alive today, the one thing she would still find in use in the kitchen would be a cast iron pan.

I don't consider my mom's cast iron skillet an heirloom. We are utilitarian, so if something is good, we keep using it, and if it's great, we use it every day, regardless of age. My mom passed away in 2011, and I now treasure her skillet. It has served our family very well.

I am going to guess the first thing I made in a cast iron skillet was bacon. I can remember hearing the sizzle as the meat heated in the pan, watching the strips brown, turning them with a fork, being careful of hot grease splatters, and, when they were perfectly cooked, taking them out of the pan and letting them drain on some folded paper. The hot grease was poured into a metal canister and saved for frying potatoes or using as the secret ingredient in my mom's homemade bread.

—*Lora Lea Misterly*

This is a basic fritter recipe you can use with your favorite veggies like sweet corn, mushrooms, or, in this case, zucchini, because, says Felicia Willett, chef-owner of Felicia Suzanne's in downtown Memphis, "Let's face it, zucchini has a long season in the South!" You can make them small for cocktail parties and add a dollop of tomato jam (Felicia sells her own, sold under the brand Flo's). For dinner, make them a little larger, add a grilled piece of meat or fish, and top with fresh salsa.

ZUCCHINI FRITTERS

1 pound zucchini (8 to 10 small or 2 large), ends trimmed
1 cup (4 ounces) grated Parmesan cheese
½ cup chopped green onions
½ cup all-purpose flour
1 tablespoon baking powder

1 large egg, beaten
Juice and grated zest of 1 lemon
Kosher salt and freshly ground black pepper
Hot sauce
½ cup olive oil

1. Preheat the oven to 350°.

2. Using the large holes of a box grater, grate the zucchini onto a clean kitchen towel. Carefully squeeze out the liquid, and discard it. In a large bowl, combine the zucchini, Parmesan, and green onions, and mix well. In a small bowl, mix the flour and baking powder well. Add to the zucchini mixture along with the egg and lemon juice and zest; mix well. Season with salt, pepper, and hot sauce.

3. Heat ¼ cup of the oil in a Lodge 12-inch cast iron skillet over medium heat. Spoon a heaping tablespoonful of the batter into the hot oil for each fritter, slightly pressing the batter down to form the cake. Fry until golden and crispy, about 2 minutes per side.

4. As the fritters finish cooking, transfer them to a parchment paper-lined baking sheet, and place in the oven to keep warm. Continue frying until all of the batter is used; add more of the remaining ¼ cup oil to the skillet as needed.
Makes 12 to 14 fritters

In this recipe from healthy lifestyle consultant, chef, and the force behind healthyeating101.com, **Megan McCarthy** has added some vibrant colors to her favorite side dish, quinoa. Red quinoa has a bit of a heartier element to it than its white counterpart but is equally delicious. Paired with roasted acorn squash, this makes for a very nice comfort food side with plenty of protein, as well as a great source of fiber and potassium.

RED QUINOA WITH ROASTED ACORN SQUASH

1 acorn squash (1 to 2 pounds)
1 tablespoon extra virgin olive oil
1 cup red quinoa, rinsed under cold running water until water runs clear

2 cups water
2 tablespoons roasted walnut oil
Fine sea salt and cracked black pepper
2 green onions, chopped

1. Preheat the oven to 400°.

2. Slice the acorn squash in half, and scrape out the seeds. Brush the cut sides with the olive oil, and place, cut side down, on a Lodge 14-inch cast iron baking pan. Bake until tender, about 45 minutes. Let cool. Peel off the skin, and discard. Cut the roasted squash into large dice.

3. While the squash roasts, combine the rinsed quinoa and water in a medium saucepan, and bring to a boil. Reduce the heat to a simmer, cover, and cook until the water is absorbed, about 12 minutes.

4. Transfer the cooked quinoa to a large bowl, drizzle with the walnut oil, and season with salt and pepper to taste. Add the roasted squash and green onions, and gently toss. **Serves 4 to 6**

Jesse Ziff Cool has been dedicated to sustainable agriculture and practices it every day in her three restaurants, Flea Street and Cool Café @ MBP in Menlo Park and Cool Café in Stanford, California. Adding parsnips and yams creates an irresistible kugel that is great on its own with a dollop of sour cream or as a side dish. The even heat from the iron skillet results in a crispy crust, which is a must in a kugel. Says Jesse, "I still use my grandmother's iron skillet. I don't think I would even consider making a kugel in any other pan."

POTATO, PARSNIP, AND YAM KUGEL

3 tablespoons vegetable oil
4 medium red- or yellow-skin potatoes
2 medium parsnips
2 medium yams or sweet potatoes
3 teaspoons kosher salt
2 medium yellow onions, peeled
6 large eggs, beaten
¼ cup unbleached all-purpose flour
1½ teaspoons chopped fresh thyme
1 teaspoon freshly ground black pepper

1. Preheat the oven to 425°. Generously oil a Lodge 10-inch cast iron skillet, and put in the oven. Save 1 teaspoon of the oil to brush on the top of the kugel before baking.

2. Peel and, using the large holes of a box grater, grate the potatoes, parsnips, and yams into a large colander. Toss with 1 teaspoon of the salt, and let drain for 15 minutes to remove excess liquid, pressing on the mixture a few times.

3. While the mixture is draining, using the large holes on the grater, grate the onions in a large bowl. When the potatoes, parsnips, and yams have finished draining, add to the onions, and toss to combine. Add the eggs, flour, thyme, pepper, and remaining 2 teaspoons salt, and mix to combine well.

4. Remove the skillet from the oven, and pour the kugel batter into the hot pan. Brush the top with the reserved 1 teaspoon oil. Reduce the oven temperature to 375°, and bake the kugel until golden brown and tender at the center when tested with the tip of a knife, about 1 hour. Remove from the oven, and let stand for 10 minutes before cutting. **Serves 8 or more**

This recipe is from Linton Hopkins, chef-owner of Restaurant Eugene in Atlanta, Georgia. The small white turnips called hakurei can be found at most farmers' markets in fall, winter, and spring. They usually come with greens, which can be sautéed with a little fatback. Pan size is key to the success of this dish. The turnips need to fit into the bottom of the pan, cut side down, in a single layer. You can also prepare this using larger turnips; peel, then cut them into 1-inch cubes.

PAN-BRAISED WHITE TURNIPS

20 white hakurei turnips (about 2 pounds)	½ cup minced yellow onion
2 tablespoons unsalted butter	1 bay leaf
	Kosher salt

1. Wash the turnips, remove, or, if desired, trim the stems and tips, and cut each one in half from stem to tip.

2. Melt the butter in a Lodge 5-quart cast iron Dutch oven over medium heat until it foams. Add the onion and bay leaf, cover, and sweat the onion until it is softened but still has no color. It is important to not add any color, as that step comes later.

3. Add the turnips, cut side down, in a single layer. Try to nestle them down in such a way that they are not on top of the sweated onion. Add enough water to come halfway up the sides of the turnips, then sprinkle over a good dose of salt, cover the pot, and bring to a boil. Reduce the heat to a simmer, and cook, covered, until the turnips are just softened; over low heat, this will take about 15 minutes. Taste a turnip. If it needs more salt, add some.

4. With the lid off, bring the water to a rapid boil over high heat, and continue to boil until all the liquid is all gone. Continue to cook over high heat until the bottoms of the turnips turn a beautiful brown. Remove from the heat, and serve immediately. **Serves 8**

Cornbread, Sausage, and
Tomato Pie, page 246

BREADS

With his passion for bread, Bill Ryan, founder of the Louisiana Dutch Oven Society, is always looking for different ways to create a great tasting roll. After tasting your first one of these, you will quickly be grabbing for more!

SPICY SAUSAGE AND CHEDDAR YEAST ROLLS

½ pound ground andouille or bulk Italian sausage

1 cup minced yellow onion

1 tablespoon minced jalapeño chile (remove seeds for less heat)

1 (¼-ounce) package active dry yeast

2 tablespoons sugar

2 tablespoons plus 1 teaspoon vegetable oil

2 cups warm water (about 110°)

6 cups bread flour

¾ cup yellow cornmeal

2 teaspoons sea salt

2 cups (8 ounces) grated white Cheddar cheese

1. Brown the sausage in a Lodge 12-inch cast iron skillet over medium heat until fully cooked. Add the onion and jalapeño, and cook, stirring a few times, for 3 minutes. Transfer the mixture to a paper towel-lined plate to drain and cool to room temperature.

2. In a small bowl, combine the yeast, sugar, and 2 tablespoons of the oil. Add the water. Mix about 4 minutes to dissolve the yeast.

3. In a large bowl, combine the flour, all but 2 tablespoons of the cornmeal, the salt, sausage mixture, and cheese. Mix until it lightly comes together, then add the yeast mixture, and mix until the dough pulls from the side of the bowl and forms a ball. Remove the dough from the bowl. Coat the bowl with the remaining 1 teaspoon oil, return the dough to the bowl, and turn it to oil all sides. Cover the bowl with plastic wrap, and let the dough rise in a warm area (70° to 75°) until doubled in size, about 2 hours.

4. Turn the dough onto a lightly floured work surface. Using your hands, gently roll it into a narrow loaf about 24 inches long. Cut the dough across into 18 equal pieces. With the palm of your hand, roll each piece into a round roll. Sprinkle the bottom of a Lodge 7-quart cast iron Dutch oven with the reserved cornmeal. Place the rolls in a single layer in the pot, spacing them 1 inch apart, cover with a clean cloth, and let rise for 30 minutes.

5. Preheat the oven to 350°. Using a sharp knife, make an X on top of each roll. Bake until golden brown, about 20 minutes. Enjoy the rolls warm from the oven. **Makes 18 rolls**

In the South, cathead biscuits are also called scratch biscuits, and nobody knows the real derivation of either name. One quaint explanation is that the craggy ridges look like a cat's ears; another is that the irregular tops resemble fur. In any case, maintains cookbook author Jim Villas, catheads must be shaped by hand, and they are baked only in heavy cast iron skillets. For the right texture, do not substitute butter or margarine for the lard in these biscuits, and serve them with plenty of butter and fruit preserves, molasses, or sorghum syrup.

CATHEAD BISCUITS

3 cups all-purpose flour
4 teaspoons baking powder
1 teaspoon salt

½ teaspoon baking soda
1 cup chilled lard, cut into pieces
1 cup buttermilk, or as needed

1. Preheat the oven to 325°. Grease two Lodge 12-inch cast iron skillets, and set aside.

2. In a large bowl, whisk the flour, baking powder, salt, and baking soda together. Add the lard, and cut it in with a pastry cutter or rub it into the flour with your fingertips until the mixture is just crumbly. Gradually stir in just enough buttermilk to form a soft ball of dough.

3. Transfer the dough to a lightly floured work surface, knead about 8 times, then shape by hand into biscuits about 3½ inches across and 1 inch high.

4. Arrange the biscuits fairly close together in the prepared skillets, and bake in the upper third of the oven until golden brown and craggy on the outsides, about 17 minutes. **Makes about 1½ dozen biscuits**

MULTIGRAIN ARTISAN LOAF

If you want authentic artisan bakery results, Leslie Mackie, chef-owner of Macrina Bakery & Café in Seattle, Washington, recommends that you bake your bread in a Lodge cast iron double Dutch oven. With its tight-fitting lid, the pot traps the moisture inside, allowing the loaf to rise as it bakes, creating a beautiful interior texture and deep golden brown crust.

1 ½ cups unbleached all-purpose flour, plus more as needed for sprinkling

2 cups lukewarm water (about 80°)

⅓ cup four-grain cereal

3 tablespoons honey

2 teaspoons active dry yeast

¾ cup stone-ground whole-wheat flour

½ cup stone-ground rye flour

2 teaspoons kosher salt

1. Line a medium bowl with a clean tea towel, and sprinkle heavily with all-purpose flour. Set aside to use later for a mold to raise the bread.

2. In a large bowl, combine the water, four-grain cereal, and honey; let soak for 1 hour.

3. Sprinkle the yeast over the surface of the liquid, and whisk gently until it has dissolved. Let stand for 3 minutes. Add the 1 ½ cups all-purpose flour, the whole-wheat flour, rye flour, and salt. With a rubber spatula, mix together for 2 or 3 minutes by pulling the spatula through the dough mixture and flipping it to simulate a kneading motion. Cover the bowl with plastic wrap, and let rise at room temperature (75°) or until the dough has doubled in size, about 2 hours.

4. Lightly sprinkle the top of the dough with all-purpose flour, and do a "baker's turn" on the dough. This is done by first releasing the dough around the edge of the bowl. Pull the dough outward, first on the right side, extending the dough out past the rim of the bowl approximately 6 inches. Bring the stretched dough back to the center of the bowl, and lay it on top. Do the same with the left side and the top and bottom portions of dough, bringing the stretched dough back to the center each time. Then flip the dough over, and cover with plastic wrap. Let rise for another 2 hours, then do another baker's turn. Cover and let the dough rise until it has doubled in size, about another hour.

5. Transfer the dough to a floured work surface, and do one more baker's turn. Invert the loaf so it is seam side down, and gently round to tighten the loaf. Place in the towel-lined bowl with the seam side up. Cover the top of the loaf with the extended ends of the tea towel. Let rise until the loaf feels like gelatin, about 2 hours.

6. One hour before baking, preheat the oven and a Lodge 5-quart cast iron double Dutch oven to 450°. Carefully remove the preheated pot, and invert the loaf onto the shallow side of the pot. Quickly "score" a 4-inch square about ¼ inch deep on top of the loaf, quickly cover the loaf with the larger part of the Dutch oven, and place in the oven. Bake, covered, for 30 minutes, then remove the top, and bake until the loaf is deep golden brown, another 20 minutes.

7. Remove from the oven, and let the loaf rest for 1 hour on a wire rack to cool. Enjoy simply eaten with butter, prepared as a tartine, or as a sandwich loaf.
Makes one 9-inch loaf

his recipe from Bill Ryan, founder of the Louisiana Dutch Oven Society, yields five mini breads, plus a larger bread. You'll need five Lodge 5-inch cast iron mini servers for this, as well as an 8-inch Dutch oven. This bread is wonderful slathered with garlic butter.

COTTAGE CHEESE DILL BREAD

2   (¼-ounce) packages active dry yeast
½   cup warm water (about 110°)
2   teaspoons plus 2 tablespoons sugar
2   cups small-curd cottage cheese
2   tablespoons minced onion

2   tablespoons dill seeds
1   tablespoon chopped fresh dill
1   tablespoon baking powder
2   teaspoons salt
2   large eggs
4   to 4½ cups all-purpose flour
2   tablespoons butter, melted

1. Combine the yeast, warm water, and 2 teaspoons sugar in a small bowl, and let stand 10 minutes.

2. In a large bowl, combine the cottage cheese, onion, dill seeds, chopped dill, baking powder, salt, the remaining 2 tablespoons sugar, and the eggs. Mix well with a stand mixer. Stir in the yeast mixture. Add the flour 1 cup at a time, mixing well after each addition. Continue mixing/kneading until the dough is smooth and elastic.

3. Turn the dough into a greased bowl, and turn once to coat it. Cover the bowl with plastic wrap, set in a warm area (70° to 78°), and let rise until doubled in size, 1 to 1½ hours.

4. Grease five Lodge 5-inch cast iron mini servers and one 8- or 10-inch cast iron Dutch oven. Punch down the dough, turn it out onto a lightly floured work surface, and form into a round loaf. Pinching off about 1 cup of dough at a time, form into a ball, and set in one of the prepared servers. Take the remaining dough, form into a ball, and place in the Dutch oven. Cover all of the dough with clean cloths, and let rise until doubled in size, 45 to 60 minutes.

5. Preheat the oven to 350°. Bake the loaves until golden brown on top, about 30 minutes. Brush the tops with melted butter, cool for 10 minutes before removing from pans, then let the loaves cool an additional 30 minutes before slicing. **Makes five 5-inch loaves and one 8-inch loaf**

This crusty bread from Jennifer Brush, owner of The Pastry Brush, a certified home bakery in Chardon, Ohio, that provides baking classes, is delicious and so very easy to make. The very wet dough is allowed to slowly ferment at room temperature, resulting in an extremely flavorful loaf. "This is my family's favorite to eat for breakfast with an omelet or for dinner with soup," says Jennifer.

CRUSTY BACON AND CHEESE BREAD

3 cups unbleached all-purpose flour, plus more for sprinkling on dough and flouring hands (Jennifer uses King Arthur)

1½ teaspoons fine sea salt

¼ teaspoon instant yeast

½ pound sliced bacon, cooked until crispy, drained, and crumbled or chopped

2 cups (8 ounces) shredded sharp Cheddar cheese

1¼ cups water

1. (Jennifer likes to mix this by hand in a 4-quart lidded plastic container so that after mixing she can just pop on the lid and leave the dough on the counter to do its thing. You can easily mix this in a medium bowl and then transfer it to a glass or plastic container with a lid. Keep in mind it will increase slightly in volume.) With a rubber spatula, mix the 3 cups flour, salt, yeast, bacon, and cheese together until incorporated. Add the water, and stir until completely incorporated. The dough should be evenly wet, with no dry spots. It will look a little "shaggy" and sticky. Cover and let stand on a counter at room temperature for 18 to 24 hours. (Jennifer likes to let it ferment for a full 24 hours if there is time.)

2. Remove the container lid. Sprinkle the top of the dough with 3 tablespoons flour. Flour your hands well. Remove the dough from the container or bowl by scooping your hands underneath the dough and lifting it out. The dough will be wet and soft. Make a ball with the dough by gently tucking the edges of the dough underneath while slightly turning it. Place the dough on a well-floured silicone baking mat or cotton kitchen towel, sprinkle the top of the dough ball lightly with flour, and cover with a cotton kitchen towel until doubled in size, 1½ to 2 hours. After the dough has risen for about 1 hour, preheat a lidded Lodge 4-quart cast iron Dutch oven to 440° in the oven. Make sure the pot is covered with the lid while preheating.

3. Remove the Dutch oven from the oven after 30 minutes. Remove the ball of dough from the bowl or towel, and place it in the pot. Cover with the lid, and bake for 30 minutes. Remove the lid, and continue to bake until golden brown, about another 15 minutes. Remove the loaf from the pot as soon as it comes out of the oven. Let cool on a wire rack for at least 1 hour before slicing.

Serves 8

a cooking secret from Jennifer

Baking in a covered cast iron pot traps the steam escaping from the moist dough and results in a soft middle and a crisp and crunchy crust.

This recipe is from Dennis Golden, cowboy poet, PBS TV host, and master Dutch oven chef. To make this, you need sourdough starter, which must be started 4 to 5 days ahead of when you want to bake your bread. If you're in a hurry, you can buy packaged starter at most specialty food or kitchenware stores or online and follow the directions.

EASY DUTCH OVEN SOURDOUGH BREAD

Sourdough starter:
2 cups unbleached all-purpose flour
2½ cups warm water (about 110°)
Sourdough bread:
4 to 6 cups unbleached all-purpose flour
1 (¼-ounce) package active dry yeast (2¼ teaspoons)

¼ cup lukewarm water (about 80°)
2½ tablespoons corn or canola oil or melted vegetable shortening
2 tablespoons sugar
1½ teaspoons salt
½ teaspoon baking soda
Nonstick cooking spray

1. Make sourdough starter: Combine the flour and water in a large glass jar or sturdy plastic container with a tight-fitting lid. Cover tightly, and set in a warm (but not hot) place for 4 to 5 days before using.

2. Make sourdough bread: In a large plastic or glass bowl, mix 1 cup of the sourdough starter with 4 cups of the flour. Stir in as much water as is needed to reach a mixable, semiliquid consistency. Cover and set in a 120° oven until the mixture is active and foamy, 45 to 60 minutes or more. In a small bowl, combine the yeast with the lukewarm water to activate. Stir in the oil, sugar, salt, and baking soda. Stir this into the sourdough mixture once it gets foamy.

3. Coat the inside of a Lodge 12-inch cast iron Dutch oven with cooking spray (including the inside of the lid). Wipe with a paper towel. Set the pot in the oven, and preheat it to 120°.

4. While the pot heats, add more flour as needed to the sourdough mixture to form a dough that is stiff enough to turn out onto a floured board. Knead and turn the dough, adding more flour as necessary, until it is stiff enough to form a round loaf and quits sticking to your hands. Don't overknead the dough; that can hamper the rising process. Transfer the dough to the prepared and preheated Dutch oven. Gently push the loaf out to the edge of the pot. It should come only halfway up the side of the Dutch oven, or even less. Cover with the lid, and place in the warm oven to rise.

5. When the dough has risen to nearly the top of the pot (after about 45 minutes), turn the oven temperature to 375° (yes, the dough is in the oven as it is preheating), and bake until golden brown, about 1 hour and 15 or 20 minutes.

6. Turn the loaf out onto a board or towel. Let it cool a bit, then slice and enjoy. **Makes one 12-inch loaf**

CRAZY FOR DUTCH OVEN COOKING

Dennis Golden

Master Dutch oven chef and cowboy poet, Reno, Nevada

Cast iron has been in my family's kitchen as long as I can remember. As I child, I helped my grandmother cook sourdough pancakes in her large cast iron skillet.

But my first vivid recollection of cooking with cast iron took place about 1948 on a hunting trip in northern Nevada. I helped my father cook sage grouse in a cast iron pot with a flat bottom and rounded lid by burying it underground in sagebrush coals. After 8 hours underground, the pot was extracted with great fanfare, and I can still remember the aroma when the lid was lifted and how we feasted like thieves on that tender, succulent bird! This method of cooking is a favorite in hunting and fishing camps and is often referred to as "bean pot cooking," which is why we always called our pot the "bean pot."

I later inherited this pot and used it to cook many meals for my own family. For years, it was used almost weekly as one of our family's most prized kitchen tools. Last year my wife and I gave it to our daughter as a wedding present.

I use cast iron frequently, because it holds heat so well and distributes it evenly. It is practically indestructible. Despite all the modern "nonstick" surfaces, cast iron continues to be superior to most . . . and it cleans up easily and quickly.

After all these years of cooking, my favorite cast iron recipe is, hands down, Dutch oven sourdough bread. It's not only a family favorite, but friends have come to expect it to be delivered at Christmastime as a holiday treat!

I keep plenty of the sourdough starter on hand so I can make bread on a regular basis. If you don't use all of the starter within 4 to 5 days, you'll need to replenish the starter and keep it healthy and active. For example, if you take 1 cup of starter, add 1/2 cup flour and 1/2 cup warm water to the jar, and repeat the procedure of leaving it in a warm place for 4 to 5 days, then refrigerate until needed again. Also, if you are a sporadic bread baker, if you haven't made bread in a month, add a couple tablespoons each of flour and water to the starter, and repeat the fermenting process before refrigerating again. With this kind of care and feeding, your starter can pretty much live forever.

CORNBREAD, SAUSAGE, AND TOMATO PIE
WITH GARLIC CREAM DRIZZLE

Lisa Keys from Middlebury, Connecticut, took home second prize at the 2012 National Cornbread Cook-Off with this delicious recipe. Lisa put a creative upside-down spin on her version of tomato pie made with fluffy sweet cornbread. Inverting the dish reveals the beautiful grape tomato topping.

Cornbread:
- ½ pound sweet Italian sausages, casings removed
- 6 tablespoons extra virgin olive oil
- 1 pint (2 cups) grape tomatoes, halved
- ½ cup chopped sweet onion
- 1 tablespoon sugar
- 1 teaspoon dried Italian seasoning
- 2 (7-ounce) packages Martha White Sweet Yellow Cornbread & Muffin Mix
- ¼ cup grated Parmesan cheese
- ½ cup milk
- ½ cup sour cream
- 3 large eggs, lightly beaten

Garlic Cream Drizzle:
- ¼ cup heavy cream, plus more as needed
- 1 teaspoon Martha White Self-Rising Enriched White Corn Meal Mix or Martha White Plain Enriched Corn Meal
- 2 garlic cloves, crushed
- 2 fresh basil leaves
- ¼ cup sour cream
- 2 tablespoons grated Parmesan cheese
- ¼ teaspoon kosher salt
- ¼ teaspoon black pepper
- Shaved Parmesan cheese and fresh basil leaves, for garnish

1. Make the cornbread: Preheat the oven to 375°. Brown the sausage in a Lodge 10-inch cast iron skillet over medium heat until no longer pink, breaking up the meat with a wooden spoon. Drain on paper towels. Add 2 tablespoons of the oil to the pan, along with the tomatoes, onion, sugar, and ½ teaspoon of the Italian seasoning. Cook, stirring occasionally, until the tomatoes and onion begin to caramelize, about 8 minutes. Spread the tomato mixture evenly over the bottom of the pan. Spoon the sausage evenly over the top.

2. In a medium bowl, stir the cornbread mix, Parmesan, milk, sour cream, eggs, remaining 4 tablespoons oil, and ½ teaspoon Italian seasoning together until smooth. Pour evenly over the mixture in the skillet. Bake until golden brown, 20 to 25 minutes. Let stand 5 minutes before inverting onto a serving plate. If any tomatoes or onions stick to the bottom of the pan, scrape them off, and replace on the cornbread.

3. Make the Garlic Cream Drizzle: Stir together the cream, corn meal mix, garlic, and basil in a microwave-safe 1-cup measuring cup or bowl. Heat on HIGH in the microwave for 45 to 60 seconds or until the mixture boils. Discard the garlic and basil. In a small bowl, whisk the sour cream, Parmesan, salt, and pepper together. Add to the cream mixture. Add 1 to 2 tablespoons more cream if needed to reach a drizzling consistency.

4. Sprinkle the cornbread with shaved Parmesan and basil leaves. Cut into wedges, and serve the Garlic Cream Drizzle on the side. **Serves 8**

how Lisa removes cornbread from the pan

1. After the cooked bread has rested for 5 minutes, place an inverted plate on top of the skillet. Gently invert the pan so that the skillet is upside down.

2. Place the plate on a flat surface and gently lift the pan upward to remove the bread from the pan.

3. Some of the tomatoes or onions may stick to the pan—just gently scrape them off and place on top of bread.

With a recipe as simple as cornbread, using quality ingredients makes all the difference. And Sean Brock uses only Southern ingredients. "If it doesn't come from the South, it's not coming through the door," declares Sean. So his cornmeal is from Anson Mills in Columbia, South Carolina, the buttermilk from Cruze Dairy Farm in Knoxville, Tennessee. Benton's Smoky Mountain Country Hams in Madisonville, Tennessee, supplies the restaurant's bacon.

HUSK CORNBREAD

2 cups fine yellow cornmeal
½ teaspoon baking soda
½ teaspoon baking powder
1½ cups buttermilk

1 large farm-fresh egg
4 tablespoons bacon drippings
2 tablespoons crumbled crisp-fried bacon

1. Preheat the oven to 450°. Place a Lodge 10-inch cast iron skillet in the oven to preheat for at least 10 minutes.

2. While the oven and skillet preheat, in a medium bowl, combine the dry ingredients. In a measuring cup, whisk the buttermilk, egg, and 3 tablespoons of the bacon drippings together. Pour into the dry ingredients, and mix until just combined. Stir in the crumbled bacon.

3. Transfer the hot skillet to the stove-top, setting it over high heat. Add the remaining 1 tablespoon bacon fat, and swirl it to coat the skillet. Make sure the batter is stirred well, then pour it into the skillet, distributing it evenly. It should sizzle. Bake until a toothpick placed in the center comes away clean, about 20 minutes. Serve from the skillet. **Serves 8**

a cooking secret from Sean

Preheating the skillet in the oven, then melting the bacon fat on the stovetop before pouring the batter into the skillet, is the key to the crisp outer edges of the bread.

BLACK OLIVE CORNBREAD WEDGES WITH CHORIZO-TOMATO GRAVY

Cornbread:

1   large egg

¾   cup buttermilk

1   (6½-ounce) package Martha White Yellow Cornbread Mix

2   tablespoons butter, melted

1   cup fresh or (thawed) frozen corn kernels

1   (2¼-ounce) can sliced black olives, drained

Gravy:

5   tablespoons butter

1   cup diced onion

2   links (about 6 ounces) Mexican chorizo sausage (see kitchen note), casings removed

3   tablespoons Martha White All-Purpose Flour

2   cups milk

1   cup diced fresh or drained canned tomatoes

½   teaspoon paprika

Garnishes:

Chopped green onions (green part only), diced ripe avocado, crumbled tortilla chips, chopped tomatoes, and/or lime wedges

This recipe, submitted by Gaynell Lawson from Maryville, Tennessee, was the second-prize winner in the 2009 National Cornbread Cook-off. Her version gets a south-of-the-border twist on the classic Southern tomato gravy—the perfect topping for crisp, olive-studded cornbread baked in a cast iron wedge pan.

1. Preheat the oven to 400°. Spray a Lodge 9-inch cast iron cornbread wedge pan with nonstick cooking spray. Place in the oven until hot, 6 to 7 minutes.

2. Make the cornbread: Beat the egg in a large bowl. Add the buttermilk, cornbread mix, melted butter, corn, and olives. Mix thoroughly. Pour evenly into the wedges of the hot pan. Bake until golden brown, 20 to 25 minutes. Remove from the oven, and keep warm.

3. While the cornbread bakes, make the gravy: Melt 2 tablespoons of the butter in a Lodge 10-inch cast iron skillet over medium heat. Add the onion, and cook, stirring a few times, until translucent, 3 to 4 minutes. Crumble the chorizo into the skillet. Cook until no longer pink, breaking up any clumps with a wooden spoon, 4 to 5 minutes. Transfer the mixture to a small bowl. Wipe out the skillet with a paper towel.

4. Return the skillet to medium heat. Melt the remaining 3 tablespoons butter. Add the flour, and whisk constantly until the mixture is golden. Slowly pour in the milk, whisking constantly, and cook until thickened, about 3 minutes, then stir in the tomatoes and paprika. Stir in the chorizo mixture, and heat through.

5. To serve, place a wedge of cornbread on each plate, and top with ½ cup of the chorizo-tomato gravy. Garnish with green onions, avocado, tortilla chips, tomatoes, and a squeeze of lime juice as desired. **Serves 8**

kitchen note:

Mexican chorizo is raw and must be cooked all the way through before eating, like Italian sausage.

SHRIMP CREOLE SKILLET CORNBREAD

I'm a very disciplined eater most of the time, but I can't imagine a Gulf Coast holiday celebration without my grandmother's luscious Shrimp Creole Cornbread," says Donna Pierce, former test kitchen director for the *Chicago Tribune* and contributing editor for *Upscale Magazine*. Donna recalls her grandmother serving these spicy wedges made with Gulf shrimp and Creole seasoning over the delicious homemade marinara sauce she learned to make from a Sicilian neighbor in Mobile, Alabama.

5 tablespoons unsalted butter
1 small yellow onion, finely chopped
1 small celery rib, finely chopped
1 small green bell pepper, seeded and finely chopped
1 small garlic clove, finely chopped
¾ pound medium (31/35 count) Gulf shrimp, peeled, deveined, and coarsely chopped
1½ teaspoons sweet paprika
1½ teaspoons coarse salt
1 teaspoon dried thyme
¼ teaspoon onion powder
¼ teaspoon garlic powder
¼ teaspoon dry mustard
Freshly ground black pepper
¾ cup all-purpose flour

¾ cup yellow cornmeal
1 tablespoon sugar
1½ teaspoons baking powder
1 teaspoon baking soda
¾ cup milk
1 (26-ounce) jar prepared marinara sauce (Donna uses a roasted garlic sauce)
2 large eggs, lightly beaten
2 ounces smoked Creole chaurice, Spanish chorizo, or Portuguese chouriço sausage, cut into ¼-inch-thick rounds, then in half (about ½ cup)
3 tablespoons chopped fresh flat-leaf parsley (optional)

1. Preheat the oven to 450°.

2. Melt 2 tablespoons of the butter in a Lodge 12-inch cast iron skillet over medium-high heat. Add the onion, celery, and bell pepper, and cook, stirring, until the vegetables begin to soften, about 3 minutes. Add the garlic and shrimp; cook 1 minute, stirring. Transfer the mixture to a medium bowl. Stir in the paprika, ½ teaspoon of the salt, the thyme, onion powder, garlic powder, mustard, and pepper to taste. Set aside. Wipe out the skillet with a paper towel.

3. In a large bowl, combine the flour, cornmeal, sugar, baking powder, baking soda, and remaining 1 teaspoon salt.

4. In a small bowl, combine the milk and ¾ cup of the marinara sauce (heat the rest of the marinara in a small saucepan; keep warm); whisk the eggs into the mixture. Whisk this into the flour mixture.

5. Melt the remaining 3 tablespoons butter in the skillet over medium heat. Stir the butter into the batter, then stir in the shrimp mixture, just until combined.

6. Return the skillet to medium heat; spread the batter evenly around the skillet with a rubber spatula. Top with the sausage slices and parsley, if using. Transfer to the oven; bake for 5 minutes. Reduce the oven temperature to 400°. Bake until golden brown and the edges begin to crisp, 20 to 25 minutes. (Cover the top with aluminum foil after 10 minutes if the cornbread begins to brown too quickly.)

7. Remove from the oven; let cool 10 minutes. Cut into wedges, and serve with the heated marinara sauce. **Serves 8 to 10 as an appetizer**

Judy Armstrong from Prairieville, Louisiana, took home third prize at the 2007 National Cornbread Cook-off for this hearty sausage and vegetable pie. By pouring her cornbread batter into a hot cast iron skillet, then topping it with sausage and Mediterranean-style ingredients, Judy ensures that the cornbread rises around the edges and creates a crust as it bakes.

ROASTED RED PEPPER, SAGE, AND SAUSAGE CORNBREAD DINNER

1	pound bulk Italian sausage	1	(14-ounce) can artichoke hearts, drained and coarsely chopped
1	medium onion, cut into thin wedges	2	roasted red peppers, chopped (about ¾ cup)
3	garlic cloves, minced		
½	teaspoon cayenne pepper		
1	(6½-ounce) package Martha White Yellow Cornbread Mix	2	plum tomatoes, diced
		1½	cups (6 ounces) shredded fontina cheese
1	large egg, beaten		
½	cup milk	2	tablespoons chopped fresh sage
½	cup store-bought red pepper pesto		

1. Preheat the oven to 425°.

2. In a Lodge 10-inch cast iron skillet, cook the sausage, onion, and garlic over medium-high heat until the sausage is no longer pink, about 5 minutes, breaking up any clumps with a wooden spoon and stirring frequently. Stir in the cayenne. Transfer the mixture to a bowl. Wipe out the skillet with a paper towel; place in the oven to heat.

3. In a medium bowl, combine the cornbread mix, egg, milk, and pesto until well mixed. Pour the batter into the hot skillet; top evenly with the sausage mixture, then the artichoke hearts, red peppers, and tomatoes. Bake until the cornbread browns around the edge, 15 to 18 minutes.

4. Sprinkle the top evenly with the cheese and sage. Return to the oven; bake until the cheese is melted, about 5 minutes.

5. Remove from the oven. Let cool for 10 minutes, then cut into wedges, and serve from the skillet. **Serves 6**

MILE-HIGH GREENS AND CREAMY CORNBREAD SKILLET

Janine Washle from Sonora, Kentucky, was named third-prize winner for this recipe in the 2006 National Cornbread Cook-off. Janine captured a favorite Southern food pairing—greens and cornbread—with this creative entry. Her crust is reminiscent of the texture of hot water cornbread piled high with wilted greens, ham, and roasted red pepper.

Cornbread:
- 1 cup Martha White Plain Yellow Corn Meal
- 1 tablespoon butter
- 1 cup boiling water
- 1 large egg, beaten
- 1 cup milk or buttermilk
- 1 tablespoon baking powder
- 1 tablespoon Martha White All-Purpose Flour
- ½ teaspoon salt
- 1 cup (4 ounces) shredded mozzarella cheese

Topping:
- 1½ tablespoons canola oil
- 1 medium onion, chopped
- 2 cups chopped cooked ham
- 1 pound kale, heavy stems trimmed and chopped
- 1 pound mustard or turnip greens, heavy stems trimmed and chopped
- ½ cup roasted red peppers, cut into strips
- Salt and freshly ground black pepper
- 1 teaspoon hot pepper sauce (optional)

1. Make the cornbread: Preheat the oven to 450°. Grease a Lodge 12-inch cast iron skillet.

2. Place the cornmeal and butter in a medium bowl. Gradually stir in the boiling water until blended and the butter is melted. Stir in the egg. Gradually blend in the milk, stirring constantly. Add the baking powder, flour, salt, and cheese; stir until blended. Pour into the prepared skillet. Bake until lightly browned, 15 to 20 minutes. Remove from the oven.

3. While the crust bakes, make the topping: Heat the oil in a Lodge 5-quart cast iron Dutch oven over medium-high heat. Add the onion, and cook, stirring a few times, until tender, about 5 minutes. Add the ham, and cook, stirring a few times, until it is browned. Spoon the ham mixture over the cornbread, leaving 1 inch around the edge uncovered.

4. Return the Dutch oven to medium-high heat, and add the kale and mustard greens in 3 to 4 additions as they wilt down. Stir in the red peppers. Cook until the greens are dark green, 5 to 7 minutes. Season to taste with salt and black pepper, and stir in the hot sauce, if using. Spoon the greens over the ham mixture. Loosely tent the skillet with aluminum foil; place in the oven until hot, 10 to 15 minutes.

5. Remove from the oven; loosen the edge with a knife. Cut into wedges, and serve from the pan. **Serves 8**

I t's not surprising that this cornbread recipe from Paula Lambert, founder and owner of The Mozzarella Company in Dallas, Texas, gets its goodness from not one but three different kinds of cheeses.

PAULA'S CHEESY CORNBREAD

5   tablespoons extra virgin olive oil
1   small onion, finely chopped
    (½ cup)
½   teaspoon minced garlic
½   cup finely chopped red bell
    pepper
1   jalapeño chile, seeded and minced
Kernels cut from 2 ears corn (1½ to
    2 cups)
1   cup unbleached all-purpose flour
1   cup yellow cornmeal

1   tablespoon baking powder
1   teaspoon salt
1½ cups buttermilk
3   large eggs, well beaten
1   cup (4 ounces) shredded pepper
    Jack cheese
1   cup (4 ounces) shredded smoked
    mozzarella cheese
1   cup (4 ounces) shredded longhorn
    cheese

1. Preheat the oven to 375°.

2. Heat 2 tablespoons of the oil in a Lodge 10-inch cast iron skillet. Add the onion, garlic, bell pepper, and jalapeño, and cook, stirring, until the vegetables begin to soften, about 4 minutes. Add the corn, and cook, stirring, for several minutes. Remove the pan from the heat; set aside.

3. In a large bowl, sift the flour, cornmeal, baking powder, and salt together. In a medium bowl, mix the buttermilk with 2 tablespoons of the oil and the eggs. Add the liquid to the dry ingredients, and stir briefly to just combine. Add the corn mixture and cheeses, and stir again to combine.

4. Wipe out the skillet well, then set over low heat for a few minutes. Pour in the remaining 1 tablespoon oil. Swirl the skillet so the oil completely coats all parts of the pan, bottom and side. Pour in the cornbread batter.

5. Bake until a toothpick inserted in the middle comes out clean and the top is golden brown, 40 to 60 minutes. Remove the cornbread from the oven, and let cool slightly in the skillet on a wire rack before cutting into wedges or squares and serving. **Serves 6 to 8**

Apple-Cranberry Pie,
page 280

DESSERTS

or Tanya Holland, cookbook author and chef-owner of Brown Sugar Kitchen in Oakland, California, this dish is a celebration of her cooking experiences. "My paternal grandmother in Virginia always fried apples in a cast iron skillet. My maternal grandmother in Louisiana always toasted pecans in her pan. Cherry clafoutis was one of the first 'exotic' desserts I made when I was taking cooking classes at Peter Kump's New York Cooking School...at 23, I felt so sophisticated just being able to pronounce it!"

APPLE-PECAN CLAFOUTIS

¾ cup pecan pieces
1½ pounds firm, semisweet apples, like Fuji or Pink Lady
¼ cup (½ stick) unsalted butter
1 cup sugar
¼ teaspoon ground cinnamon
4 large eggs

1 cup whole milk
1 tablespoon apple brandy
1½ teaspoons vanilla extract
Pinch of salt
2 cups unbleached all-purpose flour
Powdered sugar (optional)

1. Preheat the oven to 375°. Pulse the pecans in a food processor until finely chopped; be careful not to process into a powder. Set aside.

2. Peel and core the apples. Slice the apples in half, then cut each half into ⅛-inch-thick half moons.

3. Heat a Lodge 10-inch cast iron skillet over medium heat; add the butter. When melted, swirl to coat the bottom. Add the apples, ¼ cup of the sugar, and the cinnamon, and cook until the apples soften, about 10 minutes, stirring a few times.

4. While the apples cook, whisk the eggs, remaining ¾ cup sugar, the milk, brandy, and vanilla together in a medium bowl. Whisk in the pecans and salt, then slowly whisk in the flour to avoid lumps. Pour the batter over the apples in the pan. Bake for 10 minutes at 375°, then reduce the oven temperature to 350°, and cook until the clafoutis is nicely puffed up and browned on top, another 35 minutes. Dust with powdered sugar, if desired. Serve immediately.
Serves 6 to 8

MOM'S PEACH COBBLER WITH SWEET PIE DOUGH DUMPLINGS

"We always knew summer was here when Mom brought home some juicy fresh peaches from the market to make her favorite cobbler," remembers Beth Allen. "This one is different from most fruit cobblers, as it has some soft, sweet dumplings hidden inside, as well as crispy, sugary ones baked on top." As with most of her mom's desserts, bigger always meant better. She would spoon the warm cobbler into soup plates, then pour cold cream over it.

2¼ cups bleached all-purpose flour
⅓ cup granulated sugar, plus 2 tablespoons for sprinkling
1 teaspoon baking powder
1 teaspoon salt
¾ cup (1½ sticks) cold unsalted butter, cut into ½-inch cubes
¾ cup cold heavy cream
2 extra-large egg yolks
3½ pounds ripe peaches, peeled, pitted, and sliced ½ inch thick, or 3½ pounds frozen peach slices, thawed and drained (you need 10 to 11 cups)

1 cup granulated sugar
¾ cup firmly packed light brown sugar
¼ cup quick-cooking tapioca
1 tablespoon ground cinnamon
1 teaspoon grated lemon zest
3 tablespoons fresh lemon juice
2 tablespoons cornstarch
1 teaspoon vanilla extract
¼ cup (½ stick) unsalted butter, melted
Chilled "pour" cream (heavy cream), for serving

1. In a large bowl, mix the flour, ⅓ cup granulated sugar, baking powder, and salt together. Cut in the cold butter with two forks or a pastry cutter until crumbs the size of peas form. In a small bowl, whisk the cream and egg yolks together, and stir into the flour mixture. Keep stirring until a ball of dough forms. Shape into two 6-inch disks, cover in plastic wrap, and refrigerate for 30 minutes.

2. While the pie dough chills, place the peaches in a large bowl. Add the 1 cup granulated sugar, brown sugar, the tapioca, cinnamon, and lemon zest; toss gently until the peaches are coated. Combine the lemon juice and cornstarch; stir until the juice is cloudy and the cornstarch has dissolved. Stir in the vanilla, and toss with the peaches.

3. Preheat the oven to 400°. Heat half the melted butter in a Lodge 12-inch cast iron skillet over medium-low heat, add half the peaches, and toss gently just until bubbles start to form around the edge. Remove from the heat.

4. Roll out one of the pastry disks ⅜ inch thick on a lightly floured work surface. Using a 2-inch round pastry cutter (a fluted one is great if you have it), cut out the dumplings, rerolling and cutting the scraps as you go. Scatter 12 dumplings on top of the peaches in the skillet. Spread over the rest of the peaches.

5. Repeat cutting out dumplings, using the second pastry disk. Scatter 18 dumplings on top of the cobbler. Drizzle with the remaining butter, and sprinkle the dumplings with the remaining 2 tablespoons granulated sugar.

6. Bake the cobbler until the peaches are tender, the filling is bubbling, and the dumplings on the top are golden brown and crispy, about 45 minutes. The dumplings inside will be soft. Serve warm with the "pour" cream. If there is cobbler leftover, refrigerate in the skillet, and serve the next day. Warm the cobbler, uncovered, in a 350° oven until the peaches begin to bubble, about 15 minutes. Do not freeze this cobbler. **Makes 6 Texas-size servings**

MY SKILLET FULL OF MEMORIES

Beth Allen

Recipe developer and cookbook author, New York, New York

It was always there, right on the back corner burner on our family range in Houston, Texas. "It" was my grandmother's cast iron skillet, used daily on her potbelly stove in southern Texas, then given to Mom when she married "Pops" (my father). It was shiny black on the outside, though slightly rough from age, well seasoned on the inside, and always wiped clean. On Sundays right after church, Mom would move the skillet to the front center burner to cook her famous fried chicken—all battered, golden, crispy, and juicy, simply The Best I have ever eaten. On Fridays, she moved it to the front burner again to fry Gulf shrimp and oysters. On special company nights, chicken and shrimp gumbo simmered in the skillet; on Sunday mornings, ham steak and red-eye gravy. And any night of the week it could be fried greens, Pops' favorite okra and tomatoes, or creamy cheese grits. Often the skillet went into the oven to bake a batch of Mom's feathery cream biscuits.

On Thanksgiving, it was used to make her iron skillet cornbread for turkey stuffing. Other nights, the skillet came out of the oven almost bubbling over with double macaroni and cheese, and, on what I liked to think of as "my lucky nights," it was homemade peach cobbler with piecrust dumplings.

After I moved to New York and married, I returned home to my Texas homestead, always on Christmas and as often as possible throughout the year, first to visit Mom and Pops, then just Mom after my father passed. On a trip one summer, I walked into the kitchen and immediately noticed something was missing. The cast iron skillet was gone; I looked everywhere, but it was nowhere to be found. I went to hug Mom, then quietly asked her caregiver if she had seen the skillet. She had. Mom had asked her to put it in my closet for me to bring back to New York. That's when I knew: Mom wouldn't be with us much longer. But her smile, devotion to her family, Southern graciousness, heirloom recipes, and loving spirit live on. So do our cherished family memories— many wrapped around and inside that cast iron skillet. It never leaves my range now. And every time I fry some chicken, bake a cobbler, or make Mom's pull-apart biscuits, I know: It's not just a skillet, it's an important part of our family.

Food journalist and photographer Susan Benton, owner of 30AEATS.com, says, "Living on Route 30A in the Florida Panhandle in the summertime means beach picnics, sweet corn, an abundance of blueberries, and ripe, fresh tomatoes." This recipe for blueberry cobbler, like a good cast iron skillet, Susan says, "was handed down to me by my mother, who got it from her aunt, and so on. Everyone in my family seems to have this recipe tucked away for safekeeping!"

FLORIDA BLUEBERRY COBBLER

¼ cup (½ stick) unsalted butter, melted
1¼ cups sugar
1 cup self-rising flour
1 cup whole milk

2 cups fresh blueberries, picked over for stems, rinsed, and patted dry
Vanilla bean ice cream, for serving

1. Place the butter in a Lodge 10-inch cast iron skillet, and put in the oven while it preheats to 400°.

2. In a medium bowl, whisk 1 cup of the sugar with the flour and milk until smooth.

3. Remove the skillet from the oven, and swirl the butter to evenly coat the bottom and sides. Pour the batter into the skillet, and sprinkle the blueberries evenly over the top. Sprinkle over the remaining ¼ cup sugar.

4. Bake until golden brown and bubbly, 45 minutes to 1 hour. Serve warm, topped with a dollop of ice cream. **Serves 6**

Cast Iron Memories

From making fried chicken and cornbread to my grandmother's pineapple upside-down cake, a Lodge cast iron skillet is versatile in so many ways. As interest continues to grow nationwide in all things Southern food, there is a natural curiosity about the heritage of the humble cast iron skillet and the family memories it can collect over decades. I'm thankful for my prized heirloom skillets passed down by generations before me, and enjoy collecting new pieces as Lodge cast iron continues to evolve and reinvent.

—*Susan Benton*

DESSERTS

GLUTEN-FREE RHUBARB-MILLET CRISP

There's no reason to miss warm fruit desserts when you have to give up gluten. In fact, here's a little-known secret from Shauna Ahern, the Gluten-Free Girl: You don't need gluten for most baked goods. Use a whole-grain flour like millet, with its slightly nutty taste, with rhubarb and orange, baked to bubbly brown in your favorite cast iron skillet. You can find orange blossom water, coconut sugar, and millet at most natural foods stores, gourmet markets, or online.

4 cups trimmed fresh rhubarb stalks, cut into 1-inch pieces
1 cup granulated sugar
Grated zest and juice of 2 large oranges
¼ teaspoon orange blossom water
½ cup millet flour

½ cup certified gluten-free oats (use quinoa flakes if you cannot tolerate oats)
⅓ cup coconut sugar (see kitchen note)
½ teaspoon kosher salt
½ cup (1 stick) cold unsalted butter, cut into 1-inch pieces

1. Preheat the oven to 375°.

2. In a large bowl, toss the rhubarb, granulated sugar, orange zest and juice, and orange blossom water together until well combined. Pour the mixture into a Lodge 9-inch cast iron skillet.

3. In a medium bowl, combine the millet flour, oats, coconut sugar, and salt. Whisk to aerate the mixture. Add the cold butter, and use your fingertips to rub it into the flour, breaking the butter down into lima bean-sized pieces. Crumble this topping over the rhubarb, covering it completely.

4. Bake until the fruit is bubbling hot and the crisp topping is golden brown, about 1 hour. **Serves 6**

kitchen note:

If you can't locate coconut sugar, substitute firmly packed brown sugar.

how Shauna makes a crisp

1. Before incorporating the dry ingredients with the butter, mix them together well.

2. Gently rub the butter into the dry ingredients mixture with your fingertips so that small lima bean-sized pieces are formed. Be sure to start with cold butter right from the fridge so that the topping won't become overmixed.

3. With your hands, sprinkle the topping over the rhubarb mixture in the skillet, making sure the fruit mixture is completely covered.

ortia Belloc Lowndes, director of Project FEAST, Inc. (a special events company specializing in food events), co-founder of Slow Food Chicago, and executive board member of Chicago Green City Market, prepares this recipe for her family at their century-old cabin in the northern woods of Wisconsin for Thanksgiving. She loves making it with her young daughters, as they can take part in many of the tasks, from ripping up the bread to breaking the eggs.

SKILLET PUMPKIN BREAD PUDDING WITH MAPLE PRALINE SAUCE

Pumpkin Bread Pudding:
- 1 cup heavy cream
- ½ cup whole milk
- ½ cup apple juice
- 6 cups torn-up French bread (about 1 loaf)
- 2 tablespoons unsalted butter, softened
- 4 large eggs
- 1 cup firmly packed light brown sugar
- 1 (15-ounce) can pumpkin puree
- ¼ cup honey
- 1 teaspoon ground cinnamon
- 1 teaspoon ground ginger
- ½ teaspoon ground nutmeg
- 2 teaspoons vanilla extract
- 1 cup raisins or sweetened dried cranberries
- ½ cup chopped pecans

Maple Praline Sauce:
- ¾ cup pure maple syrup
- ¼ cup firmly packed light brown sugar
- ¼ teaspoon salt
- ½ cup heavy cream
- ½ cup chopped pecans
- ¼ cup (½ stick) unsalted butter, cut into tablespoons

1. Make the bread pudding: In a measuring cup, combine the cream, milk, and apple juice. Put the torn-up bread in a large bowl, and pour the cream mixture over it. Let soak for about 30 minutes, stirring occasionally.

2. Preheat the oven to 375°. Butter the bottom and sides of a Lodge 12-inch cast iron skillet with the softened butter. In a medium bowl, whisk the eggs, brown sugar, pumpkin, honey, spices, and vanilla together, then stir in the raisins and pecans. Pour the pumpkin mixture over the soaked bread, and stir to blend. Pour the mixture into the prepared skillet, and bake until set, 45 to 60 minutes.

3. While the bread pudding bakes, make the Maple Praline Sauce: In a heavy, medium saucepan, combine the maple syrup, brown sugar, salt, and cream, and cook over low heat, stirring until the sugar dissolves. Raise the heat to high, and bring to a boil. Let boil until the mixture thickens and reaches 220° on a candy thermometer, stirring constantly. Stir in the pecans and butter until the butter is fully incorporated. Remove from the heat. You can use this sauce warm or cold. It will keep, tightly covered, in the refrigerator up to 1 week.

4. Serve the bread pudding drizzled with Maple Praline Sauce. **Serves 8**

WHITE CHOCOLATE STRAWBERRY BISCUIT PUDDING

David Cunningham, executive chef of restaurant V Seagrove on County Highway 30A in Seagrove Beach, Florida, prepares and serves many dishes using Lodge cast iron.

Comfortable elegance is the theme at V Seagrove, and David says, "Lodge cast iron has a rustic charm that patrons identify with." His Strawberry Biscuit Pudding, prepared with fruit from Akers of Strawberries in nearby Baker, Florida, is a twist on an old Southern favorite.

Strawberry coulis:
30 ounces fresh strawberries, hulled and pureed until smooth
1½ cups sugar
½ cup honey
5 tablespoons cornstarch
5 tablespoons water
Biscuits:
1 cup all-purpose flour
1 tablespoon sugar
1 teaspoon baking powder
⅓ teaspoon salt
⅓ cup unsalted butter
⅓ cup buttermilk, or as needed

White chocolate pudding custard:
2½ cups heavy cream
1¼ cups whole milk
1 cup sugar
12 ounces white chocolate
6 large eggs
White chocolate bourbon sauce:
1 quart heavy cream
26 ounces white chocolate
1 cup bourbon
To assemble:
2 cups sliced fresh strawberries
Sugar

1. Make the strawberry coulis: Combine the strawberry puree, sugar, and honey in a medium, heavy saucepan over medium heat, and bring to a simmer. In a small bowl, make a slurry with the cornstarch and water, then whisk this into the strawberry mixture. Return to simmer briefly, then remove from the heat. Strain through a fine mesh strainer, and let cool to serve; discard solids. This can be prepared a day ahead; refrigerate, tightly covered.

2. Make the biscuits: Preheat the oven to 350°. In a medium bowl, sift the flour, sugar, baking powder, and salt together. Cut the butter into dime-size pieces, and gently mix with the dry ingredients, being careful not to break the butter up too much. Form a well in the center of the mixture, and add the buttermilk. Lightly mix it into the flour mixture. You should end up with a sticky dough; if it's dry, add a little more buttermilk.

3. Place the dough on a lightly floured work surface, and flatten it to a 1½-inch thickness. Cut biscuits out with a 3-inch round cutter, and set in a pie tin so they are close but not touching each other. Bake until lightly golden, 12 to 15 minutes. Remove from the oven, and set aside, up to 2 hours before serving.

4. Make the white chocolate pudding custard: Heat the cream, milk, and sugar together in a large, heavy saucepan over medium heat, stirring until hot but not steaming and the sugar dissolves. Remove from the heat, add the chocolate, and stir until melted and smooth.

5. In a large bowl, whisk the eggs until smooth. Add a generous ladleful of the hot cream mixture to the eggs in slow, steady stream, whisking constantly. Slowly add that mixture to the rest of the hot cream mixture, whisking constantly until smooth. Keep warm.

6. Make the white chocolate bourbon sauce: Heat the cream in a medium, heavy saucepan over medium heat until hot but not steaming. Remove from the heat, add the chocolate, and stir until melted and smooth. Let cool to room temperature. Whisk in the bourbon.

7. Assemble the pudding: Preheat the oven to 375°. Butter six Lodge 12-ounce cast iron round mini servers. Crumble the biscuits into large pieces, and use them to cover the bottoms of the servers by 1 inch. Ladle ¼ cup of the custard over the top of each, covering the crumbled biscuits. Arrange sliced strawberries in a single layer to cover the biscuit crumbles. Ladle another ¼ cup of custard over the strawberries. Add another layer of biscuit crumbles to almost fill the servers. Ladle a final ¼ cup custard over each, and sprinkle with sugar.

8. Cover the servers with aluminum foil, and bake for 35 minutes. Remove the foil, and bake until the pudding has a golden brown color and is firm to the touch, about another 20 minutes. If a toothpick is inserted in the pudding and comes out clean, it is done. Serve warm with the White Chocolate Bourbon Sauce and Strawberry Coulis offered on the side in small pitchers. **Serves 6**

THE GREATEST INHERITANCE

Rebecca Lang

Cookbook author and cooking instructor, Athens, Georgia

Some women inherit land, some grand diamonds, others are left with nothing more than memories. Along with a lifetime's worth of recollections of tastes and aromas in the kitchen, I inherited my grandmother Tom's prized cast iron skillet. It's well over 100 years old, yet it finds a modern home on my stainless steel stove on most days.

Skillets fall into the same category as fine china, heavy sterling silver, and family linens. They are made to pass down from generation to generation. Respecting the skillet is quintessentially honoring the previous generation. Tom cooked for so many years in this pan; it's pitch-black in color and as shiny as polished granite.

I watched Tom cook her fried chicken perfectly, complete with a browned "kiss" from the skillet after the first turn of the meat. Of all the things I remember about her kitchen, where the tools were kept and Southern staples stored, I can't recall the skillet ever being

put away. It was on the stove and in the oven so much, I don't think that it ever needed a designated spot in the cabinet. It was this skillet filled with fried chicken that first taught me how comfort and love could be tasted and shared without saying a word.

On days that I miss her, which is more often than not, I simply have to wrap my fingers around the handle of her skillet and I instantly feel she's not far away. It's amazing how iron mined from far beneath the ground has bridged a gap between the lives of two cooks who loved each other dearly. I know she loved her cast iron pan, and she knew I loved her. Tom was completely at ease with it on the stove heated to crazy-high temps with hot grease sizzling away. She could turn out a batch of cornbread in it with her eyes closed. She was a woman who was comfortable in the kitchen, a master of her skillet, and she was mine.

CAST IRON NATION

Rebecca's grandparents on their first Thanksgiving after being married

Rebecca Lang uses any excuse to serve dessert at her table. She loves that with these little skillets, there's no need to share. Her warm and rich chocolate creations are as comforting as they are dreamy.

GOOEY CHOCOLATE SKILLETS

1 (9-ounce) package chocolate wafers (such as Nabisco Famous Chocolate Wafers)	¾ cup sugar
	⅓ cup all-purpose flour
	1½ teaspoons vanilla extract
¾ cup (1½ sticks) unsalted butter	2 large eggs, beaten
¾ cup bittersweet chocolate chips (60% cacao)	Vanilla ice cream, for serving

1. Preheat the oven to 325°.

2. Process the wafers in a food processor fitted with the metal blade until crushed, or seal them in a zip-top plastic bag, and crush with a rolling pin. Melt ¼ cup (½ stick) of the butter in a medium saucepan. Add to the wafers; pulse to combine, or work into the crumbs with your fingertips. Press the wafer mixture into the bottom of six Lodge 5-inch cast iron skillets.

3. Melt the remaining ½ cup (1 stick) butter and chocolate chips together in the same saucepan over low heat. Remove from the heat, and whisk in the sugar, flour, and vanilla. While whisking, add the eggs, and beat well. Divide the mixture evenly between the prepared skillets. Bake for 18 minutes (they will not look set at this point). The centers will be slightly gooey. Do not over-bake.

4. Serve each lucky guest their own chocolate skillet, topped with a scoop of vanilla ice cream. **Serves 6**

a cooking secret from Rebecca

This simple fudgy dessert gets its rich, intense chocolate flavor from bittersweet chocolate chips, so it's important to use high-quality chocolate—one with at least 60% cacao.

GRANDMOTHER'S APPLE CAKE

San Francisco-based pastry chef Emily Luchetti collects cast iron pans to cook in her wood-fired oven, including many vintage pieces. Says Emily, "It's the one antique you can use and not worry about breaking!"

This recipe comes from her father-in-law's grandmother, who made it for him over 75 years ago. Baking the cake in a cast iron pan gives it a delicious brown bottom, but be careful not to overcook it or it will be dry. The cake is best warm, but it can be made a day in advance; wrap in plastic wrap, and store at room temperature. Reheat in a 350° oven for 5 minutes.

9   tablespoons sugar
1   cup all-purpose flour
½   teaspoon salt
1   teaspoon baking powder
1   large egg
2   tablespoons milk
1   teaspoon vanilla extract
¼   cup (½ stick) unsalted butter, softened
3   medium Golden Delicious apples
½   teaspoon ground cinnamon
Chantilly Cream (recipe follows)

1. Preheat the oven to 400°. Coat the bottom of a Lodge 10-inch cast iron skillet with cooking spray. Sprinkle 2 tablespoons of the sugar over the bottom of the pan.

2. In a small bowl, sift the flour, salt, and baking powder together. In another small bowl, whisk the egg, milk, and vanilla together.

3. In a large bowl, cream the butter and 4 tablespoons of the sugar together until light, about 1 minute with a stand mixer or 2 minutes with a handheld mixer. By hand, stir in one third of the flour mixture and then one third of the milk mixture just until mixed. Add the remaining flour and milk mixtures in two more additions. Spread the batter in the prepared skillet. It will be thick and a little sticky. If difficult to spread, wet the back of a spoon or your fingertips to push the batter out to the edge.

4. Peel and core the apples. Cut them into slices ⅛ inch thick. Starting from the outer edge of the cake, arrange the slices in concentric circles, slightly overlapping, over the top of the batter, completely covering it. In a small bowl, mix the remaining 3 tablespoons sugar with the cinnamon, and sprinkle it over the apples.

5. Bake until a skewer inserted in the middle just comes out clean, 20 to 25 minutes. Do not overcook or the cake will be dry. Let cool on a wire rack for 10 minutes. Loosen the edge and bottom of the cake from the pan using a large metal spatula. Place a large plate on top of the cake. Invert the pan and plate together, then remove the pan. Place another plate on top of the cake, and invert it again so it is right side up. Serve with Chantilly Cream. **Serves 8**

CHANTILLY CREAM

1   cup heavy (whipping) cream
3   tablespoons sugar
½   teaspoon vanilla extract

1. Combine all the ingredients in a medium bowl, and beat with an electric mixer on medium-high speed until soft peaks form. Refrigerate until you are ready to use. This can be made a couple of hours in advance. It may thin out, especially near the bottom. If it does, whisk briefly to thicken. **Makes 2 cups**

FRESH PEACH UPSIDE-DOWN CAKE

2 cups small-diced peeled ripe peaches
½ cup firmly packed light brown sugar
2 tablespoons salted butter, melted
1 cup plus 1 tablespoon bleached all-purpose flour
½ cup (1 stick) salted butter, softened

½ cup vegetable oil
1 cup granulated sugar
3 large eggs
½ cup masa flour
1 teaspoon salt
1 teaspoon baking powder
½ cup whole milk
1 teaspoon vanilla extract

1. Preheat the oven to 350°. Coat a Lodge 9-inch cast iron skillet with cooking spray.

2. In a medium bowl, combine the peaches, brown sugar, melted butter, and 1 tablespoon flour.

3. In a medium bowl, beat the softened butter, oil, and granulated sugar together with an electric mixer fitted with a whisk attachment on medium speed until light and fluffy. Add the eggs, one at a time, beating well after each addition.

4. In a small bowl, sift the remaining 1 cup all-purpose flour, the masa flour, salt, and baking powder together three times. Alternating with the milk, add it to the batter, beating with the mixer until smooth. Use a rubber spatula to scrape any batter down from the side of the bowl. Add the vanilla, and mix until smooth.

5. Spoon the peaches evenly over the bottom of the pan; pour the batter over the fruit. Place the skillet on the middle rack of the oven, and bake until the center of the cake springs back when touched or a toothpick inserted in the center comes out clean, 30 to 35 minutes.

6. Remove the skillet from the oven, and let cool on a wire rack for 10 minutes. Invert the cake onto a serving platter, and cut into wedges to serve.

Serves 8

This upside-down recipe is the go-to cake for Felicia Willett, chef-owner of Felicia Suzanne's in downtown Memphis. "I love that this cake can be on your counter all year long, made with whatever fruit is in season and looks the best, like peaches, blackberries, and blueberries. Baking this in a cast iron pan is perfect too," says Felicia. "The heat from the pan caramelizes the fruit, creating an amazing Southern dessert."

a cooking secret from Felicia

You can find masa (corn flour) at most Hispanic markets, but if it's unavailable, increase the amount of all-purpose flour to 1½ cups.

Cast Iron Memories

Living on a tight budget during my university days in Australia, all I could afford was a cast iron pan I found for sale in a camping shop. It was badly rusted and obviously neglected for years.

Not wanting to set off smoke alarms seasoning the pan, I sat in the car park under a hot Australian summer sun. With a portable stove, pork fat, and leeks, I seasoned the pan like the Cantonese do their woks.

The first time I used it after the seasoning was done, it browned a prime aged steak beautifully, and I was hooked. There is no sweeter symphony of sizzles than that of meat hitting searing hot cast iron. It was a revelation.

That trusty cast iron pan fed many friends in the following two years, frying and sautéing up many a memorable meal. Brushed down with only hot water and a bamboo wok brush, the older the pan got, the tastier the food cooked in it!

I gifted that pan to my house-mate when I graduated so that it could continue to give pleasure to impoverished students. My seren-dipitous encounter with cast iron changed the way I cook, and I've been in love with it ever since.

—*Nick Lam*

This recipe comes from Nick Lam, a pâtissier-chocolatier from Singapore and New York cooking teacher. Halfway between a pound cake and chiffon cake, the recipe for this kasutera (Japanese sponge cake) spread around the globe during the Age of Discovery. Originating in Portugal and perfected by the Japanese, it can be found today in Hawai'i, where Portuguese and Japanese influences are strong. Feel free to substitute ground-up Earl Grey, Ceylon, or any other tea of your fancy for the maccha (green tea powder).

HONEY-MACCHA KASUTERA TEA CAKE

1 tablespoon maccha (green tea powder) or any other powdered tea of choice
1 cup plus 1 tablespoon unbleached bread flour
½ teaspoon baking powder
1 cup plus 1¼ tablespoons eggs (around 5½ large eggs)

⅔ cup sugar
2½ tablespoons whole milk
3 tablespoons honey, preferably sourwood honey
2 tablespoons light corn syrup
Pinch of salt

1. Preheat the oven to 325°. Line a Lodge 10 x 5 x 3-inch cast iron loaf pan with parchment paper. Do this by cutting a strip that will line the bottom and run up the two narrow ends of the pan, and another strip that will cover the bottom and run up the two longer sides of the pan.

2. In a small bowl, combine the green tea powder, flour, and baking powder. Sift it three times to ensure all the particles are evenly dispersed.

3. Place the eggs and sugar in a large metal bowl set over barely simmering water in a large saucepan. Whisk continuously until the mixture reaches 140° on an instant-read thermometer or is slightly hot to the touch. (This stabilizes the mixture for the whisking phase.) Remove the bowl from the saucepan, and, using an electric mixer fitted with the whisk attachment, whisk on medium-high speed until the mixture is ribboned, 12 to 15 minutes. (To test for the ribbon stage, drip some of the mixture in a figure 8 onto the surface of the rest of the mixture. It should hold its shape for at least 10 seconds before sinking. If it sinks prematurely, continue to whisk, checking it every 2 minutes. Reaching this stage is important for the success of the cake.)

4. In a small microwave-safe bowl, combine the milk, honey, corn syrup, and salt, and heat it in a microwave until it is warm and runny but not hot. Drizzle the milk mixture into the ribboned eggs with the mixer on medium speed, and beat just until combined. Fold in the flour mixture, adding it in three additions, folding each time until it is just mixed and no flour is visible.

5. Pour the batter into the prepared loaf pan. Run a rubber spatula across the top of the batter to break any large air bubbles. Place the pan on the middle rack of the oven. After 4 minutes, remove it from the oven, and run the spatula

once in a zigzag motion along the length of the pan, agitating the mixture to remove any large air bubbles. Return to the oven, and bake until the top starts to brown, about 12 minutes.

6. Place a sheet of parchment paper on top of the cake, and set a baking sheet on top of the pan. This will serve as a lid to flatten the top of the cake and let it brown evenly. Continue to bake until a cake tester inserted in the center comes out clean, another 30 to 35 minutes.

7. Remove the pan from the oven, and remove the parchment. Cover the loaf pan with a fresh sheet of parchment, and cover again with the baking sheet. Invert the loaf pan and baking sheet. Remove the loaf pan, and let the cake sit upside down on the baking sheet until it cools down just enough that you can handle it. Wrap tightly with plastic wrap to lock in the moisture, and refrigerate for 12 hours before serving in slices. **Makes one loaf cake; serves 8 to 10**

PEAR TARTE TATIN

1 cup all-purpose flour
½ teaspoon fine sea salt
2 tablespoons sugar
6 tablespoons (¾ stick) unsalted
  butter
2 to 4 tablespoons ice cold water

4 small pears, or more as needed
Juice from 1 lemon
1¼ cups sugar
¼ cup water
2 tablespoons unsalted butter

1. Make the piecrust: In a bowl, combine the flour, salt, and sugar, using a wire whisk to blend well. Cut the butter into ¼-inch cubes. Using a pastry cutter, cut the butter cubes into the flour until the lumps are the size of peas. Add the ice water, 1 tablespoon at a time, and toss with a fork. Pinch a bit of the mixture between your fingers; if it holds together, you have added enough liquid.

2. Pour the mixture onto a lightly floured work surface. Cuddle the mixture into a ball by holding your hands on the counter and pressing the outside of the ball. You don't want to overhandle the dough. Using your hands, flatten the ball along the sides to push it into a square shape. (It will crumble and that is okay.) Using a pastry or regular knife, cut the dough into thirds, and stack the thirds in a tower. Press to flatten, then cut and stack 5 more times. The last time, flatten and round the dough by cuddling your hands around the edges. Wrap the dough tightly in plastic wrap, and refrigerate while you prepare the filling, or make ahead and chill overnight.

3. Preheat the oven to 425°. Peel the pears, then cut in half lengthwise. Remove the cores using a melon ball scoop. Place on a sheet pan or in a large flat bowl in a single layer. Sprinkle with the lemon juice and ¼ cup of the sugar.

4. In a Lodge 9-inch cast iron skillet, combine the remaining 1 cup sugar and the water. Bring to a boil. Reduce the heat to medium-low, and simmer, stirring occasionally to be sure all the sugar dissolves. Cook until the sugar turns a rich brown caramel color, 6 to 8 minutes. Use a spoon to check the color, since, in the dark pan, it will be difficult to see. Remove from the heat; stir in the butter until it is incorporated into the caramel. Let cool for 5 minutes.

5. Remove the pears from the pan or bowl, leaving the liquid behind; reserve the liquid. Cut the pears lengthwise into ½-inch-thick slices almost, but not quite through, the stem end. Arrange the pears on top of the caramel, cut side up, in a fan around the edge of the pan and along the center of the pan.

6. Remove the dough from the refrigerator, and place on a lightly floured work surface. With a floured rolling pin, roll the dough out to a 10-inch round. Place over the pears, tucking the dough in along the side of the pan. Prick several times with a fork. Bake on the middle rack of the oven until the crust is golden brown, 25 to 30 minutes. Let cool 10 minutes. Carefully tilt the skillet, and use a baster to drain the liquid into a saucepan. Add the reserved liquid from the raw pears to the saucepan. Bring to a boil, and reduce to make a thickened caramel sauce that will coat the back of a spoon.

7. Invert a plate over the skillet, and turn the plate and skillet over together quickly and carefully. Drizzle the top with the thickened caramel sauce.

Makes one 9-inch tarte tatin; serves 6

lassic tarte tatin is made using apples, but for an elegant and delicious alternative, Belinda Ellis, editor of *Edible Piedmont* magazine, likes to prepare it using fresh pears. "Making a tarte tatin is easier than making a pie," counsels Belinda. "There's no soggy crust to worry about because it's baked on top. The only scary part is turning it onto the plate, but when you do, the results are simply beautiful." Be sure to use ripe Green Anjou or Bosc pears.

HOW TO COOK IN A CAMP DUTCH OVEN

A Camp Dutch oven is specifically designed for outdoor cooking. It has three stubby legs that lift it off the ground just enough so that hot coals can be set underneath it, as well as a flat, flanged lid so coals can be set on top of it with no worry that they will roll off. You can choose between shallow and deep Dutch ovens; they range in size from 8 to 16 inches in diameter. The shallow Dutch ovens are also known as "bread ovens," as they are the preferred pot when cooking bread or biscuits. The deeper Dutch ovens are perfect for chili, stews, and meat dishes of all sorts.

Camp Cooking 101

1. Prepare your cooking area. You want to choose a site with as much wind shelter as possible. If need be, build up a windbreak around where you will set your pot, using patio stones, brick, or concrete block. If you are using a Camp Dutch oven in your backyard, be sure to clear the cooking area of twigs and other flammable materials. You may also want to lay out an area of brick to use for your fire site.

2. Determine how many briquettes you'll need for the temperature you want and get them going in a chimney starter. (See chart below or your recipe.)

3. Place the hot coals. Draw an outline of the bottom of your Dutch oven where it will be cooking. Using the chart (or your recipe) as your guide, place the appropriate number of bottom briquettes in a checkerboard fashion within that outline. Set the oven over those coals. Then place the top coals in a checkerboard fashion on the lid of the oven.

4. Rotate your oven. To maintain an even oven temperature and prevent hot spots, lift and rotate the oven a quarter turn every 15 minutes. Then rotate the lid a quarter turn in the opposite direction. You'll find that a pair of welding gloves and a lid lifter are necessities for camp cooking.

baking in your Dutch oven

Oven Size	Briquettes	325°	350°	375°	400°	425°	450°
8"	Total briquettes	15	16	17	18	19	20
	Top/bottom	10/5	11/5	11/6	12/6	13/6	14/6
10"	Total briquettes	19	21	23	25	27	29
	Top/bottom	13/6	14/7	16/7	17/8	18/9	19/10
12"	Total briquettes	23	25	27	29	31	33
	Top/bottom	16/7	17/8	18/9	19/10	21/10	22/11
14"	Total briquettes	30	32	34	36	38	40
	Top/bottom	20/10	21/11	22/12	24/12	25/13	26/14
16"	Total briquettes	37	39	41	43	45	47
	Top/bottom	25/12	26/13	27/14	28/15	29/16	30/17

Dutch Oven Diva Lesley Tennessen was inspired to make this pie when she was given a bottle of rum-infused maple syrup from Burton's Maplewood Farm in Medora, Indiana. It ended up being a winner at an Iowa Dutch oven competition.

MAPLE COCONUT OATMEAL PIE

1 cup sweetened flaked coconut
¾ cup old-fashioned rolled oats
½ cup granulated sugar
½ cup firmly packed brown sugar
½ cup (1 stick) unsalted butter, melted

¾ cup pure maple syrup (the real stuff, and preferably rum-infused)
2 large eggs, beaten
¾ cup whole or 2% milk
1 (10-inch) piecrust (recipe follows)

1. In a large bowl, mix the coconut, oats, both sugars, melted butter, maple syrup, eggs, and milk together. Pour the filling into the piecrust in the Dutch oven. Put the lid on the oven. Set the Dutch oven on 8 coals, and set 17 coals on the lid (see "How to Cook in a Camp Dutch Oven," opposite). Bake for 15 minutes.

2. Reduce the interior temperature by removing 3 coals from the lid. Continue to bake until the center is just set, 30 to 40 minutes.

3. If you used parchment strips and a disk, let the pie cool for 10 to 15 minutes before holding the strips and lifting the pie onto a serving dish. Or, let the pie cool completely in the Dutch oven before slicing. **Makes one 9-inch pie**

PIECRUST

3 cups all-purpose flour
1 teaspoon salt
1 teaspoon sugar

1 cup vegetable shortening
1 large egg
Milk as needed

1. In a large bowl, sift the dry ingredients together. Add the shortening, and cut in with a pastry blender until the pieces are about the size of peas. Place the egg in a measuring cup, beat with a fork, then add enough milk to make ½ cup, and stir to mix. Slowly add to the flour mixture. Stir with a fork until thoroughly mixed and the dough holds together. Roll the dough into a ball, and cover with plastic wrap. Chill for 30 minutes.

2. Roll the ball out between 2 well-floured pieces of parchment paper into a 12-inch circle. Line a Lodge 10-inch cast iron Camp Dutch oven with two strips of parchment paper placed in an X and a parchment paper circle cut to fit the bottom of the oven. Transfer the piecrust to the Dutch oven, and smooth the dough over the bottom and about 2 inches up the side of the oven. Crimp the edge of the dough by pinching it between your thumb and index finger. Chill until ready to pour in the filling. **Makes one 9-inch piecrust**

APPLE-CRANBERRY PIE

This is from the recipe box of Bill Ryan, founder of the Louisiana Dutch Oven Society. This recipe won Bill his third Louisiana State Dutch Oven Cook-off in 2011.

8 ounces all-purpose flour (about 1½ cups plus 2 tablespoons)
1 tablespoon sugar
½ teaspoon salt
½ cup (1 stick) cold butter, cut into ¼-inch pieces
2 tablespoons vegetable shortening
2 tablespoons ice water, plus more as needed

2 cups fresh or frozen cranberries, picked over for stems
1½ cups sugar
4 tablespoons cornstarch
2 tablespoons water
5 cups cored, peeled, and sliced Granny Smith apples (5 medium)
½ teaspoon ground cinnamon
¼ teaspoon ground nutmeg

1. In a large bowl, sift the flour, sugar, and salt together. Using your fingertips, work the butter and shortening into the flour until the mixture resembles coarse crumbs. Add the ice water, and work it in with your fingertips until incorporated and the dough comes together. Add 1 tablespoon of water at a time as needed to make a smooth dough, being careful not to overwork it. Form the dough into a disk, wrap in plastic, and refrigerate for at least 30 minutes.

2. Combine the cranberries, 1 cup of the sugar, 1 tablespoon of the cornstarch, and the water in a medium, heavy saucepan. Bring to a boil over high heat, boil for 5 minutes, remove from the heat, and let cool 15 minutes.

3. In a large bowl, combine the apples, the remaining ½ cup sugar and 3 tablespoons cornstarch, the cinnamon, and nutmeg, tossing until the apples are well coated. Stir in the cranberry mixture.

4. Take a piece of parchment paper, and cut out a circle that will fit into the bottom of a Lodge 10-inch cast iron Camp Dutch oven. Cut five strips of parchment paper 1½ inches wide. Position them so they all cross in the center of the bottom of the Dutch oven and run up the side of the oven all around. You can fasten them in place using clothespins. Fit the parchment circle in the bottom of the oven on top of the strips. Spray the inside of the oven with cooking spray.

5. Divide the dough in half. On a lightly floured work surface, roll out one half to fit the bottom and go 1½ to 2 inches up the side of the Dutch oven.

6. Spoon the filling into the crust. Roll out the other half of the dough so it is large enough to generously cover the top of the pie in the Dutch oven. Trim the crusts, then crimp the top and bottom crusts together to seal. Cut four 1-inch slits through the top crust to vent the pie while cooking. Put the lid on the Dutch oven. Set the oven on 9 coals, and set 18 coals on top of the lid (see "How to Cook in a Camp Dutch Oven," page 278). Bake until the crust is golden brown, 40 to 50 minutes. If the edges start to brown too much, cover them with aluminum foil. When the pie is done, remove the lid and coals, and remove the pot from the coals. Let the pie cool for about 10 minutes, then, with assistance, grab the parchment strips, and lift the pie out of the oven onto a serving plate. Let the pie completely cool before slicing. **Makes one 9-inch pie**

Nothing says spring better than fresh strawberries. Campfire cooking expert Johnny Nix says, "Add a few strawberries to this moist bread, and you've got a perfect dessert or anytime coffee cake."

FRESH HOMEMADE STRAWBERRY BREAD

2 cups sugar
2 pints fresh strawberries, hulled and chopped
3 cups bleached all-purpose flour
2 teaspoons ground cinnamon

1 teaspoon baking soda
1 teaspoon salt
4 large eggs, beaten
¼ cup vegetable oil
1 cup chopped pecans

1. In a medium bowl, sprinkle 1 cup of the sugar over the chopped berries, stir to mix, and let stand until juice forms, about 45 minutes.

2. In a large bowl, combine the flour, cinnamon, baking soda, salt, and remaining 1 cup sugar. Add the strawberries, eggs, and oil, and stir just until the dry ingredients are evenly moistened. Gently stir in the pecans.

3. Pour the batter into a well-greased Lodge 12-inch cast iron camp Dutch oven, and cover. Set the Dutch oven on 8 coals, and set 17 coals on the lid (see "How to Cook in a Camp Dutch Oven," page 278). Bake until a knife inserted in the center comes out clean, about 1 hour and 20 minutes, replenishing coals as needed. Remove the pot from the coals, uncover, and let cool before slicing. **Serves 8 to 10**

a cooking secret from Johnny

Cooking bread in a Dutch oven with the lid on prevents moisture from escaping and delivers a moist and tender texture. When cooking, remember to watch for hotspots in your campfire and rotate your oven by a quarter or half turn to prevent portions of the bread from becoming overly browned.

CARING FOR CAST IRON

All of the cast iron that Lodge sells (not including their enameled line, of course) is preseasoned at the foundry, using vegetable oil. As a result, seasoning the pan, the traditional first step in cast iron cookware ownership, is now not necessary. But your preseasoned cookware still benefits from correct care. Here's what to do:

1. Rinse your cast iron cookware with hot water. If there is any stuck-on food, use a stiff brush to remove it. Do not use soap, as any type of detergent will break down the oil-based seasoning.

2. After rinsing, dry the cookware immediately inside and out. If water remains on the surface, rusting can occur, even with a seasoned piece.

3. While the piece is still warm from being washed, use cooking spray or a paper towel soaked with melted vegetable shortening to give the interior and exterior surfaces of the pan (including the underside of the lid if the piece has one) a light coating of oil.

4. Store in a cool, dry place. If the piece has a lid, folded paper towels should be placed between the lid and pot to allow air to circulate.

WHEN YOU NEED TO RE-SEASON A PAN

It happens sometimes—a friend helpfully puts your cast iron skillet in the dishwasher without your knowing it or takes a steel scrubbing pad to it, stripping the seasoning from its surface. Or you inherit or acquire an older piece of cast iron that needs refurbishing. Here's how to do it:

1. Preheat the oven to 350°. If you have three racks in the oven, remove one and move the others so they are in the two lowest positions.

2. Prepare the piece for re-seasoning by washing it in hot, soapy water, using a stiff brush to remove any stuck-on food. If the pan has surface rust, remove it using fine steel wool or an abrasive soap pad such as Brillo® or S.O.S.® (If a piece is severely rusted, you'll need to take it to a local machine shop to have it sandblasted. It will then need to be re-seasoned IMMEDIATELY.) Rinse and towel-dry the pan immediately and thoroughly.

3. Coat the piece with oil as instructed in step 3 above, making sure to also include the handle.

4. Place a large sheet of aluminum foil on the lowest oven rack. Set the pan upside down on the rack above it. Bake for 1 hour.

5. If the piece has a lid, set it beside the pan. Close the oven door, turn off the oven, and leave until the pieces cool off. Store as directed above.

METRIC EQUIVALENTS

The information in the following charts is provided to help cooks outside the United States successfully use the recipes in this book. All equivalents are approximate.

Equivalents for Different Types of Ingredients

Standard Cup	Fine Powder (ex. flour)	Grain (ex. rice)	Granular (ex. sugar)	Liquid Solids (ex. butter)	Liquid (ex. milk)
1	140 g	150 g	190 g	200 g	240 ml
¾	105 g	113 g	143 g	150 g	180 ml
⅔	93 g	100 g	125 g	133 g	160 ml
½	70 g	75 g	95 g	100 g	120 ml
⅓	47 g	50 g	63 g	67 g	80 ml
¼	35 g	38 g	48 g	50 g	60 ml
⅛	18 g	19 g	24 g	25 g	30 ml

Liquid Ingredients by Volume

¼ tsp =				1 ml
½ tsp =				2 ml
1 tsp =				5 ml
3 tsp =	1 Tbsp =		½ fl oz =	15 ml
	2 Tbsp =	⅛ cup =	1 fl oz =	30 ml
	4 Tbsp =	¼ cup =	2 fl oz =	60 ml
	5⅓ Tbsp =	⅓ cup =	3 fl oz =	80 ml
	8 Tbsp =	½ cup =	4 fl oz =	120 ml
	10⅔ Tbsp =	⅔ cup =	5 fl oz =	160 ml
	12 Tbsp =	¾ cup =	6 fl oz =	180 ml
	16 Tbsp =	1 cup =	8 fl oz =	240 ml
	1 pt =	2 cups =	16 fl oz =	480 ml
	1 qt =	4 cups =	32 fl oz =	960 ml
			33 fl oz =	1000 ml = 1 l

Dry Ingredients by Weight

(To convert ounces to grams, multiply the number of ounces by 30.)

1 oz	=	1/16 lb	=	30 g
4 oz	=	¼ lb	=	120 g
8 oz	=	½ lb	=	240 g
12 oz	=	¾ lb	=	360 g
16 oz	=	1 lb	=	480 g

Length

(To convert inches to centimeters, multiply the number of inches by 2.5.)

1 in			=	2.5 cm		
6 in =	½ ft	=		15 cm		
12 in =	1 ft	=		30 cm		
36 in =	3 ft	=	1 yd	=	90 cm	
40 in			=	100 cm	=	1 m

Cooking/Oven Temperatures

	Fahrenheit	Celsius	Gas Mark
Freeze Water	32° F	0° C	
Room Temperature	68° F	20° C	
Boil Water	212° F	100° C	
Bake	325° F	160° C	3
	350° F	180° C	4
	375° F	190° C	5
	400° F	200° C	6
	425° F	220° C	7
	450° F	230° C	8
Broil			Grill

INDEX

INDEX

INDEX

©2014, 2018 by Lodge Manufacturing Company

Images ©2014, 2018 by Time Inc. Books

ISBN-13: 978-0-8487-4226-3
ISBN-10: 0-8487-4226-5

Library of Congress Control Number: 2013956264
Printed in the United States of America
Eleventh Printing 2021

Oxmoor House
Vice President, Brand Publishing: Laura Sappington
Editorial Director: Leah McLaughlin
Creative Director: Felicity Keane
Brand Manager: Vanessa Tiongson
Senior Editor: Andrea C. Kirkland, M.S., R.D.
Managing Editor: Elizabeth Tyler Austin
Assistant Managing Editor: Jeanne de Lathouder

Lodge Cast Iron Nation
Art Director: Christopher Rhoads
Project Editor: Lacie Pinyan
Senior Designer: Melissa Clark
Assistant Designer: Allison Sperando Potter
Recipe Developers and Testers: Wendy Ball, R.D.;
   Victoria E. Cox; Tamara Goldis, R.D.; Stefanie Maloney;
   Callie Nash; Karen Rankin; Leah Van Deren
Assistant Test Kitchen Manager: Alyson Moreland Haynes
Food Stylists: Margaret Monroe Dickey,
   Catherine Crowell Steele
Photography Director: Jim Bathie
Senior Photographer: Hélène Dujardin
Senior Photo Stylist: Kay E. Clarke
Photo Stylist: Mindi Shapiro Levine
Assistant Photo Stylist: Mary Louise Menendez
Production Managers: Theresa Beste-Farley,
   Tamara Nall Wilder

Contributors
Writers: Pam Hoenig, Mark H. Kelly
Illustrator: Steven Noble
Copy Editors: Donna Baldone, Rebecca Benton
Proofreader: Jasmine Hodges
Indexer: Nanette Cardon
Fellows: Ali Carruba, Frances Gunnells, Elizabeth Laseter,
   Amy Pinney, Madison Taylor Pozzo, Deanna Sakal,
   April Smitherman, Megan Thompson, Tonya West
Food Stylists: Tami Hardeman, Erica Hopper
Photographers: Caroline Allison, Beau Gustafson
Photo Stylists: Mary Clayton Carl

For information on bulk purchases, please contact IPG at specialmarkets@ipgbook.com or call (800) 888-4741.

Cover: Skillet Roast Chicken, page 112;
      Pan-Roasted Spring Vegetables, page 212

*Lodge Manufacturing is a proud sponsor of the Tennessee Aquarium's Serve & Protect program.

Recipe Contributions:
Hard-Shell Clams with Parsley Pesto, page 200, from *The New York Times*, January 31 © 2007 The New York Times. All rights reserved. Used by permission and protected by the Copyright Laws of the United States. The printing, copying, redistribution, or retransmission of this content without express written permission is prohibited.

Country Ham and Fig Pizza, page 156, reprinted with permission from *Pizza on the Grill* by Elizabeth Karmel and Bob Blumer, The Taunton Press, 2008.

Photo Credits:
Page 29: Courtesy of Raul Serna; Page 188: Courtesy of Skip Hopkins; page 198: John Bamber Photography; Page 259: Courtesy of JR Dawkins

note to reader
The publisher of this book has made every reasonable effort to ensure that the activities in this book are safe if conducted as instructed and performed with reasonable skill and care. However, the publisher cannot and does not assume any responsibility or liability whatsoever for any damage caused or injury sustained while performing any of the activities contained in this book. You are solely responsible for taking all reasonable and necessary safety precautions when performing any of the activities contained in this book.